THE
SMALL BUSINESS
INFORMATION HANDBOOK

THE
SMALL BUSINESS
INFORMATION HANDBOOK

Gustav Berle

John Wiley & Sons

New York · Chichester · Brisbane · Toronto · Singapore

DEDICATION

Across the width of America, five million men and women each year turn on the light of inspiration. They see themselves as entrepreneurs—in business for themselves, independent, self-reliant, making their own decisions, creating their own successes. Out of those five million, only 12 percent actually take the next step leading to the fulfillment of their entrepreneurial dream: they step out into a business of their own. But these 12 percent number 600,000 and they are a formidable and adventurous cadre of small business people, a new generation of taxpayers, breadwinners, and innovators. Not all will make it. Only about 40 percent of this select group are prepared sufficiently to remain in business successfully. To these successful entrepreneurs and to the many others who, I hope, can join them because of the information and advice in *The Small Business Information Handbook*, this book is dedicated with gratitude and good wishes.

Entrepreneurship isn't an event, it's a career. True entrepreneurs do it over and over again, whether they succeed or fail.

CHARLES HOFER
Professor, University of Georgia

Every entrepreneur needs an avocation. But don't be like the football nut whose business wound up in the hands of a receiver.

An entrepreneur's foremost ability is *reliability!*

An entrepreneur rarely watches the clock, because he does not want to be one of the hands.

The true entrepreneur knows that he must get off his bottom if he wants to rise to the top.

Curiosity is one of the permanent and certain characteristics of a vigorous intellect.

SAMUEL JOHNSON

INTRODUCTION

Business bankruptcies are usually the sad legacy of unpreparedness. While insufficient capitalization, sudden and overwhelming competition, national and sectional trends over which the entrepreneur has no control, often inexplicable changes in fashions and preferences, and even acts of God play vital roles in entrepreneurial demise, all too often the bottom line reads: Mismanagement.

To counter this counterable cause of bankruptcies, this book takes a look at what can be done to prevent them. It does not point an I-told-you-so finger at those who did not listen to advisors, or take advantage of the many preventive business measures that are available, or back up their imagination and innovation with patience, preparedness, and sound business principles.

Very generally, two types of businesses escape being in the often quoted statistic of an 80 to 85 percent demise of new businesses within the first five years of their life. The two exceptions are new franchises and purchased businesses that have been successfully operating under a former owner.

Why will only 100,000 new businesses survive the first five years, out of 600,000 that start up in any one year? It requires no deep analysis: most businesses taken over by a new owner, or businesses that are set up by a franchisor who has a proven track record of successes, have a 5:1 better chance of long-term survival than most small enterprises started from scratch. A large portion of the statistical percentage is secured in that ratio. Some states have better business survival records than others. The Small Business Administration, in a survey made during the first six months of 1988 (the latest figures available at the time of writing), identified the top-10 states for "survival" (defined as a decline in bankruptcies from the previous year):

		Percent
1.	Maryland	68.5
2.	Wyoming	67.1
3.	Mississippi	64.4
4.	New Jersey	46.3
5.	Ohio	42.5

6.	Missouri	41.6
7.	Kansas	37.6
8.	West Virginia	37.4
9.	California	37.3
10.	Iowa	36.6

During the same year, however, other statistics released by Cognetics, Inc., a research firm, and published in *INC.* magazine indicated that the city with the highest number of startups was Austin, Texas. Among the top-10 hot spots were Dallas, El Paso, and San Antonio—all in the Lone Star State. Not one of the states shown in the SBA's greatest-declines-in-bankruptcies list was even included. In a related list, also by Cognetics, Inc., places where startups have the greatest chance of growth were topped by the Manchester-Nashua, NH area, but Austin was among the top-10.

Statistics obviously need to be interpreted and mixed with a great portion of personal preferences and prejudices. However, there is one inescapable common denominator: Knowledge and experience are the foundation of good entrepreneurial management.

A survey by a group of members of SCORE (Service Corps of Retired Executives) had significant results. Only 5 percent of all those attending workshops on small business received immediate encouragement, or a "green light," from their SCORE counselors. In fact, only 12 percent of those attending SCORE workshops actually went into businesses of their own. They had a far higher survival ratio than those who did not receive SCORE encouragement and training. The 5 percent who were thought to be prepared, fared well and survived; the next 7 percent, who were judged to be not prepared but went into business anyway, either sent up "help" signals at later stages or joined the sad statistics of small business bankruptcies.

The moral is clear: *Be prepared.*

It is hoped that *The Small Business Information Handbook* will help its readers in being prepared, in surviving, and in avoiding the small business failure statistics.

Gustav Berle

Silver Spring, Maryland
July 1990

SOURCE FINDER

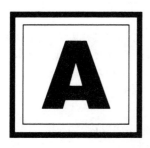

ACADEMY OF SENIOR PROFESSIONALS An organization of about 125 retired professors, military officers, doctors, lawyers, government officials, businesspeople, and theologians has been formed into a think tank sponsored by Eckerd College of St. Petersburg, Florida. Members pay for the privilege of belonging to this elite group. They are on call for their input and opinions and occasionally take on teaching assignments. The Academy's annual activities usually include more than two dozen presentations that are open to the public and cover developments in science, technology, sociology, literature, and business. Some members team up with faculty staff instructors as "discussant colleagues" and coteach a variety of cultural courses. Students get the benefit of their pragmatic contributions, but the senior participants receive "the real prize" of the retiree-educator program: the opportunity to interact with young people. Arthur Peterson, the Academy's director, has commented: "These older people have all had active intellectual lives and they want to extend that through the young people."

ACCOUNTANT An accountant is one of a team of professionals—together with an attorney, a banker, and an insurance representative—who are vital in the proper organization of a new business. A highly trained and intensively educated professional, an accountant sets up the financial record-keeping needed by a business and helps the business owner to understand what the "books" and figures mean. An accountant must pass a stringent three-part exam, usually in the state in which he or she is in professional practice, in order to become a Certified Public Accountant (CPA). Independent accountants' functions include preparing tax returns for corporations, other businesses, and individuals, and auditing companies' financial records (inspecting and verifying their validity). A bookkeeper implements the record-keeping system, once it is set up. The accountant analyzes the figures and financial statements; advises the client on ways to improve business transactions, cash flow, and tax procedure; and assists in the preparation of financial statements, annual reports, and analyses needed to buy or sell enterprises. Along with attorneys and insurance representatives, the accountant is a key professional for the fiscal portions of an enterprise's operation. While accountants may arrange for a single-project fee, they usually work with long-term clients, on a monthly retainer basis.

ACCOUNTING

The accounting system of an enterprise provides quantitative, but usually not qualitative, analysis of a business's financial situation. The system in most companies is set up by a licensed public accountant, who may be a Certified Public Accountant (CPA). (See *Accountant.*) An accounting system may be set up on either an accrual basis or a cash basis. The accrual method lists all transactions as they earn revenue or incur expenses, whether any cash has changed hands or not; the cash or bird-in-the-hand method, used by most small and individual entrepreneurs, recognizes earnings and expenses only when the actual income is received or the bills paid. It is often vital for entrepreneurs to understand that an accountant can be even more useful than a lawyer or banker. Accounting encompasses writing the business plan, designing an accounting system that is suited to the business's needs and personality, analyzing cash flow, and developing compensation plans that tend to retain good employees and minimize tax bites. How much will accounting services cost? Fees depend on the size of the accounting firm, customary charges in the area, and a business's requirements. Annual average fees, based on companies' gross sales, are:

Gross Sales	Annual Fee
Under $1 million	$ 3,600
$1 million to $2.5 million	$ 6,000
$2.5 million to $5 million	$12,000

ACCOUNTS RECEIVABLE

A record of what is owed to a company by all of its customers or clients is called its accounts receivable (A/R). Even though the company does not have the payments in hand, all the money that is owed, as shown in its A/R, is considered an asset. For accounting purposes, it is as good as money in the bank, but for A/R to become real rather than paper assets, they must of course be collected. The entrepreneur should know at almost any time what outstanding A/Rs are, to have a realistic idea of the cash flow and the worth of the business. Equally important is the age of each and every A/R; when an overdue account becomes too old, it will be more difficult to collect. If an entrepreneur asks to borrow money from a bank or factor against the company's accounts receivable, the age of each account will be taken into consideration. Any account more than 90 days overdue will usually not be accepted as collateral, or will be sharply discounted in value. For more specific information, see *Small Time Operator,* rev. ed., by

Bernard Kamoroff (1989), available from the author at 702 South Michigan Street, South Bend, IN 46618; and *The Small Business Bible* by Paul Resnick (230 pp.; New York: John Wiley & Sons, 1988).

ADVENTURE CAPITAL Speculative investment is usually put up by entrepreneurs who are interested in other entrepreneurs, like their proposition, and have hopes (or faith) that they are going to make a lot of money—and their investors will share in their profits. Most of these lenders know that they are on a "crap shooting expedition," but they will go along for the ride because they figure that the innovation, management, and hard work of the entrepreneur are going to be successful. They are not, however, purely altruistic or charitable. They will want their "pound of flesh"; a high percentage of profits must be shared with these "angels." Investors of this type are not easily found. They are not in any directory, but they exist across the country. They have quietly become a major source of capital, especially for speculative startup enterprises. Robert Gaston, who was commissioned by the Small Business Administration (SBA) to find these investors and determine their input to the entrepreneurial loan picture, determined that their annual contribution to the nation's startup entrepreneurs is about $27 billion (Robert Gaston, *Finding Private Venture Capital for Your Firm*, New York: John Wiley & Sons, 1989). The known, listed *venture* capitalists during Gaston's year of investigation (1987) invested only about $1 billion! How can these informal investors be found? Through connections, friends, business contacts, networking, or referrals. This national source of startup wealth has been around for decades: Henry Ford borrowed $40,000 from adventure capitalists in 1903. Some adventure capitalists back only startups, looking for a 20 percent return. When the new enterprise is running smoothly and making money, they turn over the "client" to more formal lending sources and bail out. Meanwhile, they offer both money and expertise, and remain a controlling interest until they decide it is time to get out.

ADVERTISING An advertisement is a paid message, in a public medium, designed to influence the purchasing behavior or thought pattern of an audience. Advertising is an effective marketing tool when used in combination with other marketing tools, such as sales promotion, personal selling, public relations, and publicity. Since 1625, when the first paid advertisement appeared in English in the *Weekly Newes of London*, the advertising business has developed into a $100 billion industry. Among the profusion of media available to an entrepreneur are newspapers (daily and weekly, paid and free), magazines (local, regional, and national), billboards, painted signs, transportation cards, television, radio, and direct mail. Selection of the medium that is right for a company's marketing efforts is a job for an expert. Unfortunately, much advertising is bought subjectively, because the entrepreneur (or spouse) favors a certain medium personally, even though the customers might read, watch, or listen to a totally different medium. To be objective, entrepreneurs need to know what media their customers or clients are exposed to and what each medium costs—not only totally but in terms of each thousand prospects reached with the message. Media representatives should have this information available. For a substantial investment in advertising, an experienced advertising agency (which will usually charge a consultation fee) should be retained. The agency will earn a 15 percent commission on all ad placement except in local newspapers and direct mail.

(A negotiated fee is usually charged for the latter; see also *Cooperative Advertising.*) To underscore the need for advertising continuity, peruse the listing of America's top advertisers of a hundred years ago, below. About 40 of them can still be recognized today as operating companies.

LEADERS IN NATIONAL ADVERTISING IN THE 1890S

A. P. W. Paper	Cuticura Soap
Adams Tutti Frutti Gum	Devoe & Raynolds Artist's
Æolian Company	Materials
American Express Traveler's Cheques	Derby Desks
Armour Beef Extract	De Long Hook and Eye
Autoharp	Diamond Dyes
Baker's Cocoa	Dixon's Graphite Paint
Battle Ax Plug Tobacco	Dixon's Pencils
Beardsley's Shredded Codfish	W. L. Douglas Shoes
Beeman's Pepsin Gum	Edison Mimeograph
Bent's Crown Piano	Earl & Wilson Collars
Burlington Railroad	Elgin Watches
Burnett's Extracts	Edison Phonograph
California Fig Syrup	Everett Piano
Caligraph Typewriter	Epps's Cocoa
Castoria	Estey Organ
A. B. Chase Piano	Fall River Line
Chicago Great Western	Felt & Tarrant Comptometer
Chicago, Milwaukee & St. Paul Railroad	Ferry's Seeds
Chicago Great Western Railway	Fisher Piano
Chocolat-Menier	Fowler Bicycles
Chickering Piano	Franco American Soup
Columbia Bicycles	Garland Stoves
Cleveland Baking Powder	Gold Dust
Cottolene Shortening	Gold Dust Washing Powder
Cook's Tours	Gorham's Silver
Crown Pianos	Gramophone
Crescent Bicycles	Great Northern Railroad

H-O Breakfast Food	Mellin's Food
Hamburg American Line	Mennen's Talcum Powder
Hammond Typewriter	Michigan Central Railroad
Hartford Bicycle	Monarch Bicycles
Hartshorn's Shade Rollers	J. L. Mott Indoor Plumbing
Heinz's Baked Beans	Munsing Underwear
Peter Henderson & Co.	Murphy Varnish Company
Hires' Root Beer	New England Mincemeat
Hoffman House Cigars	New York Central Railroad
Huyler's Chocolates	North German Lloyd
Hunyadi Janos	Old Dominion Line
Ingersoll Watches	Oneita Knitted Goods
Ives & Pond Piano	Packer's Tar Soap
Ivory Soap	Pearline Soap Powder
Jaeger Underwear	Peartltop Lamp Chimneys
Kirk's American Family Soap	Pears' Soap
Kodak	Alfred Peats Wall Paper
Liebeg's Extract of Beef	Pettijohn's Breakfast Food
Lipton's Teas	Pittsburgh Stogies
Lowney's Chocolates	Pond's Extract
Lundborg's Perfumes	Postum Cereal
James McCutcheon Linens	Prudential Insurance Co.
Dr. Lyon's Toothpowder	Quaker Oats
Mason & Hamlin Piano	

Reproduced from Frank Presbey, *History and Development of Advertising* (Garden City, NY: Doubleday, 1929), p. 361.

ADVERTISING MEDIA SELECTION

PROS AND CONS OF MAJOR ADVERTISING MEDIA

Medium	Advantages	Disadvantages
Newspapers	Good flexibility Reasonable cost Short deadlines Good market coverage Pinpointed targeting	Competition from other ads Crowded pages Marginal reproduction (especially photos) Waste circulation of major dailies
Magazines	Long life of ad Good quality reproduction Good market selectivity Availability of color Diverse readership Good attention value (especially for full-page ads)	Deadlines far ahead High cost per thousand Expensive production Waste circulation (of general magazines) Inflexibility for tight scheduling

Medium	Advantages	Disadvantages
Radio	Short deadlines Flexibility Relatively inexpensive Good market selectivity Provable audience loyalty Low production cost	Brief life of ad message Limited only to hearing High competition among stations in same market area Difficult to merchandise
Television	High impact Quick results Dramatic demonstration and action possibilities Wide market coverage Fairly flexible scheduling	High cost of air time High production cost Brief message exposure Bunching up of several commercials Difficult to merchandise
Direct mail	Most penetrating medium Longest sustained impact Targetable to specific audience Controllable size and timing Excellent product demon- stration possibility Total cost adjustable to any budget	High cost per thousand for large audiences Competition from "junk mail" Complex medium, too often seen as "child's play" Costly returns, from high mobility of audience

ADVERTISING SUCCESS FORMULA There are seven essential steps to making advertising pay off. These steps can be applied to writing ads, sales letters, mail-order promotions, radio or TV commercials, or sales talks. Their basic psychology has worked for generations. They will work for entrepreneurs now!

1. Get attention. State a believable promise and direct it to the right audience. A picture of the product in use or of the reward from its use can add extra impact.

2. Hold attention. To extend the promise or benefit, use a subhead, a second illustration, or a strong first paragraph that continues the most potent promises.

3. Create desire. Pull out all the stops on the benefits. One of them must hit the reader's wallet.

4. Make the message credible. Use specific statistics, guarantees, testimonials, test reports, and proofs of popularity.

5. Prove the value. All the world loves a bargain—which need not be a price reduction, as long as the reader perceives value in the proposition.

6. Make it easy. Tell the reader whether to buy at a store or office, how to order by mail or phone, and exactly how to get what is being offered.

7. Give a reason for acting now. Because prospects forget easily or are distracted by countless other offers, there is need for assuring their quick action. Do this by indicating a limited-time offer, limited quantity, special bonus, or reward for promptness, or by encouraging enjoyment of benefits now instead of later.

AGRIBUSINESS

The business of agriculture in the 1990s is becoming widespread and sophisticated Big Business. The number of family farms is shrinking, but some back-to-the-soil movement is also evident. The remaining farms are bigger and are often run by agricultural-college-trained children of the original owners or by professional farm managers. Of 1.7 million United States farms, 458 are large farm corporations and nearly 6,000 are farm cooperatives. This fairly formidable "industry" is serviced by over 30,000 farm implement dealers, nearly 8,500 tractor and machinery dealers, and over 16,000 farm supply and feed dealers. Farm magazines catering to this audience number 386, and nearly 350 daily newspapers think farming is important enough to have farm editors. Of the 1.7 million farms, 161,000 raise dairy cows, nearly 380,000 raise beef cattle, and 234,000 raise hogs; corn is grown on 533,000, soybeans on 376,000, and wheat on 322,000. About 20 percent of America's farms use computers to manage their spreads. Today's high-tech generation of agriculturists use microchips to help them decide what to plant, based on future supply and demand, or which dairy cows to sell as beef, to take advantage of market prices in the auction halls of Kansas City and Chicago. The Data Transmission Network Corporation of Omaha has 43,000 farm subscribers for up-to-date information on the latest price shifts and weather conditions. Specifically tailored software guides farmers on the most productive ways of raising calves into feedlot cows, the moment when a piglet can be converted into a "cash crop," or when a flock of chickens becomes worth more than the eggs it produces. Red Wing Business System, in Red Wing, MN, can give herd owners birth-to-slaughter-house statistics on growth, feed, lactating, calving, and similar live-stock data. For some younger farmers, computers have become as important as combines.

AGRICULTURAL LIBRARY, NATIONAL

The nation's agricultural trade and marketing information center, the National Agricultural Library, is a part of the United States Department of Agriculture (USDA). It can be contacted at Room 304, Beltsville, MD 20705, phone: (301) 344-3719. The Library houses agribusiness, barter, export, and trade development information—principally for farmers, agricultural experts and specialists, and those involved in the export of agricultural products. The resources of the Library are truly worldwide. It organizes and disseminates information and facilitates communication and cooperation among the USDA, private institutions and organizations, and users interested in agricultural pursuits, research, and allied enterprises. Relevant agricultural trade and marketing literature is indexed and made accessible worldwide through a number of services. AGRICOLA, the Library's computerized data base system, offers an index to more than 2 million books and articles relating to all aspects of agriculture. Access to the AGRICOLA data base is possible through office and personal dial-up computer terminals, public or university libraries, and commercial search services.

AMERICAN HOTEL AND MOTEL ASSOCIATION (AHMA)

Founded in Chicago in 1910, the AHMA is an umbrella federation for about 10,000 hotel and motel organizations located in 50 states, the District of Columbia, Puerto Rico, and the Virgin Islands. The AHMA speaks for a $52 billion lodging industry, comprising around 1.4 million rooms; its members can obtain information on any lodging industry management problem by calling (202) 289-3155 in Washington, DC. Each state has its own chapter, sometimes allied to tourism and restaurant groups. A national monthly, *Lodging Magazine*, and an annual buyers' guide are sent to members in good standing. Available also are: a 75,000-circulation directory of the entire industry; a travel club that assures members a 50 percent reduction on accommodations; an insurance and retirement program; a 40-year-old Educational Institute, the world's largest source of hospitality industry training material; and a certification process leading to an MHS designation. Entrepreneurs considering any phase of the hospitality industry, whether as providers or suppliers, can contact their state chapter or the AHMA directly, at 1201 New York Avenue, NW, Washington, DC 20005-3917, phone: (202) 289-3100.

AMERICAN SOCIETY OF TRAVEL AGENTS (ASTA)

More than one-third (12,000) of the 30,000-plus registered travel agencies in the United States are members of ASTA. In addition, ASTA has about 5,000 members from allied services: travel suppliers in hotels, car rental firms, airlines and cruiselines, and other related companies. About 2,000 international members also display the ASTA symbol. In 1989 almost 8,000 members met in Hungary for ASTA's annual convention. ASTA's consumer affairs department fields thousands of inquiries from members and consumers, provides continuing training programs, coordinates legislative and regulatory activities, disseminates research and statistical data (salary, benefits, and profitability surveys), and publishes a series of public relations pieces. ASTA members are located in major cities (39 percent), in suburbs (40 percent), and in rural areas of small towns (21 percent). About 70 percent of the members run agencies reporting under $1 million gross. Business activities of ASTA members are divided as follows: 55 percent handle leisure travel; 17 percent, commercial travel; and 28 percent, some of each. More than 75 percent of the members are women; 80 percent of ASTA agency owners are college graduates; more than 50 percent of owners and 70 percent of managers have been in the travel business for at least five and 10 years, respectively. More than 95 percent of all member agencies have at least one online computer reservation system. Membership dues range from $85 to $325, with a $35 first-time fee. ASTA headquarters are at 1101 King Street, Alexandria, VA 22314, phone: (703) 739-2782.

AMERICAN WOMAN'S ECONOMIC DEVELOPMENT CORPORATION (AWED)

Formed with a federal grant in 1976, AWED explores, analyzes, and implements programs that will help women with management training and technical assistance—the most useful tools for women beginning business ownership. AWED's programs include:

- "Starting Your Own Business"—group sessions for women who know the business they want to go into and need help in learning how to proceed.
- "Building Your Own Business"—an 18-week training and counseling program for new entrepreneurs.
- "Managing Your Own Business"—an 18-month management training and technical assistance program for women who have been in business at least one year.
- "Chief Executive Roundtables"—a two-year training program for women whose businesses gross more than $1 million a year.

Tens of thousands of women have been counseled by AWED since its inception; about one-fifth of them were from minority groups. Of the women who participated in the long-range training programs, only about one percent subsequently declared bankruptcy. Because of its timely and effective work, AWED has received financial support from numerous large industries. Participants also contributed from $240 to $1,100, depending on the program. AWED has two unique telephone assistance programs: telephone counseling sessions, following a formal application, in which a knowledgeable counselor is made available (at a charge of $35); and a 10-minute hotline counseling session to respond to a single query ($10), phone:

(800) 222-AWED, Monday through Friday, between 10 A.M. and 5 P.M.). Sylvia Porter has attributed AWED's success to "its ability to bring women with similar experience and problems together." AWED is headquartered at 60 East 42nd Street, Suite 405, New York, NY 10165.

APPRAISAL

An estimate of the value of a business or property is usually rendered by a professionally licensed appraiser whose report will be taken as proof by banks, government agencies, buyers, and sellers, and as evidence in a court of law. An estimate by an appraiser is used as a starting point for buy–sell negotiations, loans or fund-raising, partnership severance, lawsuits, insurance claims and settlements, insurance policy determination, or processing of an individual's estate. Appraisers are involved most frequently in real estate, jewelry, art, and personal estate value determinations. The Yellow Pages lists local appraisers; referrals are often given by attorneys or bankers. Some business brokers are also appraisers. For an entrepreneur in the market to buy a business rather than start one, it would be advisable to obtain a "second opinion" from an independent appraiser. Brokers, sometimes cast in a dual role, tend to quote too high a price for a business. (See *Buying a Business.*)

ARBITRATION

This procedure is a form of judgment in the event of a conflict that cannot be resolved by the two opposing parties. An arbitrator, an impartial person, is chosen by the two parties in the dispute, to determine an equitable settlement. The costs to launch a claim or counterclaim investigation through an approved arbitrator—a member of the American Arbitration Association (AAA)—run from $250 to $850 per party, depending on the amount of the claim. The AAA and a similar body, the Associated Specialty Contractors Association, have a 10-page explanation of the rules under which arbitration takes place. The mediator is a neutral person who may expedite a peaceful settlement even before an arbitrator becomes involved, but who does not have authority to make a binding decision or award. Once the dispute comes before the arbitrator(s), however, the disputants agree to abide by and perform any award rendered by the arbitrator(s). Following that decision, "a judgment of the court having jurisdiction may be entered upon the award." The final fee, upon the settlement of a claim or counterclaim, ranges from a minimum of $200 (for claims of $1 to $20,000) to a maximum of $1,800 plus .0025 percent of the excess over $160,000. Since the maximum claim in an arbitration is $5 million, the top arbitration fee would be $13,900. Faster resolution of disputes, without the trauma and delay of open court, is the principal advantage of submitting disputes to arbitration. The American Arbitration Association has 31 regional directors in all areas of the country.

ARTICLES OF INCORPORATION   Before a corporation legally exists and is allowed to do business, a legal document that sets forth the purposes and regulations for the corporation must be approved by the appropriate state office. Each state has different requirements and the procedures are fairly complicated. Despite published claims that you can do it yourself for the mere cost of the filing fee, it is usually necessary to engage a lawyer who specializes in corporate law to set up and get approval for a corporation. The Articles of Incorporation (in some States they are called a Certificate of Incorporation) are usually filed with the Secretary of State at the State House or the Corporation Division of the State in which the new business resides. The filing fee for a domestic corporation is often accompanied by another fee called the franchise tax. The total costs can be as low as $26 as in Arkansas, or go up to $265 and more in California. A few states peg the franchise tax to a percentage of net income, Louisiana has a tricky formula that levies $1.50 per $1,000 of stock issued.

ASIAN AMERICANS, NATIVE AMERICANS, AND OTHER MINORITIES   This growing segment of the American population generated nearly $200 million in fiscal support from the Small Business Administration (SBA) during 1988, in 893 separate loans. Additionally, they received almost $800 million in SBA awards through the Section 8(a) program during the same year. The Section 8(a) program sets aside funds for procurement awards to eligible socially disadvantaged firms in the minorities categories; 640 such firms signed up for the program in the United States and Puerto Rico during 1989. A total of 8,100 firms owned by these minorities have signed up with the SBA's Procurement Automated Source System (PASS) so that the potential for the future goes well above the 1988 figures. Of these firms, 92.3 percent or 236,058 were sole proprietorships. Only 2.2 percent were corporations but they accounted for 27.5 percent of gross receipts. More than 60 percent of the firms were in retailing and selected services; this group included more than 10,000 food stores, over 17,000 eating and drinking establishments, and in excess of 20,000 in various other services. As expected, California led as the location of these minority-owned businesses, with 95,982, followed by Hawaii with 29,040. The cities with the largest number of firms owned by Asian Americans, Native Americans, and other minorities were (in round numbers):

Los Angeles	17,000
Honolulu	14,000
New York	13,500
San Francisco	8,000
Chicago	4,600
Houston	4,600
San Jose	3,500
Oakland	2,000
Seattle	1,800
San Antonio	1,700

ASIAN FINANCING (HUI) This ancient method of raising capital for many small enterprises is relatively new in the United States. Immigrants from Korea, Hong Kong, Viet Nam, and Chinese outposts have, over the past two decades, made it noteworthy. *Hui* is a self-help method that calls for membership in an investment club, often years before the entrepreneur actually goes into a business. Members contribute as much as they can while they are working, or even later when they earn money as owners. These loan clubs or loan pools are not gigantic, but may reach $500,000. In ancient times, *huis* paid for local town improvements, businesses, weddings, and other important expenses. Now, entrepreneurs who wish to borrow money for a new business, or for the expansion of an existing one, petition the *hui* at one of its monthly meetings. The applicant also indicates how much interest can be paid. All bids are then opened and announced, and the highest bidder receives the loan. The neediest may bid the highest and get the earliest "pot." The person who organizes the pool usually has first choice of a loan and gets it interest-free. This invisible venture capital method of financing has been going on for generations and is entirely safe. No credit checks are made. Defaults are rare; to cheat on neighbors and fellow-lenders would mean social suicide. Whether this system of "internal" financing will continue in the United States and Canada is problematic. As the Asian communities grow and become "Americanized," close relationships get diluted and risks are increased. Meanwhile, the *hui's* informality, legal simplicity, and payback assurance make it the envy of bankers who are familiar with the way thousands of Asian small businesses have gotten their start in this country.

ASSETS Anything of value that is owned by you or owed to you and contributes to the worth of your business is an asset and can be pledged as collateral for a loan, property, or equipment purchase. Assets include: money in the bank, cash on hand, accounts receivable, securities held in the name of the business, property or buildings, equipment, fixtures, merchandise for sale or in the process of manufacture, supplies, insurance policy equity, or valuables that can be used for payment of debt or as collateral. Fixed assets (also called real or tangible assets) can be used as collateral for loans—perhaps not at their full value, but at a value of at least 75 percent. Soft assets include such intangibles as good will, patents, formulas, and capitalized research and development (R&D). Soft assets are not always accepted as collateral; they are, in fact, thought to distort a business's value and are regarded by investors as a danger signal. To some bank examiners, assignation of a high R&D value flies a red flag over an entrepreneur's business plan.

ASSOCIATED BUILDERS AND CONTRACTORS (ABC)

This trade organization began in Maryland in 1950 with six contractor-members and has grown to include nearly 20,000 companies. An entrepreneur considering entry into the construction field should get to know this association. The thrust of ABC is that it promotes the merit system of free enterprise in cooperation with both open-shop and union companies. There are 80 chapters from coast to coast. ABC member companies reserve the right to manage according to merit-shop policies and goals: each worker is paid and promoted on the bases of his or her skills, desire for individual achievement, and overall performance. An outstanding feature of ABC is its apprenticeship training programs, available in many four-year colleges and in over 200 schools that offer two-year construction courses. The field that ABC represents, as any entrepreneur who is planning to enter it should know, has a predicted value of $1.5 trillion over the next 10 years. This will include more than 1 million new classrooms, 375,000 new bridges, more than $500 billion in new industrial, commercial, institutional, and public works, and expansion and maintenance of interstate road programs. Various free publications, videos, and information about membership and training courses are available from ABC, 729 15th Street, NW, Washington, DC 20005, phone: (202)637-8800.

ASSOCIATED SPECIALTY CONTRACTORS (ASC)

The ASC includes the following constituent organizations:

The Mason Contractors Association of America (MCA), est. 1950; conducts the International Masonry Institute.

The Mechanical Contractors Association of America (MCA), est. 1889.

National Association of Plumbing, Heating, and Cooling Contractors (NAPHCC), est. 1883; includes 300 state and local groups.

The National Electrical Contractors Association (NECA), est. 1900; has 6,000 members in 134 chapters.

National Insulation Contractors Association, est. 1953; more than 1,600 members internationally, seven regional groups.

National Roofing Contractors Association (NRCA), est. 1886; more than 2,800 members in all 50 states and 22 foreign countries. The National Roofing Foundation is its college-level affiliate.

Painting and Decorating Contractors of America (PDCA), est. 1884; has 250 local chapters, 32 regional councils.

The Sheet Metal and Air Conditioning Contractors National Association (SMACNA), est. 1943; represents 2,400 contractors.

The ASC has published a text entitled *Contract Documents*, which contains general contractor–subcontractor guidelines, details about subcontracting, owners' and subcontractors' guides, AIA documents, subcontract forms, prime contract information, and virtually everything else needed to function profitably in these allied fields. The book is $20 (approximately 200 pages) from the ASC. Any entrepreneur seeking to enter one of the fields covered by the ASC would be well advised to contact this organization at 7315 Wisconsin Avenue, NW, Bethesda, MD 20814-3299, phone: (301) 657–3110; Daniel G. Walter, President.

ASSOCIATION OF COLLEGIATE ENTREPRENEURS (ACE)

Founded in 1983 at Wichita State University (Kansas) by Robert King, then a student, this organization now has 100 chapters in the United States and networking contacts with twice that many throughout the world. ACE has been instrumental in starting entrepreneurial organizations in 35 countries, including Russia and China. Its 1988 conference, held in Washington, DC, was attended by more than 1,000 students and the response was repeated in San Francisco in 1989. Membership in ACE is open to entrepreneurs of all ages, though the focus is on those under 30 years of age. Current ownership of a business is not a prerequisite for membership. By providing an association for young entrepreneurs, ACE helps alleviate two problems common to young businesspeople: a perceived lack of credibility, and lack of business contacts. ACE helps young business-minded and actively engaged entrepreneurs to network with each other and with academicians and professionals. Current membership stands at about 4,500. Annual membership, which includes the "ACE Action" newsletter and a subscription to either *INC.* or Entrepreneur magazine is $29. Contact: ACE, Box 147, 1845 North Fairmount, Wichita, KS 67208. (See also *Young Entrepreneurs' Association.*)

BAD DEBT Money owed that cannot be collected is a bad debt. It is useless to moralize on how and why bad debts get onto the books of a business. Many bad debts are incurred by customers and clients who fall on hard times or who go bankrupt. Having a cash-only policy or charging only on no-recourse charge cards will prevent bad debts. The popularity of credit cards attests to businesspersons' realization that they can collect from the credit card company even when the customer may turn out to be a deadbeat (there are limits to this procedure, of course). Bad debts come in various sizes and conditions. Some very fashionable stores that sell only to high-income big-spenders need to carry charge accounts because wealthy people rarely carry cash; yet, even the very rich can go bankrupt if their considerable fortunes become deflated in a stock market crash. At the other end of the spectrum are merchants who deal with workers in highly unstable and volatile industries or farmers whose income comes in at the end of a growing season. It is customary to extend credit to these customers, and, while they are usually exceptionally honest, unforeseen economic reverses can create bad debts. The entrepreneur must analyze each situation and method of operation. Through experience, and reports from trade and government bureaus, the entrepreneur can establish a fairly reliable bad-debt ratio. If, on an average, bad-debt loss is 2 percent of gross volume, then 2 percent must be tacked on to overall markup on all products and services, as compensation.

BAKERIES: RETAIL BAKERS OF AMERICA (RBA) Of the nearly 30,000 bakeries and bakery suppliers in the United States, 2,817 are members of this trade organization. Unless an entrepreneur plans to purchase a franchise from one of the several franchisers offering shopping-mall instant bake shops or cookie factories, it would be well during the start-up phase to learn from a trade association. The RBA was founded in 1918 and is the "professional" representative of this $12 billion industry. Dues are $75 to $500, depending on self-declared gross volume. RBA publishes a "Fresh Baked" newsletter, and a monthly *Research and Merchandising Bulletin,* and maintains a hotline for quick answers to members' problems and a government affairs office in Washington, DC. Workshops, national promotions, an annual suppliers' directory, and journeyman and master certification are available as member benefits. RBA is located at 6525 Belcrest Road, Suite 250, Hyattsville, MD 20782, phone: (301) 277-0990.

BALANCE SHEET

A business record that shows what a business owns and owes at any one time is called a balance sheet: its two parts, like the scales of justice, are supposed to be equal. On one side is a list of the business's assets and their present value; on the other side is a list of the dollar amounts of its liabilities. The liabilities are all debts that the business owes, including the net worth of the business, which the business "owes" its owners. The two sides, like a scale, should be equally balanced. When an owner looks at the balance sheet, it is like looking at a current snapshot-by-the-numbers of the business. A simplified balance sheet might look like this:

Cash	$ 5,000	Charge accounts	$ 5,000
Vehicles	15,000	Merchandise owed	20,000
Furniture	5,000	Equipment loan	10,000
Property	50,000	Mortgage	30,000
Securities	5,000	Equity	15,000
Total assets	$80,000	Total liability and equity	$80,000

BANK LOAN APPLICATION

Any bank that receives an application for a loan from an owner of a small business will require information on eight characteristics of the business. The application will have better success and a quicker reply if this information is ready in detail:

1. *Description of business*—A written description of the existing or proposed business, including information regarding:

Date of information	Proposed future operation
Type of organization	Marketing area
Location and zoning	Competition
Product or service	Customers
Brief history of business	Suppliers

2. *Management's experience*—Background (résumé) of each owner and/or of those who will manage the business.

3. *Personal financial statements*—Recent financial statements (owners may use a bank form) for each owner of the existing or proposed business, and copies of federal, state, and local income tax returns for the prior year.

4. *Money requirements*—A brief, *specific,* written statement indicating how the funds are to be used in the business, and the dollar amounts.

5. *Loan repayment*—A written statement indicating how the loan funds are to be repaid, including repayment sources and time required, and copies of cash flow schedules, budgets, and other appropriate information.

6. *Business financial data*—

   Existing business: The past three years' financial statements plus currently dated balance sheets and profit and loss statements.

   New business: A pro forma balance sheet reflecting sources and uses of both equity and borrowed funds. (Equity money must be proven.)

7. *Projections*—Projections of future operations for at least the following year: expected income and expenses and the bases for the estimates.

8. *Collateral*—Assets or possessions offered to secure the loan.

The Small Business Administration (SBA) Office of Public Information issues this advice in its publication on *SBA Business Loans:*

1. Prepare a current financial statement listing all assets and all liabilities of the business; do not include personal items.

2. Prepare an earnings (profit and loss) statement for the previous full year, and for the current period to the date of the balance sheet.

3. Prepare a current personal financial statement of the owner, or each partner or stockholder owning 20 percent or more of the stock of the business.

4. List collateral to be offered as loan security, with your estimate of the present market value of each item.

5. State amount of loan requested, and explain exact purposes for which it will be used.

6. Take the above financial information with you to your banker. Ask for a direct loan. If the direct loan is declined, ask the bank to (a) give you a loan under SBA's Guaranty Loan Plan, or (b) participate with SBA in a loan. If the bank is interested, ask the banker to discuss your application with the SBA. In most cases, SBA deals directly with the bank on these two types of loans.

7. If neither the guaranty nor the participation loan is available to you, visit or write your nearest SBA office. Take your financial information with you on your first office visit, or include it in your first letter.

BANK LOANS   When an owner's money resources and those of his or her immediate family are exhausted, there are other choices: sell some of the owner's equity, take in a partner, discuss fiscal needs with possible outside investors, or go to a bank and talk to a loan officer. Asking a bank for a loan is essentially asking it to become a partner for a specified period of time and guaranteeing it, as a partner, a predetermined rate of earnings. Not all banks loan money, and in any bank the loan depends on the circumstances. Hence, it is good for an owner to get to know a bank officer. If the officer's bank cannot accommodate a request, the owner can at least rely on its recommendation to try another bank or to explore a loan that is guaranteed by the SBA. Certain preparations are needed before a loan is applied for. How much money is really needed? What is it needed for? What terms can be afforded? How long will it take to pay back the loan out of the profits of the business? Will the loan really do the job it is expected to do? What papers does the bank need and is the necessary information available? A business plan, a financial statement, a profit and loss statement, a cash flow statement, an inventory of all assets, property, and investments—all these are the basic ingredients that can bring results. Bank executives, especially in the current banking climate, are fairly hard-boiled. They've heard all the hard-luck stories before and are not really interested. They want to help you but only if their bank can profit in the process and be *assured* that it will get back its money plus a profit (interest). Loans are the product that banks sell. They want to lend money. But they also must make sure that they will get their money back.

BANKRUPTCY   When a business goes broke; when a state of insolvency develops; when bills pile up beyond the capacity to pay them; when an enterprise's liabilities become greater than its assets; when creditors gang up and force a business to close its doors and liquidate its assets in order to pay its bills—all of these are descriptions of bankruptcy, which strikes 400,000 starry-eyed new entrepreneurs each year. Its principal cause is lack of sufficient expertise in managing the business. The 1978 Bankruptcy Act offers two types of legal bankruptcy: Chapter 7 or involuntary bankruptcy, when creditors petition a court to close up an insolvent business; and Chapter 11 or voluntary bankruptcy, when owners petition the court, explain why the enterprise must cease doing business, and propose how they will attempt an orderly and equitable settlement of their just financial obligations. A federal District Court administers both types. The most common reasons for business management failures include:

1. Not keeping adequate records of business transactions.
2. Disregarding or misinterpreting financial statements.

3. Not controlling costs properly; letting the output become greater than the input.

4. Allowing poor internal control that invites thievery.

5. Being too short-sighted—not planning ahead.

6. Not emphasizing sales sufficiently.

7. Having insufficient working capital; overbuying; overpaying.

8. Not carrying enough insurance for emergencies.

9. Failing to train employees, especially those who are in contact with customers.

10. Not recognizing a need for professional help and delaying in getting this help when it is needed.

BAZAARS   Popular as fund-raising events, bazaars are usually sponsored by nonprofit organizations like churches, charities, and service and civic clubs, but they are equally adaptable to entrepreneurial enterprises. Shopping centers have promoted successful bazaars for both merchants and nonprofits by placing carts, booths, or kiosks in the mall. Reminiscent of country fairs, bazaars are economical to produce, require few fixtures, and invariably draw considerable crowds. In downtown Philadelphia, a Christmas bazaar has been held annually since 1928. Nearly 40 organizations set up individual booths in the ballroom of a local hotel and raise from $440 to $1,800 each during this two-day event. One participating agency held a "Santa's Pack" raffle and raised $6,300. The element of chance is traditional and increases profits in bazaar operations. The merchandise that sells best at bazaars includes new and unusual gifts, items geared to the season during which the bazaar is held, low-priced white elephant "treasures," plants, and, of course, foods. If a business takes trade-ins during normal business operations, then these items (if in good condition or spruced up) can be displayed for sale at bazaars. As a rule, useful items sell better than decorative ones and unusual items that are not available locally get the greatest attention. A commercial enterprise might select a local beneficiary—a charity or church or school—and donate a portion of a bazaar's proceeds to it, to help traffic and profits. Merchandise might even be obtainable on consignment, unsold items would be returnable right after the event. Bazaars are good grist for the publicity mills and fun for all participants.

BLACK ENTREPRENEURSHIP   This highly charged, supersensitive topic is best defined in terms of several black entrepreneurs who have "made it." Blacks represent the largest single minority and their estimated total spending power is in excess of $200 billion a year. If they were a separate economy, American blacks would be the world's ninth largest nation. In Los Angeles, which boasts America's largest concentration of black businesses and a hefty black political power base, there is not a single black commercial bank. Alonzo Wallette tried to start one but was forced to abandon the effort—famous and rich black entertainers and sports figures would not join in. His friend, well-to-do real estate developer Bondie Gambrell, pointed out that L.A.'s newer Asian community controls 30 commercial banks in the area: "The Koreans have figured out that the real color of freedom is green." Other latecomers to the American economy are Hispanics, who own 50 percent more enterprises than blacks; Asians now control nearly four times as many businesses as blacks do. Gambrell added, "Blacks have not had the mentality to do what the Koreans and Hispanics are doing . . . they have relied on others to make opportunities." Ironically, integration has helped to kill black entrepreneurism, with the exception of black West Indian immigrants who have fared very well in small businesses. American blacks in Miami deserted established black shops in droves when flashier Cuban franchises and supermarkets opened near their neighborhoods. Tony Brown, a New York TV personality, has stated, "Black-owned businesses dropped from 13.5 percent to 7 percent in the past 20 years." According to *Black Enterprise* magazine, lack of black community support has killed most black enterprises. (See *INC.* magazine, September, 1986, pp. 81–86.)

A more positive report on black participation in new businesses appeared in *Ebony* magazine (November 1987). Quoting the Small Business Administration, the article stated that an estimated 339,239 black businesses have produced roughly $12.5 billion in annual sales. *Ebony* offered the following steps as general guidelines for starting new business ventures:

1. Evaluate yourself to see if you should be a business owner (managerial and technical skills, personal finances).

2. Develop a salable idea that satisfies a need.

3. Study the potential market carefully, including customers' buying habits and strength of competition.

4. Seek advice from those who know—especially other established entrepreneurs.

5. Develop a comprehensive business plan, which provides both the entrepreneur and the investor with a blueprint.

6. Be persistent in seeking startup money; it will help to have absolutely credible projections.

7. Choose business partners carefully and use an attorney to draw up any agreement.

8. Establish good record-keeping procedures and an understanding of what they mean.

9. Assure a quality product or service, for good public relations—it is the simplest and most effective tool for business growth.

10. "If at first you don't succeed," and there are extenuating circumstances over which the entrepreneur has little control, don't give up—try again!

The above advice (and the proof of the Johnson publishing empire, which owns *Ebony*) reemphasizes that the rules of success are the same for all who enter the American entrepreneurial economy. Success is not colored white, black, or yellow—it's *green*.

BLACK-OWNED BUSINESSES

(See also *Black Entrepreneurship*.) In 1988 the Small Business Administration (SBA) provided, through its various programs, a total of 579 direct and guaranteed loans to black-owned small enterprises. These loans were worth $71 million. Through the Section 8(a) program, 1,800 contracts worth $1.4 billion were awarded that year to black-owned firms. More than 1,400 black-owned firms are in the Section 8(a) program, but more than 10,000 are listed in the computerized PASS operation. At the time of the 1980 census, there were 340,000 black-owned businesses in the United States. Of these, over 68 percent were in retail and service trades and the vast proportion of these firms (95 percent) were sole proprietorships. They accounted, however, for only 53 percent of black gross receipts. Black-owned automotive dealers and service stations led all other black industry groups in gross receipts—an achievement duplicated among Hispanic-owned small businesses. Businesses owned by Asian Americans were concentrated in the food and services sectors. California led in the number of black-owned business establishments (45,000 during the 1980 census). Illinois was second, not in numbers but in gross receipts, indicating that Chicago-area black-owned businesses were, on an average, larger in size. The 10 cities with the largest number of black-owned businesses were:

New York	17,350
Los Angeles	12,200
Chicago	10,300
Houston	10,000
Washington, DC	9,000
Detroit	6,800
Philadelphia	5,000
Dallas	4,900
Baltimore	4,000
Oakland	3,600

Brainstorming

A brainstorming session gathers a group of entrepreneurs from different business disciplines. New ideas are expressed to solve a business situation, formulate corporate policy, create a new concept or innovation, or stimulate one's own or others' ideas. The key to good brainstorming is to stimulate each group member to contribute ideas. Alex Osborne of Batten, Barton, Durstine & Osborne Advertising, Inc., a large New York advertising agency, is credited with having originated formal brainstorming sessions which, according to one agency principal, produced 44 percent more new ideas than the usual individual, "ivory tower" thinking. The chain reaction that often results from a good brainstorming session is contagious, stimulating, and beneficial to all participants. In arranging for a brainstorming session, certain ground rules should be observed:

- Only specific problems are to be discussed.
- No criticism of contributors is allowed.
- Quantities of contributions are the aim.
- Strive for improvements or elaborations on ideas already brought out.
- Focus attention on all participants and avoid small splinter groups and discussions.
- Keep reportorial, not verbatim records.

To function advantageously, a brainstorming session must have strong leadership in an almost formalized setting. The purpose of this technique is to come up with original ideas, or a combination of old ones that appear to be new, arising from the gut feelings of the participants and expressed without inhibitions.

Bureau of Industrial Economics

This agency of the Department of Commerce can be contacted at Room 4878, Washington, DC 20230, phone: (202) 377-1405. The Bureau maintains a staff of about 100 analysts who monitor specific industries. For anyone who plans to go into business in almost any industry, there will no doubt be a specialist at the Bureau who will share the available information and research. Some of the sections staffed by analysts are listed below. If a particular category is not listed, the telephone number above should be called to find an expert in the area of interest or enterprise.

Advertising

Aerospace equipment

Agricultural, construction, materials handling equipment

Aluminum, metals, materials

Building materials and products

Commercial printing

Computers; business and photographic equipment

Cutting tools, generators, welding and rolling mill equipment

Dairy products, tobacco, sugar, and grain products

Electronic components and accessories

Fertilizers

Foods and confectionary, retail and wholesale

Footwear, leather, luggage, leather goods

Franchising

General merchandise retailing

Glass and metal containers, plastic packaging

Hotel, motel, and recreation wholesale trades

Household furnishings, appliances, lamps

Housing construction

Lumber products

Machine tools, metal forming

Medical, surgical, dental, and opthalmic supplies

Metalworking machinery and equipment

Newspapers, publishing

Paper products, packaging

Pharmaceuticals and chemicals

Rubber and rubber products

Scientific and electronic instruments

Ship and boat building and repairs

Soaps, detergents, toilet preparations

Solid wastes

Textiles

Toys, games, silverware, ceramics, novelties, jewelry, musical

Truck and bus equipment

Water resources, waste water equipment

BUSINESS DEVELOPMENT CORPORATION (BDC)

A BDC is a business financing agency or corporation, usually made up of the financial institutions in an area or state and organized primarily to assist industrial concerns that have equipment and property but are unable to obtain assistance through normal channels. BDCs operate under the approval and guidance of the Small Business Administration. The risk of loans made by BDCs is spread among various members, and the interest charged on loans may vary somewhat from those charged by traditional institutions—that is, the BDC loans are usually a little higher, to take into account higher risk factors. Because BDC loans are made on collateral of real estate and equipment, appraisers determine the loan amount, the purpose of the loan, and the good that the requested loan can do for the community in increased employment, goods production, or exports. There are several hundred BDCs throughout the country. Because their activity changes periodically—sometimes charters are withdrawn by the SBA because of inactivity—entrepreneurs should check in with the nearest SBA field office for an up-to-date list of local or area BDCs.

BUSINESS DEVELOPMENT PUBLICATIONS

This series of pamphlets is produced by the Small Business Administration (SBA) for public purchase. Current charges range from $0.50 to $1.00 for each of the 60 titles currently available. The following topics are covered:

	Number of Available Pamphlets
Crime prevention	3
Financial management and analysis	13
General management and planning	28
Marketing	11
New products, ideas, inventions	2
Personnel management	3

The complete list of current SBA business development publications appears as Appendix C. Any of the booklets may be ordered, with payment by check or money order, from the United States Small Business Administration, P.O. Box 15434, Fort Worth, TX, 76119. Most of the titles may be purchased at SBA and SCORE offices, which are listed in Appendix A and can be found in the telephone-book blue pages under Small Business Administration.

BUSINESS MEETINGS

Getting together with prospective or active customers and clients, a lawyer or accountant, a trade or civic group, a supplier, a ladies' kaffee-klatsch, or a political cabal, can be fun and profitable if the purpose of the meeting is always kept in mind. Since time is part of an entrepreneur's stock-in-trade, it is wise to hew to a preset timetable. Some points to keep in mind when planning and attending business meetings are:

- There will usually be some people who come late. That's their tough luck. Suggest that they be brought up-to-date during intermission by one of the other attendees.

- Limit the number of people attending. Five is ideal; one dozen should be tops. Beyond that number, the meeting becomes a conference.

- Unless the meeting stretches beyond a manageable time, say 90 minutes, don't plan for any intermissions.

- If at all possible, use a tape recorder during discussions and comments. Let participants know that they are being taped.

- Analyze which meetings are important and which you can read about in subsequent reports; which ones are really necessary for you to attend and which you can have attended by a surrogate; which ones must be held and which are better covered by a memorandum. All of these judgments are important to save your precious time.

- If you ask questions, make them count. Ask only those that produce comments and discussions, not yes–no replies.

- Ask questions that contain only one point, and entertain questions from others that cover only one point. Some questioners like to hear themselves talk.

- Avoid confrontations with people who ask questions or make comments. Ask what their reason is for certain action, rather than a blunt, confrontational Why.

- Try to be neutral in your questioning; reserve opinions for later; mull over objections and disagreements till you have time to rationally and objectively formulate an answer.

- In case of an unsolvable conflict, ask more questions or turn the matter over to a small committee for further study.

BUSINESS NAME   Giving a name or title to a business, product, or company, and promoting it to identify it with the business seems like a simple task but can be most troublesome because it is fraught with all kinds of legal implications. Ernest and Julio Gallo are famous California winemakers. Their brother Joseph, who is not in the wine business with them, opened a cheese factory and called it Gallo Cheese Co. The winemakers promptly sued and won their case. A judge ruled that Joseph deliberately tried to cash in on the good will and advertising value of his brothers' long-established business. Had he named his cheese company the Joseph Gallo Cheese Company, chances are he would have gotten away with it. Had Joseph's tradename application included "not affiliated with any other Gallo company," it might also have been approved. While there is no hard and fast rule that determines proper use of a name—even if it is the owner's name—judges do look at the longevity of the first user's tradename, the territory in which the initial user does business, how conflicting the new business might be with the earlier one, and how well the original name is implanted in the minds of consumers. Some considerations in picking an effective trade name are:

- Don't be cutesy, unless you're a small gift shop or beauty salon.
- Don't use your children's names or a combination thereof.
- Don't use a name nobody can pronounce or remember.
- Don't use a name that sounds like it ought to belong to a totally different product or service.
- Don't use a blatant imitation of another, established name.
- Do use a name that is easy to say, easy to remember, pertinent to the product or service, and easy to reproduce on a sign or letterhead.

BUSINESS ORGANIZATIONS

The three types of business organizations can be compared for their relative advantages and disadvantages as follows:

	Advantages	Disadvantages
Proprietorship	Easiest to start	Unlimited liability of owner
	Most freedom	Death or illness of owner endangers business
	Maximum authority	
	Tax status	Growth limited to personal energy and skill
	Social security benefits for owner	Personal affairs easily mixed with business
Partnership	Joining of two or more skills, talents	Dissolution with withdrawal or death of partner
	Higher capital contributions	Bad partner creates unsolvable problems
	Improved credit rating	Often difficult to define authority, duties
	Reduced strain for each owner	Can limit growth

	Advantages	**Disadvantages**
Corporation	Limited liability of stockholders	Considerable legal formality
	Assured and greater continuity	Can be expensive to start
	Easy transfer of shares	Power limited to charter
	Management unaffected by ownership change	Limited freedom to make changes
	Easier to raise capital	

Business Plan

To plan and operate a successful business, it has always been necessary to have a business plan. In recent years it has re-emerged as a major topic of business talk, as if it were a unique discovery. What is a business plan? It is the guidepost for a business's existence, the road map that shows how to go forward on the road to success, the blueprint for building an enterprise, and the key that can open the door to a bank loan. Without a viable, complete, credible business plan, an owner is groping in the maze of entrepreneurship. With a business plan, the entrepreneur becomes a professional. It can lead to riches, or it can reveal pitfalls that have been ignored. Revealed pitfalls are not unconquerable stumbling blocks—they are incentives to do more research, learn more, do more checking, rein in enthusiasm until knowledge catches up with it. A business plan is the heart of a business's start and should contain:

1. Identification of the business, the owner, and all the people who are working on the startup

2. Goals of the proposed business and proof that they can be reached, including the need for and proposed uses of loans

3. Detailed description of the business, competition, and helpers

4. The market: Who, where, and how; prospects for growth

5. Competition, and how and why this business is as good or better

6. Location: Cost, zoning, growth feature, market access

7. Management: Detailed résumés, duties, incomes

8. Financial information on the owner and the supporters and their collective ability to pay back any loans

For more detail, see Gustav Berle, *The Do-It-Yourself Business Book* (New York: John Wiley & Sons, 1989), pp. 59–70. See also *Startup Advice.*

BUSINESS STARTUPS   It should be rare to have an entrepreneur who says: What kind of a
business do I want to start? Which kind would grow the most? Which
one will likely be in existence five years down the road? Where do I
want to start that business? Many entrepreneurs pose exactly these
questions, not knowing how and where to start; operating by the seat
of their pants; flying, so to speak, in a pea-fog. For those who need to
be prodded by some real facts, here are *statistically* proven answers to
some of these common questions. The listings are given in descending
order of importance.

Which businesses are started most frequently?
   Business services, eating and drinking establishments, shopping
   goods other than traditional retail merchandise, automotive repair
   shops, home construction, machinery and equipment distributors,
   real estate offices, retail stores, furniture and home furnishings,
   computer and data processing services.

Where are the best places to start a business?
   Manchester/Nashua, NH; Raleigh/Durham, NC; Nashville, TN;
   Boston, MA; Washington, DC; South Bend/Benton Harbor, IN;
   Atlanta, GA; Fort Wayne, IN; Orlando, FL; Austin, TX.

What industries offer the highest growth potentials?
   Commercial banking, electronic component manufacturing, paper-
   board container manufacturing, computers and office machines,
   paper products, plastic products, basic steel products, pharmaceuticals, communication equipment, partitions and fixtures.

Which businesses have the highest survival rates?
   Veterinary services, funeral services, dentists, commercial savings
   banks, hotels and motels, campgrounds and trailer parks, physi-
   cians, barbershops, bowling and billiards, grain crops.

BUY–SELL AGREEMENT   This pact between two partners,
or among the several partners or
stockholders of a company, spells out how those remaining in the
enterprise will buy out the interests of those who wish to sell their
interest and leave, or whose participation is terminated by death.
Almost like a prenuptial agreement between spouses, the buy–sell
agreement is used for sole proprietorships, partnerships, and close
corporations. If a partner dies and the business had the foresight to
take out partnership insurance, then this policy can buy out all or
most of the deceased partner's interest. This "continuity insurance" is
available for all types of enterprises. Any agreement between partners or stockholders, or even between a sole proprietor and a key
employee, must be signed by all parties involved and must specify the

use of any insurance policies. In case of death, the respective families would be required to abide by the agreement. Another reason for a buy–sell agreement is to provide for any exigency, such as a partnership dissolution. Differences in personalities, working habits, skills, spending, or methods of operating a business or of hiring help could all be causes for unhappiness among partners. The agreement should provide for these possibilities and must include a way in which a disinterested professional can appraise and evaluate the business at the time of the desired dissolution. A buy–sell agreement made at the time of the original business formation will minimize problems in the future and assure the continuance of the business and optimum cash retention by all parties.

BUYING A BUSINESS

The difference between a quick start to entrepreneurship or the acquisition of somebody else's headache depends on how assiduously a proposition is researched. A young entrepreneur might prefer to start a business or buy a franchise; an older one might be more inclined to buy a going business that requires less time to develop, especially if personal funds are available to invest. Two basic considerations must be considered: (1) Why does the seller want to get rid of the business? (2) Is this the kind of business that I can run and in which I will be happy? If an entrepreneur is satisfied that a business is being sold for personal reasons and not because of financial reverses or economic and demographic changes, then the first consideration is satisfied. The second question has an entirely personal answer that involves the necessary temperament, education, skills, and experience to take over a business and keep it running successfully. A third consideration is money—sufficient capital to make the down payment or meet whatever payments are agreed upon, capital to operate the business until cash flow develops adequately, and then perhaps another 25 percent to cushion against unforeseen circumstances that no amount of investigation and researching can predict. The source of information about a business could also have a bearing on the ultimate decision. If the buyer works through a business broker, is there an exclusive listing or are several brokers trying to sell the business? What are the bottom-line price and terms? Ultimately only a direct discussion with the seller or the estate representative will do. (See William A. Cohen, *The Entrepreneur and Small Business Problem Solver*, 2d ed. (New York: John Wiley & Sons, 1990), chapter 6.

CHECKLIST

The following points should be considered and answered satisfactorily before any formal commitment is made to purchase someone else's business.

1. What does the asking price actually cover? Inventory? Equipment? Good will? Receivables? Cash on hand?

2. Since good will is an intangible that is often overvalued by the seller, is this item negotiable?

3. How personal is this business? Will it suffer by the present owner's withdrawal? Will he or she be available for a while?

4. If the business shows a negative cash flow, why? Management? Product? Location? Economics? Fashion trends? Marital problems? Partnership problems? Security leaks? Owner's death?

5. What does the competition say about this business?

6. What is "the trade's" opinion about the business?

7. Will the seller retain some equity position so that the buyer's cash or loan requirements are minimized?

8. Will the seller keep the accounts receivables, or sell them at a substantial discount? How old are they?

9. What is the turnover of merchandise? The age of various parts of the inventory?

10. What kind of contracts exist? For the lease? Key employees? Major lines of merchandise? Raw material? Discounts?

11. Are there other innovative financing methods that will make the acquisition more economical and less dependent on outside financing?

12. Is the seller willing to let the buyer or the buyer's accountant examine at least the last three years' tax returns?

13. How good are the resources needed to continue the business? Payment terms? Discounts? Shipping details?

14. What forecast can be made about the future prospects of this business? Obsolescence? Trends? Popularity? Growth?

15. What recourse is there in the worst-scenario situation—the buyer cannot continue running the business but it is not yet paid off?

COSTS AND RED FLAGS

Type of Business	Price Offering Range	Watch Out for . . .
Apparel shops	.75 to 1.5 times net + equipment + inventory	Location/competition company image/specialization/shopping patterns/obsolete inventory/parking

Type of Business	Price Offering Range	Watch Out for . . .
Auto dealerships	1.25 to 2 times net + equipment	Type or brand/factory allocation policy/location/reputation/reliability of mechanics
Auto service stations	$1.25 to $2 per gallon pumped each month, including equipment	Traffic pattern/length of lease/lease terms/location/competition/gas supplier relations/gallons per month
Beauty salons	.25 to .75 times gross + equipment + inventory	Staff turnover/image/location/reputation/age of equipment
Fast-food stores	1 to 1.25 times net	Street traffic/service space/seating space/location/competition/lease terms/ franchise/maintenance
Grocery stores/ Supermarkets	.25 to .33 times gross including equipment	Nearby competition/lease terms/location/condition of facilities/alcoholic beverage permit/percentage of nongrocery lines
Insurance agency	1 to 2 times annual renewal commissions	Agent turnover/client mix/carrier characteristics/demographics of clients/transferability of clients
Local newspapers	.75 to 1.25 times gross, including equipment	Economic profile of circulation area/demographics/economic conditions/competition/advertiser loyalty
Manufacturers	1.5 to 2.5 times net including equipment + inventory	Single major customer/competition from abroad/relations with dealers or distributors/condition of plant and equipment/market position/labor relations

Type of Business	Price Offering Range	Watch Out for . . .
Personnel agency	.75 to 1 times gross (including equipment)	Staff turnover/reputation/ specialization/client relations
Real estate office	.75 to 1.5 times net + equipment + inventory	Intensity of competition/ tenure of sales associates/ reputation/franchise agreement
Restaurants	.25 to .50 times gross including equipment	History of previous failures/ location/reputation/ competition/lease/liquor license
Retail stores	.75 to 1.5 times net + equipment + inventory	Chain competition/lease term/location/competi- tion/company image/ specialization/shopping patterns/ obsolete inventory/parking
Travel agencies	.04 to .10 times gross including equipment	Where revenue comes from/ general climate for travel (international)/reputation/ location/relationships with key employees/member- ships (IATA, ASTA, etc.)
Video stores	1 to 2 times net + equipment	Obsolescence of tapes/chain store competition/location– traffic/customer match to inventory

CABLE TV (CATV) Community Antenna Television, the CATV system's actual name, was born in Pennsylvania in the 1970s and has reached its greatest heights in California. Cable television is an affordable advertising medium for small entrepreneurs; regular TV, with its larger audiences, has largely out-priced itself for businesses with small budgets and narrow markets. Cable TV usually offers better reception, a larger number of available channels, more focused local programming, and lower costs because of localized, limited audiences. For the small entrepreneur, these are advantages. For larger advertisers, cable TV can be too limiting. There are now more than 8,000 cable systems in the country; each is limited to a specific community. In the nation's top markets, the average cable TV penetration is 67 percent. The top 10 cable TV states are: Wyoming, Connecticut, Hawaii, Delaware, West Virginia, New Jersey, Kansas, Massachusetts, New Hampshire and Kentucky; all have from 57 to 71 percent cable TV coverage. The top 10 cities with cable TV subscribers are: Marquette, MI; Erie, PA; Bakersfield, CA; Palm Springs, CA; Syracuse, NY; Santa Barbara, CA: Wichita, KS; Laredo, TX; San Angelo, TX; and Biloxi, MS, in that order. All have between 77 and 88.5 percent cable TV ownership. Some marketing experts feel that owners of cable TV are people who are more innovative, more receptive to new ideas and marketing via the television screen. Costs can be reasonable if announcements are bought as a package of 10, 20, or more over a period of time. Production can be economical if owners, who know their product or service best, do their own "pitch."

CAPITAL   The money available for investment in an enterprise and the total of accumulated assets on hand for production of goods or acquisition of property is called capital. When entrepreneurs begin a business, their capital is the total of their property plus the money resources they can make available for the business (their own savings, borrowings, and loans) plus whatever they will need to live on while the business gets going. Once their enterprise is making money, it will accumulate capital in the form of surplus cash, securities, property, goods, and sound accounts receivable. The need for capital ("capital requirements") is invariably more than anticipated. Some financial advisors suggest that entrepreneurs make a list of all capital requirements and then add 25 percent—the margin of the unexpected. One of the most important and often overlooked expense items is personal living costs. Entrepreneurs can tighten their belts only so much. Appearances must be kept and owners must remain healthy and happy while they develop the business. Developing a business may take longer than anticipated. Expected customers may not come through; others who promised quick payment may demur or claim hard times. A sudden illness in the family, an automobile accident, or a burst water heater at home may demand extra cash. For innumerable reasons, cash reserves are needed. Capital needs are like grandmother's chicken soup recipe: for every ingredient, add a spoonful for the pot. Entrepreneurs should always add something extra for the pot.

CAR LEASING

To buy or to lease a car is a decision that small entrepreneurs have wrestled with for years. One major advantage of leasing is that, with a good leasing contract, a small business can conserve some up-front capital. Automotive authorities have estimated that a 4-year-old car costs $1,900 a year to operate (or less than $160 a month) while the average new car costs closer to $3,500 (or nearly $292 a month). Weighing all the costs and benefits entailed in leasing, here are some pros and cons pointed out by an accountant:

For leasing:
- Lessees no longer lose a tax deduction for interest they would have paid on a car loan, since the deduction for personal interest is being phased out.
- Monthly leasing payments are often lower than car loan payments.
- At the end of a lease, lessees can usually opt to buy the car at a specified price based on "blue book" value.

Against leasing:
- Car leases often set a specified annual mileage allowance and make additional charges if this preset allowance is exceeded.
- Some leases mandate maintenance that could be in excess of what lessees normally give a car.
- Minor cosmetic damages could be chargeable at the conclusion of the lease.
- Premature lease cancellation is usually accompanied by a substantial penalty.
- Comprehensive insurance must be carried on behalf of the lessor and this expense is included in the cost of the lease.

For current updates on tax advantages and disadvantages of leasing vs. ownership, especially if only one or two vehicles are involved, entrepreneurs should check with an accountant.

CARD DECKS

A method of promoting or merchandising books, publications, stationery, office equipment, or anything that can be sold by mail is to prepare and mail card decks. This direct response advertising approach utilizes a number of postcard-size advertising pieces that are mailed together, usually in a sealed plastic pouch, to a large list of prospects who have purchased merchandise by mail or bought subscriptions to trade and professional magazines. The Standard Rates and Data Service publishes the telephone-directory size *Business Publication Rates and Data, Part II,*

Direct Response, which lists all the companies that sell participation in card deck mailings. A major publisher of business books promotes selected titles periodically, each described on one mail-in order card, to a list of about 300,000 executives and claims an average of 4 percent response. While it costs from $1,000 to $3,000 for a single card to be included, card deck mailings are targeted advertising that can produce direct, traceable results. As an example of available mailings in which an entrepreneur can participate, one company offers the following availabilities: 16,000 security item dealers, 62,000 local government purchasing agents, 30,000 boating dealers, 55,000 building industry specifiers and buyers, 30,000 members of the small commercial airline industry, 37,000 fire chiefs, 80,000 real estate investors, 28,000 buyers in the robotics industry, 17,000 swimming pool builders and servicers, and 28,000 executives in the waste industry. (See also *Standard Rates and Data Service.*)

CASH FLOW   The amount of money actually available to make purchases and pay current bills and obligations is one of the most vital functions of fiscal control. If cash flow projections show a shortage at some periods during the year, owners need to take steps in advance to implement their cash flow. Maintaining a good cash flow chart is one way to avoid unpleasant surprises and to have an instrument for discussion of a possible shortfall with a banker when applying for a short-term loan. Here are a half-dozen steps to increase the health of cash flow:

1. Take advantage of discounts offered by your suppliers.
2. Control buying to goods that are cost-effective and necessary; sell underutilized inventory already on hand.
3. Keep close control on inventory (unsold inventory costs money for storage and increases obsolescence).
4. Bill as soon as goods are delivered or services rendered; don't wait till some future time or the end of the month.
5. Improve collection proceedings by offering discounts for early payment, adding penalties to late payments, and keeping meticulous track of payment deadlines.
6. Tighten up credit policies as much as circumstances (valued customer, competitive practices) allow and be more selective in extending credit.

Cash flow control is especially important when a business is highly seasonal. Many businesses do a substantial amount of their business during the Christmas season; others need to purchase raw material all at once, during certain times of the year, in order to obtain their

CASH FLOW CHART

	Jan	Feb	Mar	Apr	May	Jun	Jul	Aug	Sep	Oct	Nov	Dec
1. Cash in bank first day of month												
2. Petty cash at first day of month												
3. Total cash (1 + 2)												
4. Expected cash sales												
5. Expected collections												
6. Other income expected												
7. Total cash receipts (4 + 5 + 6)												
8. Total cash and receipts (3 + 7)												
9. All cash paid out in month												
10. Cash balance at end of month (8 − 9 = 10). Starting cash for following month.												

needed supply at best prices. Some owners depend on unexpected "close-out" purchases to increase their sales and profits. On-hand cash or a good credit line at the bank is essential. The cash flow chart at left will help to document these needs.

CENSUS DATA   The Bureau of the Census, an information collection agency within the United States Department of Commerce, employs more than 3,500 people and an annual budget of $38 million to gather, process, and disseminate data about our population. Entrepreneurs are well advised to make use of Census information that may help their planned or projected business operations. Section chiefs can be contacted by mail or phone for free statistical information. User fees are charged for some reports or computer data. The general contact is: Bureau of the Census, Department of Commerce, Washington, DC 20233, phone: (301) 763-5190. The principal *economic* divisions of the Bureau are:

	Phone
Agriculture—crop and livestock, farm economics	(301) 763-5230
Business	(301) 763-2360
Construction—special trades, building permits, starts, sales	(301) 763-7163
Governments—revenue sharing, taxation	(301) 763-7366
Manufacturers—durables, nondurables, exports	(301) 763-7666
Retail trade	(301) 763-7561
Service industries	(301) 763-7039
Transportation	(301) 763-1744
Wholesale trade	(301) 763-5281

The Census Bureau has 12 regional offices that offer user assistance:

	Phone
Atlanta, GA	(404) 881-2271
Boston, MA	(617) 223-2327
Charlotte, NC	(704) 371-6142
Chicago, IL	(312) 353-6251
Dallas, TX	(214) 767-2621
Denver, CO	(303) 234-3924
Detroit, MI	(313) 226-7742
Kansas City, KS	(913) 236-3728
Los Angeles, CA	(213) 209-6616
New York, NY	(212) 264-3860
Philadelphia, PA	(215) 597-4920
Seattle, WA	(206) 442-7828

CENTER FOR FAMILY BUSINESS This small organization, located in Cleveland, Ohio, since 1962, focuses on the success and survival of small, family owned enterprises and facilitates their being passed on to a younger member of the family upon the retirement or demise of the elder owner. The Center is operated by Leon A. Danco, Ph D and Katy Danco. Several times a year they conduct a seminar, in Cleveland, on "Managing Succession Without Conflict." A number of books they have written on the subject can be ordered directly from the Center. Considering the very personal and emotional problem of passing the gavel in a family business, the advice of this expert outside source could be very valuable indeed. Contact: P.O. Box 24268, Cleveland, OH 44124, phone: (216) 442-0800.

CERTIFIED DEVELOPMENT COMPANIES (CDC) These are private–public investment companies composed of private or local lenders, banks, and local Small Business Administration (SBA) offices. They provide small businesses with financing for periods of up to 20 years, for the acquisition of land, buildings, machinery, and equipment; construction; or modernization, renovation, or restoration. A CDC is nominally a nonprofit company set up by Public Law 504 and monitored and backed by the SBA. Usually, a local CDC, interested in fostering business and adding to employment in its area, sells authorized debentures in order to raise money for a business making a loan application. The SBA guarantees up to 40 percent of the project, the local lending institution backs 50 percent, and the loan applicant is expected to come up with 10 percent. The CDC operates in the locale or region defined by its charter and numbers 25 or more members who share an interest in their community. Membership is composed of representatives of government, private-sector lending institutions, business concerns, and community organizations. At least one of the directors must have commercial lending experience and at least five directors must meet quarterly. The SBA requires that at least two loans be placed annually in order for a CDC to remain functional under its guarantee loan program. Loans can go up to $750,000 under this program, but one basic criterion must be followed: for each $15,000 of a CDC loan, one new job must be created or an old job retained. There are, on an average, 400 CDCs active nationwide at any one time. Addresses are available at commercial banks or the nearest SBA office.

CDCs must have a full-time staff to market the P.L. 504 program and to close and service the CDC loan portfolio. The program allows funds to flow into community businesses through the sale of 100 percent SBA-guaranteed debentures to private investors, in amounts of up to 40 percent of a project or a maximum of $750,000. Most projects supported are in the $1 million to $2 million class. The minimum amount of CDC participation is $50,000. Since a proprietor applying for a CDC debenture puts up 10 percent of the loan equity, and a private lender institution advances 40 percent, collateral is usually as follows: a mortgage on the land and the building being financed; liens on machinery, equipment, and fixtures; and lease assignments. The private-sector lender is secured by a first lien in the project and the SBA holds a second lien. Fees are set by prior agreement of the SBA with the CDC. Eligible businesses should have net worths not exceeding $6 million and average after-tax profits of not over $2 million. Contact: The nearest SBA office.

CHAMBER OF COMMERCE

Local business people can form an association called a Chamber of Commerce when they group together to promote private enterprise, their community, and their trade or profession. There are about 4,500 chambers of commerce in the United States and many more in other countries. About 60 percent of these local chambers are members of the national United States Chamber of Commerce, which conducts professional and legislative programs on a national and international level. Local chambers in major business communities are often managed by paid professionals, aided by local volunteers. They conduct activities, programs, seminars, and exhibits to promote business; conduct local legislative campaigns in favor of the chambers' aims and viewpoints; help members to promote their businesses; act as local information bureaus for visitors and newcomers; and disseminate information favorable to entrepreneurship and their community. Membership in a local chamber of commerce can be particularly useful to new enterprises, to get to know other businesspeople and competitors and to network products and services. A chamber decal on the door of a store or office and a mention of membership on business stationery have real and psychological impact that can be worth the cost of membership. Most states have a central chamber of commerce, which acts as a clearinghouse for local chambers (see Appendix A). About 135 chambers across the country house chapters of the Service Corps of Retired Executives (SCORE). (See also SCORE.)

COENTREPRENEURS

Coentrepreneurs are the 1990s' version of a "mom-and-pop business." Usually a couple but not always married, they start and operate an up-to-date, modern, and, as often as not, professional or high-tech type of enterprise. Since Americans are prone to association-forming, it is not surprising that in Eugene, Oregon, Frank and Sharan Barnett formed the National Association of Entrepreneurial Couples (NAEC) and in 1989 published a book on the subject: *Working Together; Entrepreneurial Couples* (available from NAEC, P.O. Box 3238, Eugene,

OR 97403-3238). In the Great Depression, mom-and-pop businesses proliferated as the result of economic necessity; during WWII and the postwar decades there was a hiatus in this kind of enterprise formation. In the 1980s, however, about a half-million couples formed and ran businesses together as coentrepreneurs—with varying success. The planning and compromising needed for a man and woman to work together as coequals are similar to the marriage itself. If the marriage is sound, the business has every chance of surviving and prospering; if the marriage is beset with problems, then the business will be prone to serious rifts. The Barnetts say that "far too many of us have acquiesced to the cultural myths and biases" that sever personal—and business—relationships. Coentrepreneuring, admittedly, is not for all spouses. Separation of responsibilities, compromise of differences, limits on the amount of work and the number of hours devoted to the business, planned private time together, including vacations and business trips to conventions and shows, and mutually agreeable ways of handling finances must be recognized and enforced, to make coentrepreneuring work. The alternatives, divorce and bankruptcy, are not viable.

COLLECTIONS   The conversion of accounts receivable to cash, known as collection, is when the buck "in the mail" becomes the buck in the hand. Every entrepreneur who extends credit to customers or clients—whether to retailers and wholesalers, for products, or consultants and professionals for services—will need to set up a policy and a system to effect the collection of money owed to the enterprise. Someone once said that cash creates no enemies. It would be wonderful if all payment for goods or services was rendered as soon as they were received. The prolific use of credit cards in recent years has made a cash economy more pragmatic. However, many customers and clients prefer being billed after a purchase or after a service is rendered, and the vendor has no choice but to bill later and hope for the best. A study showed that doctors who bill immediately after service have a collection rate of close to 100 percent; doctors who bill at the end of the month have a 65 percent collection rate. Collection agencies, the recourse for entrepreneurs owed long-overdue debts, put "red flags" on these situations and people:

- A client pledges his or her own accounts to a factor or bank.
- Other suppliers have brought claims against or obtained judgments against a client or customer.
- Financial information sought is being refused.
- Frequent changes are noted in a bank account.

- If called for inquiry about the money, the customer shows considerable annoyance.
- The customer makes promises to remit, but reneges.
- The customer's purchases are beyond normal needs.
- Normal payments are slowing down and excuses are speeding up.
- If the customer has a credit rating, it has suddenly declined.

Entrepreneurs should try to effect collections within 60 days; after that, they become difficult. Turning collections over to a collection agency not only cuts out 25 to 50 percent of receipts but loses the customer.

COMMERCE DEPARTMENT (UNITED STATES DEPARTMENT OF COMMERCE)

One of the federal government's largest and most useful agencies, this Department's purpose is to encourage, promote, and serve the economic development and technological advancement of American business. The Department employs nearly 26,000 people, has an annual budget of more than $1.5 billion, and has under its umbrella no less than 13 major divisions which can be of help to the entrepreneur. For information on available help and the name of someone who can advise on application procedures for possible assistance, contact: Office of Business Liaison, U.S. Department of Commerce, 14th and Constitution Avenue, NW, Room 5898C, Washington, DC 20230, phone: (202) 377-3176. Check also: Matthew Lesko, *Information U.S.A.* (New York: Viking-Penguin, 1986).

The major Commerce Department divisions are:

International Trade Administration, Room 3850, phone: (202) 377-2867. Promotes trade development, especially American exports.

National Oceanic and Atmospheric Administration, Room 5813, phone: (202) 377-2985. Environmental concerns; predicts conditions.

U.S. Travel and Tourism Administration, Room 1524, phone: (202) 377-3811. Collects, analyzes, and disseminates tourism data.

Minority Business Development Agency, Room 5053, phone: (202) 377-1936. Provides market opportunities for minority business.

National Institute of Standards and Technology, Gaithersburg, MD 20899, phone: (301) 921-1000. Has 15 centers for technological research and assistance, including a 21st-century robotics shop; makes research and applied systems available to private enterprises.

Patent and Trademark Office, phone: (703) 557-3158. Examines and issues patents, registers trademarks; maintains scientific library and search files for applicants' use.

Bureau of the Census, phone: (202) 763-5190. Collects, tabulates, and publishes data for the evaluation of economic programs.

National Technical Information Service (NTIS), 5285 Port Royal Road, Springfield, VA 22161, phone: (703) 557-4660. Sells a wide variety of government-sponsored research, engineering reports. Publishes excellent *Directory of Federal and State Business Assistance* (PB88-101977).

COMMERCIAL LOANS

The 14,500 commercial banks in the United States are the major source of business capital; they issue about 85 percent of the loans granted to operating small businesses. Credit is the lifeblood of most entrepreneurs, providing them with the financial means to get started, obtain equipment, build inventory, develop new lines of merchandise, or expand. The banks that are the sources of most of this capital are in the business of lending money to well-managed, creditworthy enterprises. However, commercial banks have set up criteria that must be met before a loan can be approved. A borrower must supply the following information:

1. Description of the business—how the loan will help.
2. Management—complete personal résumés for each principal.
3. Equity—how much owners can put into the business; if they borrow from others, too, how they will pay back.
4. Collateral—current appraisals that will support a potential bank loan.
5. Financial information—a three-year financial statement or, for a future business, accurate projections.
6. Use of funds—a breakdown of the intended use of the loan and corroborating claims or statements.
7. Personal financial statement—for each owner or partner, or any stockholder owning more than 20 percent.

The amount requested should be only enough to be used effectively. This is vital: Loans have to be paid back, with interest, and the business operation must generate sufficient cash flow to assure the loan officer of its capability to make stipulated payments. The collateral put up has to have a greater value than the amount borrowed, liquidity, and a stable economic life. Personal guarantees are invariably required as well. (See also *Loans.*)

COMMERCIAL MORTGAGES

An owner who plans to buy, construct, or enlarge a building or to purchase a piece of unimproved property (land) will probably need a loan in the form of a mortgage. Usually the property is appraised by the bank's or another licensed appraiser and 75 to 80 percent of the resulting evaluation is lent for a period of 10 to 20 years. The cost of the appraisal is charged to the applicant. Property that has a loan value can be mortgaged to gain additional cash or to obtain a second mortgage, against the new property. The interest rate on the second property will not be affected by the interest on the first property. Generally, second mortgage rates are higher than first mortgage rates, because the risk is higher. The other types of commercial mortgages are:

Chattel mortgage—a lien against personal property such as equipment, tools, or machinery. Since the Uniform Commercial Code (UCC) covers this type of transaction, it is identical throughout the United States and its possessions (Louisiana is the only exception).

Adjustable rate mortgage (ARM)—allows the interest rate to be flexible, changing with general market conditions, until the loan matures and is paid off.

Closed-end mortgage—executed under a deed of trust (a formal agreement) that prohibits both repayment before maturity and repledging of the same collateral without the permission of the mortgage holder. Open-end mortgage—opposite of closed end. The borrower may secure additional funds from the lender, usually below a stipulated ceiling amount that can be borrowed.

COMMITTEES

Groups that meet regularly for discussion and policy directives can be designated as committees. Managing by committee is popular in large companies, political and social organizations, and government. Entrepreneurs generally do not manage by committee, although the use of management teams, advisors, consultants, and boards of directors are not only commonplace but desirable. One of the world's pioneer entrepreneurs, Dr. F. Porsche, who developed the famed German car that carries his name, once commented: "Committees are, by nature, timid. They are based on the premise of safety in numbers; content to survive inconspicuously, rather than take risks and move independently ahead. Without independence, without the freedom for new ideas to be tried, to fail, and ultimately to succeed, the world will not move ahead, but live in fear of its own potential." The ideal committee that a small business could explore might consist of a lawyer, an accountant, a banker or financial expert, a representative of the end-use of the small company's product or service, and anybody who can lend stature, reputation, encouragement, and ideas to the enterprise. Board members who have stature, name recognition, and professional expertise will be valuable public relations or image assets to the enterprise. Their names are impressive on the letterhead and useful when recommendations to suppliers, lenders, and potential customers or clients are needed.

COMPETITION

Rivalry in the marketplace, or competition, is part of a capitalistic economy; the public tends to reward the more efficient producer or supplier. Factors that can make a competitor superior are: better quality, service, promotion, lower pricing, improved display or packaging, timing, new or additional benefits, location (convenience), and the nebulous, often indefinable ingredient called image. Some products win with aggressiveness, cutthroat competition, wild claims, and inordinate incentives to their salespeople. However, these techniques are not suited to every entrepreneur's personality and they sometimes become counterproductive and backfire in the long run. Competition's inroads can be blunted in some perfectly permissible and legal ways:

- Buy a competitor's product, analyze it, dissect it, evaluate it, and find its weak points.
- If the competitor does any advertising or promotion, try to get a copy of the material for scrutiny.
- Peruse trade or professional publications, computerized information services clipping bureau output, stock brokerage reports on competitors' stocks, or reports on patent applications in the "Official Gazette."
- Ask stock brokers and other security analysts for information on presently traded stocks or upcoming issues.
- Hire a professional investigator, market researcher, or consultant familiar with the field.
- Establish a security policy and modus for your own company that covers all of your employees.
- Have big ears—at trade shows, business meetings, and even in the office elevators; have big eyes—in the business pages, watch for contracts received and personnel changes.

COMPUTER ABUSE AND PROTECTION AGAINST IT

Computer crime causes an estimated $40 billion damage annually, yet only 1 percent is detected and prosecuted. For long-term help, get a copy of *A Small Business Guide to Computer Security* (LF-001) from any Small Business Administration Office of Business Development. Here are eight initiating steps to prevent computer abuse:

1. Assign a computer password and security code to anyone who uses the computer.
2. Train employees in the importance of security measures; change passwords frequently, on an irregular basis.
3. Keep a meticulous computer log and review it occasionally to make sure employees not authorized to work in certain areas do not overstep their limitations.
4. Insist that employees log in and log out each time they use the computer, no matter how briefly.
5. Create a system of checks and balances. An employee who records or signs checks should not be same one who works on the accounts payable.
6. Shred or otherwise destroy sensitive material from the computer printout. Keep diskettes and other vital data in a safe, locked compartment.
7. Make backup copies of all vital material. Store them in fire-proof, waterproof containers, preferably off the premises.
8. Spot-check usage of computer by employees, to reveal possible abuses of the system and keep pertinent employees on their toes.

COMPUTER APPLICATIONS FOR SMALL BUSINESSES

Accounts Receivable	Keeping a daily register of invoices. Keeping a daily record of adjustments. Keeping a daily record of cash receipts. Preparing customer statements. Summarizing due and past-due accounts.
Accounts Payable	Storing vendors' names, addresses, and purchases. Keeping schedules of open accounts. Registering transactions and general ledger disbursements. Making out checks and remittances. Keeping a list of paid items.
Inventory Control	Maintaining perpetual reports on stock status. Producing physical inventory worksheets. Listing items and quantities in stock. Recording receipts and adjustments. Printing out low-stock reports.

Payroll	Maintaining master inquiry files on employees.
	Making out payroll checks and earnings statements.
	Preparing W-2 and other tax forms.
	Tracking vacations, holidays, and sick days.
	Transferring information to proper registers.
General Ledger	Maintaining the ledger.
	Running up trial balances.
	Preparing balance sheets.
	Preparing statements of financial condition.
	Preparing income statements.
	Listing transactions and charts of accounts.
Planning	Creating spreadsheets for proper analysis of company performance.
	Analyzing different scenarios to see how they would affect the numbers (material cost, employee changes, style changes, etc.)
Non-Accounting Functions	Correspondence.
	Record-storage.
	Promotion response record.
	Commission-vs.-sales ratios.

COMPUTER SECURITY

The proliferation of computer use by all sizes of businesses has increased the need to protect these vital information systems. Small businesses use primarily micro- and minicomputers, but even these are subject to losses for which the usual protection against theft, fire, or embezzlement is inadequate. Even though Congress has enacted the Computer Fraud and Abuse Act, and most states have laws that specifically protect against computer fraud, high-tech criminals have found ways of using computers for devious and illegal purposes. Computers store a small business's entire operational information—personnel records, tax records, inventories, accounts receivable, accounts payable, shipments, bank accounts, and all other vital data—on small diskettes that easily fit into a pocket; their advantages of size and capacity increase their vulnerability. Still, a small to moderate size enterprise should not hesitate to computerize its operation. The advantages in streamlining a business far outweigh the possible dangers. Security measure can be overdone and become too costly. A balance between the threats to which a computer system is exposed and the cost of addressing those threats can be found with proper analysis and/or advice from computer experts. Protection against theft and fire is simple: know the real cost of producing computer records and take out coverage to compensate for those real costs in the event of a tragedy. More subtle and insidious are the unseen dangers: outsiders who can gain access to private information, or disgruntled employees who can access proprietary information, divert money or goods, or destroy records—with surprisingly small chance of being caught. Being knowledgeable about computers and sensitive to potential losses are an entrepreneur's first steps. (See *Computer Abuse and Protection Against It.*)

COMPUTERS   For many entrepreneurs starting out in a business during middle age, the computer is an obstacle comparable to a Marine qualification course but one of the most valuable obstacles they will ever overcome. (See *Computer Applications for Small Businesses.*) The world of the 1990s seems to be hooked on computers but first-time users still need to employ some cautions in making the leap. Several questions need to be answered:

1. What kind of computer should be selected? The kind of computer selected depends on the answer to question 2. Most newcomers to the world of chips, bytes, and rams use the WYFANU method: "What your friends and neighbors use." If they are happy with theirs and it does about the same job as the one envisioned, then the selection method is as good as any.

2. What functions should the computer have? Make a list of the functions needed and go over it with an informed friend or teacher or a computer sales rep.

3. Who will operate the computer? It would be wise for any owner to learn how to use the computer expertly, even if someone is hired to run it. No entrepreneur wants to be at the mercy of a machine or its operator. And never forget: The computer is a machine. It needs a human being to instruct it what to do. Knowing its proper functions is a protection against its fraudulent use.

4. What is the alternative to the computer? The human brain. No matter how great, the computer does not have the intelligence of the human mind. If anything goes wrong with it, if the "file" gets lost, or a power outage closes down a business, files and brains remain.

5. Should a computer be purchased or rented? New users who are not quite sure of computers' uses should rent, to try before they buy.

CONSULTANT   When corporate executives, civil service administrators, or Pentagon potentates retire or are given their golden parachutes, they often become consultants— independent contractors who are specialists in some field and provide advice for a fee. There are consultants in accounting, finance, management, merchandising, and marketing. Nearly 100,000 consultants cover just about every need, and half of them are one-person operations. Their number is growing at an estimated rate of 10 percent annually. They, too, are entrepreneurs, most flexible entrepreneurs. Their startup costs are the price of some good stationery, possibly a separate business telephone, and "sincere" business attire. Consultants can work out of their home, their garage, a telephone-equipped car, a shared secretarial suite, or a fancy office. What do consultants need? Lots of contacts, perhaps those made during corporate, military, or government careers; previous associations might offer customer connections, reference points, and credibility. The consultant's tasks are to convince a client that the latter has a problem and that the consultant is the one to solve that problem—for a price, of course—and then to come up with an idea and a written proposal for a solution. It is difficult to determine a fair fee: $25 to $100 an hour or $200 to $1,000 a day are not unusual. Charges depend on the problem, the wealth of the client, the consultant's reputation and track record, and the length of the assignment. Since having the right connections is a consultant's stock-in-trade, belonging to the proper organizations is a basic decision and a major investment. Remember that Lord Chesterfield's first assignment to his new bank clerk was, "Come and walk down the street with me!"

CONSULTANT, HOME-BASED

Consulting is a business that can be and most frequently is conducted from the entrepreneur's home. A consultant's clients are elsewhere anyway and the consultant goes to see them, not vice versa. This business can be conducted full- or part-time; by the hour, the day, or the week; directly or through another company; as an independent or as a moonlighter still employed by a larger company. Along with all its advantages, working out of a home as a consultant has certain restrictions, requirements, and parameters. Anyone serious about it should have a separate business telephone line and an answering device or service, and a comfortable and efficient working space that is distinctly separated from living and family activity quarters. The separate space is important for both efficiency and tax purposes. Children should be kept out of the office and away from the telephone. Stationery and business cards should be the affordable best; they are sales tools, reminders, part of an image. Some highly specialized personnel agencies hire consultants, especially in high-tech fields, by the day or longer. A startup consultant may want to be registered with one or more of them. Joining professional, social, and business organizations where networking is possible can be very profitable. (Dues are tax-deductible.) Membership in the chamber of commerce and volunteer work with ACE and the active sector of

SCORE will produce some gratuitous consulting, but will usually line up contacts and paid work. Look into lecturing at a local community or four-year college or be available as a guest lecturer. For tax purposes, all business-related expenditures must be documented; no deductions can be claimed without a receipt or other proof.

CONSULTING The ways to start a successful consulting enterprise continue to be important for profitability throughout the life of the firm:

1. Be visible by writing a book, authoring articles in professional or trade publications, or giving talks before important groups.
2. Think and act positively; enthusiasm and confidence show.
3. Believe in yourself and trust that others will want to buy the knowledge and skills you possess.
4. Network through professional and trade groups to make sure you are well known in your field.
5. Create a business plan for yourself. Maintain lists of potential clients, create good stationery, develop your sales approach, and determine all your charges and billing.
6. Make sure you have enough savings; weeks may pass before you get enough business to survive or between assignments.
7. Be sure you have an idea, even before you start, where your business will be coming from.
8. Keep your overhead low until you are established. If you need reliable help, get it from freelancers, graduate students, or moonlighters.

Two recommended books on this subject are: *Consulting: The Complete Guide to a Profitable Career*, by Robert E. Kelley (New York: Charles Scribner's Sons, 1986); and *Marketing Your Consulting and Professional Services*, by Richard A. Conros, Jr. (New York: John Wiley & Sons, 1985).

CONTRACT LABOR Part-time employees who are hired temporarily for specific tasks, pay their own taxes and other withholdings, furnish their own tools, and work their own hours are contract labor. Other than being instructed by the contractor or company, they are independent. Contract labor offers the advantages of a reduction of employer responsibility for payroll taxes and bookkeeping burden, avoidance of payment for idle time and vacations, and the absence of health and insurance benefits and of provision of transportation and equipment. Many small entrepreneurs resort to contract labor, especially in home improvements and home services industries and when they need temporary office help, consultants of various types, and handicraft workers who produce units of goods at their homes. If contract labor sounds too convenient, the entrepreneur or prime contractor must be aware of numerous restrictions imposed by the IRS and possibly by federal and state departments of labor. In the worst-case scenario, the IRS can come back at some future time and penalize the entrepreneur for back taxes and benefit payments that the contract laborer forgot to pay. The degree of control exercised by contractors is crucial. The latter must not specify when and how the work is to be done, if they wish to preserve their status as contractors with limited tax obligations. Similarly, contractors cannot perform their own solicitation of work and then turn the performance of such work over to an outside contract laborer without assuming tax liabilities. For a detailed reading of the law, see U.S. Department of Labor, *Regulations, Part 530—Homeworkers,* or consult an attorney familiar with labor law.

COOPERATIVE ADVERTISING

This form of advertising can be divided into two types: (1) advertising for which the manufacturer or supplier pays, usually jointly with a retailer, and (2) advertising that is produced and financed by a group of merchants in a neighborhood or shopping mall. If a merchants' association exists in a neighborhood or shopping center and has an operating promotion program, including a joint or cooperative advertising program, it would pay a new entrepreneur—especially an independent merchant—to join this effort. Coop ads are more economical, have a larger circulation than any solo promotion, and—as it says on our coins—*e pluribus unum.* Loosely translated, this means there's strength in numbers. Attractions of one store rub off on the others, and vice versa, which is the reason for leasing space in a shopping center in the first place. The cooperative advertising method should be investigated and watched carefully. Many manufacturers and suppliers have built into the price structure of their product or service a small percentage for cooperative advertising. Some of that percentage is rebated when the manufacturer's or supplier's product or service is advertised, but, if the ad appears in a newspaper or magazine, a tearsheet (the full page containing the ad) must be submitted with the invoice. The ad must conform with the rules set up by the supplier. The amount rebated usually depends on either a special arrangement (such as when a new product is first introduced) or a fixed percentage of purchases. Make sure to use this coop money or a larger competitor in the same market will absorb the promotional allowance. A media rep or advertising agency can explain how to get the most out of any cooperative advertising contract.

CORPORATION   A legal entity that is chartered by a state or the federal government, a corporation is separate and distinct from the person or persons who own it. A corporation may own property, borrow money, incur debts, enter into contracts, sue, or be sued. Its owners or shareholders are generally protected from liability and can lose only the money they have invested in the corporation. A corporation can sell stock that can easily be resold and transferred. Regardless of who runs the corporation or holds stock in it, people can be changed as needed and the organization continues with their replacements. Corporations generally obtain credit and loans more easily than individuals do. Twenty percent of all businesses are incorporated, but they hold 90 percent of all business revenue and 75 percent of them report profits. Corporations can be formed as S corporations, which have limited liability for stockholders and enjoy the advantages of other, conventional corporations. The added advantage of the S corporation is that it allows shareholders to absorb all corporate income or losses as partners. If these shareholders are well-to-do, or if the corporation is still quite new and cannot afford tax payments, then this method has tax advantages on both sides. The wealthy individual can declare initial corporate losses on his or her personal return and save on income taxes. Forming a corporation is costly, cumbersome, and subject to numerous restrictions. A lawyer should be retained during its formation, especially for spelling out responsibilities to shareholders and planning corporate activities for future years.

COST BENEFIT ANALYSIS   This method of measuring the benefits expected from a business decision answers questions such as: How much does the decision cost? What will the advantages be? Who will benefit from it and how? What is the company profit that might be derived from the decision? Does the benefit thus derived exceed the cost and effort? These questions must be weighed when considering the purchase of new equipment, fixtures, or vehicles, the hiring of a new employee, expansion into extra space, investment in a new sign, or institution of a health or profit-sharing program. When government departments use this method, the question is: Do this new program's benefits warrant the expenditure of tax dollars and the effort of the staff? Being analytical in managing a business is one of the assets of a successful entrepreneur. Everything needs to have a reason—even though many decisions are based on "gut feelings." If a supplier offers a 2 percent discount for paying in 10 days, but no money is available, will a bank grant a short-term loan until the collections come in—normally 30 days—and thus allow the entrepreneur to *make* money? Assume the order is for $10,000; a 2 percent discount amounts to $200. To take out a 30-day loan at 15 percent amount to $125 ($1,500 ÷ 12). Obviously a quick $75 results from taking out the loan and paying the invoice within the discount period. There are two additional benefits: (1) the supplier will note the quick payment; credit rating will be improved and future service enhanced; (2) the bank will consider the borrower a regular customer; in turn, the borrower establishes good credit with the bank for possibly larger loans in the future. Cost benefit analysis of the situation has found a solution that is beneficial all around.

Cost control

There are at least four controls that can make or break a business: (1) personal expenditures; (2) overbuying of merchandise that may not be needed; (3) spending on business expansion that may not be warranted; and (4) internal leakage. If money is borrowed to operate the business, add: (5) borrowing money unnecessarily or at a rate higher than the business can afford. Accumulated surplus funds should be invested wisely to produce optimum returns. If the business has operated for a while, cost controls can be checked for effectiveness; if a startup, controls should be set up that permit the owners to live within the parameters of available funds. Once the controls are established, add another 25 percent to estimated expenses, for unforeseen exigencies, price increases unknown at this time, slow collections, losses of customers or clients, increased fees and taxes, sudden insurance or security needs, unexpected new trends that require unscheduled expenditures, loss of a key employee (to cover the time and money needed to acquire and train a replacement), breakdown of machinery or motor vehicles, and so on. There are probably as many "unforeseens" as there are fixed and controllable expenses; in some circumstances, a 25 percent buffer may not even be enough. To assure workable cost control, a proper accounting setup and the continuing help of a knowledgeable, practical accountant are valuable. However, the setup and monitoring of effective controls depend on the owner's understanding the need for them and providing sufficient details. Like sticking to a diet, cost control works only if the prescription is followed daily.

Counseling—Givers

When a counselor gives advice or makes suggestions, the implementation of the advice or suggestions is left up to the person being counseled. Counseling is somewhat different from consulting, which implies a stronger, more positive relationship and definite recommendations to be followed. Counseling to entrepreneurs, for instance, is done by the Small Business Administration through its affiliated agencies (see *Small Business Administration* and *SCORE*). The advantages of sound advance counseling in starting a business and continuing counseling during the developing stages of a business become apparent from these statistics: Out of a group of 500 SCORE clients who attended going-into-business workshops or were counseled on this subject, only 12 percent (60 men and women), actually went into business. Of the group of 60, only 25 received their SCORE counselors' recommendations to go ahead with their plans. The others were advised to bide time, accumulate more capital, get more experience, or do some more studying. The 35 others who were thought to be not ready went ahead and started businesses anyway. Within three years, about 20 were bankrupt. Of the first group of 25 whom SCORE counselors advised and among whom a readiness for independent business was perceived, only one went bankrupt during this test period. Counseling, especially continual counseling, does pay off.

COUNSELING—SEEKERS

From the perspective of the entrepreneur, counseling is a method of seeking advice on business problems from a person in whom the entrepreneur has confidence, who is believed to be an expert in the area of interest, and who will treat problem(s) in a professional and confidential manner. Counselors can be a business's triumvirate of professionals: its lawyer, accountant, and banker. Counselors might also be financial planners, business advisors, academics at a nearby university, or other businesspeople or professionals who are not direct competitors. The Small Business Administration and its affiliates are available with pertinent literature, research, and counseling— usually free or at a very moderate cost. SCORE can be especially valuable to a startup entrepreneur or one who has run into an unexpected snag. To get the most out of counseling, the entrepreneur should be definite and detailed in describing the problem and the targets to be achieved. Counselors are pragmatic men and women; they are not mind-readers. If feasible, ask for a counselor who has had the kind of experience that will be helpful; ask, too, about available literature and about other clients who might have encountered, and resolved, similar problems. The following advice covers the ingredients of good counseling:

1. *Analyze the problem.* The counselor is no mind-reader; be sure to write down or tell all the counselor needs to know in order to be able to help.

2. *Prepare for counseling.* Have all pertinent data available in clean and legible form—description of a possible business, bookkeeping and accounting information, leases and equipment contracts, drafts or attempts at publicity and promotional material, any available sales figures on the business and on competitors.

3. *Establish rapport.* Have confidence in the counselor; like the counselor sufficiently to trust him or her with problems; be

comfortable in the meeting's physical environment; move aside any physical barriers.

4. *Follow up.* Be prepared to take notes. Realize that problems that have been weeks, months, and years in developing cannot be resolved in a one-hour session. Ask for another meeting at a time when additional materials might be reviewed, or after the counselor's requests or suggestions have been tested.

5. *Ask and study.* If all concerns are not discussed or answered by the counselor, don't be afraid to ask questions that focus on real concerns. Ask about any literature that might be available from the counselor's organization, the government, the library, or a trade or professional association, and about beneficial courses of study at a local college.

6. *Don't be disappointed.* Not all counseling works, nor will it always live up to expectations. Seek another counselor, perhaps within the same organization, with more direct experience or with a more empathic personality. Counseling is not a plop-plop-fizz-fizz panacea. It can, however, be a short-cut to answers, prevent further problems, and occasionally even save tremendous time and money. Seekers usually get out of counseling what they put into it.

CREDIT The amount of available funds an entrepreneur can draw from an outside resource—money from a bank or goods from a supplier—is the business's available credit. A good credit standing depends on reputation, past dealings with the bank or supplier, and the real assets pledged to secure the credit—securities, real estate, salable assets, or title to goods being purchased. It is always good to have credit at a bank, even if it is not needed. Need for money can often come suddenly and unexpectedly, and the establishment of credit at a bank does not happen quickly; it depends on a lengthy relationship with the bank and its manager or loan officer. Making loans and paying them back promptly is one good way to establish credit with a bank. Doing business with a manufacturer or other supplier over a period of time and paying bills promptly (i.e., taking discounts, if these are available) is a way of building credit with trade sources. Conversely, an entrepreneur may be in a position where credit is extended to clients or customers. The gigantic increase of credit card use has minimized the risk that retailers and professionals formerly had to bear, but the assurance and convenience have a price. Credit card companies charge 2 to 6 percent for their services, and business operators need to take this cost into consideration—as they would if they were extending credit personally. Over the past 20 years most businesses have switched to utilizing "plastic credit" as a simpler, surer, quicker way of getting their money. Personal credit extensions to customers survive mainly in department stores and prestigious, high-markup retailers. (See William A. Cohen, *The Entrepreneur and Small Business Problem Solver,* [New York: John Wiley & Sons, 1990], chapter 7.)

CREDIT UNIONS These not-for-profit financial institutions are usually formed by employees of a company, members of a labor union or religious group, or a division of government. There are about 9,000 credit unions. Most have less than $5 million in assets, but some that have aggressive management, like the Puerto Rican Police Co-op, develop assets of over $50 million. Credit unions probably began with the formation of an employees' lending organization at the Boston Globe in 1892. They received a boost from Edward Filene, the Boston department store magnate, who encouraged his employees to start one in 1915. Credit unions may offer a full range of services and may pay higher rates on deposits and charge lower rates on loans than commercial banks do. They are, however, regulated by the Federal Credit Union Administration. Credit unions have even lent their expertise and financial muscle to subsidize the poor in projects such as halfway houses in Massachusetts and the Arizona Council for the Blind in Phoenix. Altogether, credit unions in the United States hold total assets of more that $200 billion; with a membership potential of 55 million, the credit union industry is a formidable segment of American finance. Even the huge American Association of Retired Persons (AARP) recently started a credit union for its members. It is conceivable that, within the restrictions of the Federal Credit Union Administration, an entrepreneur can explore a major credit union as a financing source.

CRISIS MANAGEMENT To manage an enterprise during a crisis requires being aware of company problems and resolving them. The first things an entrepreneur needs to do if problems are suspected or noted are: listen, and communicate. Much can be learned from business associates and advisors; solutions often are suggested by conversations with key employees and outside professionals. Sometimes problems arise due to personal upsets; sometimes thorough planning has been lacking, which is a critical fault. Having a sound business plan to refer to can be of immense help. Here is a random checklist of problems or pitfalls that can happen in almost any business:

- *Overreach:* Has the enterprise encountered or fulfilled the Peter Principle? Gone beyond the available skills and expertise of available or affordable management?

- *Change:* Changes have occurred outside the business—sudden changes in technology or competitiveness, or changes in consumer preferences for different products or services.

- *Inflation:* Though tolerable in government, inflation is often lethal in business. By keeping inventory, lending limits, and cash flow flexible, a business can pull in its belt when needed.

- *Oversupply of personnel:* It can be a rock around the corporate neck if employees do not produce a surplus, or if the company is stuck with inflexible labor contracts.

- *Costs:* Keep an eye on the cost-effectiveness of locations—local taxes, high labor costs, changes in traffic flow, tough new competition. Trim when necessary. Only survival counts.

- *Fiscal alliances:* Risky relationships with unconscionable suppliers or too-tough bankers/lenders can shove an entrepreneur against a wall. Keep funding elastic. Have some resources in reserve.

- *Undiversified customer base:* Depending on one giant customer can be Russian roulette. There are too many classic cases in which a giant retailer absorbed the small supplier. Never put more than 40 percent of the company's eggs into one basket.

- *Disharmony:* Internal conflict can dissipate entrepreneurial vigor. Partnerships or corporations can be rent apart by conservative vs. aggressive management.

CUSTOMER CARE Could there be anyone more important than a customer, the person who buys products or services and is the reason for being in business? Yet mistreatment of customers is cited as the first or second reason when customers leave and seek out another purveyor who is more appreciative of their money. Example: when Wendy's, the huge chain of fast-food restaurants, suffered its first annual operating loss recently, the chain's founder, R. David Thomas, analyzed the possible reason and declared honestly, "We probably forgot the customer. . . . We got too many computers." In addition to increased impersonal treatment, traceable causes of customer alienation are: tremendous turnovers in personnel, inept sales people (increased training costs-reduced training periods), and emphasis on automatic merchandising and self-help. Each entrepreneur should figure out how much it costs to attract a customer or client. If sales are $500,000 and total advertising, promotion, display, training, and packaging costs are 10 percent, $50,000 a year is spent to attract customers. How many customers? 500? 5,000? 25,000? The "customer-attraction" cost then would be $100, $10, $2 respectively. Each time a customer is dissatisfied and leaves to go to a competitor, from $2 to $100 is lost. Conversely, how much training and effort are required to reverse this trend? Nordstrom, a Seattle-based department store chain, declared a 36 percent increase in business during a recent year and attributed it to implementation of a slogan all the way through its many units: "Coddle the customer!" Customers should be asked about the treatment they are receiving from the company. Owners should meet some of them personally, check telephone handling, install a continuing training program, start an improved image program, or post this reminder of the importance of customers:

Credo for Increased Profits:

Customers are the most important people we serve.

Customers are human beings with feelings like our own.

Customers deserve our courteous and attentive treatment.

Customers do not interrupt our work; they are the purpose of it.

Customers bring us their needs; it is our job to fulfill them.

Customers do not depend on us; we depend on them.

Customers are our business.

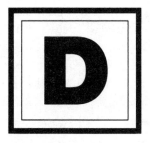

DAYCARE   Entrepreneurial concern for female employees' young children is not merely an ethical and social responsibility; providing babysitting while a mother works is a very practical concern. More than half the workforce is female, and of these a growing number are young mothers and single parents. Large corporations may provide built-in daycare centers or join with other companies in the area in subsidizing or totally supporting such facilities. On a reduced scale, the small entrepreneur must be aware of the need for such physical environments. If a business will need or already requires employees, making daycare facilities available or giving consideration to their need in the hiring process will immensely broaden the availability of personnel and the loyalty of those hired. The cost of a daycare facility to the mother should be a factor in discussing salaries, and can be an incentive for an employee to remain with the company. Examples of annual daycare costs in various parts of the country are:

New York City	$9,000
Boston	5,700
Hempstead, NY	5,000
San Francisco	4,300
Chicago	3,900
Los Angeles	3,500
Tampa, FL	2,400

To put the issue of daycare on a practical basis, suppose a fashion manufacturing business planned to open in the Los Angeles area, and attracting reliable women employees was an important problem. The prevailing wages ranged around $200 a week. Out of 12 applicants, three had preschool children aged 2, 4, 4, and 5. The children represented daycare for a total of nine child-years at $3,500 each or an investment of $31,500 over a four-year period. Would it be worth retaining good employees?

DEBT RATIOS   Three important mathematical formulas are of interest to bankers (lenders) when gauging a company and its strength. These debt ratios are given special focus in the American Bankers Association guidelines for evaluating a business:

1. *Total debt to total assets:* This ratio looks at the ability of a business to repay long-term debt. In this example:

   $100,000 (Total debt): $200,000 (Total assets) = 2:1 or 50 percent

   the assets are twice as large as the debts. The company therefore presents a healthy financial picture.

2. *Total debt to net worth:* This ratio measures the extent to which a firm relies on borrowed funds. It provides an indication of the company's ability to repay debts.

3. *Total debt to current debt:* This ratio shows the proportion of a company's debts within the present operating year—the current debts. It further shows whether the company might be exposed to unusual financial strains from debts maturing during the current year. Such strains indicate that a repayment schedule could be jeopardized or, at best, that the loan should be extended. If a higher risk is indicated, then a higher interest rate on the loan might be requested.

DEDUCTIONS   Under the Internal Revenue Code taxpayers are allowed to subtract some permitted expenses, often within limits, from their Gross Income or Adjusted Gross Income. Knowing all the various deductions that can legitimately be used to reduce tax payments can be as important to an entrepreneur as making a profit on mercantile or financial transactions. "Little" deductions can add up to big savings. Few of these little deductions mean as much in the aggregate as all those little daily expenditures that are often overlooked: postage, literature purchased to enhance one's business education, legitimate entertainment, attendance at business-related functions, automobile and other transportation needed in the conduct of the business, uniforms or other modes of dress that contribute to increasing business income, use of telephone and other instruments in the conduct of business, depreciation of equipment bought for business use and, in the case of a business that is exclusively operated from home, the accurate percentage of the overall space that is used for the business and the cost of its maintenance. The keys to making the most out of these deductions are (1) keeping immaculate records and (2) having proof of all of them as backup for claims, in case of an IRS audit. It is advisable to get a receipt of each expenditure, to keep a daily auto log, and to have some sort of convenient system of keeping track of and totaling petty expenditures each month. Even a small, one-person enterprise can easily run up $200 a month in miscellaneous, often out-of-pocket expenses. With income of $50,000 a year, petty expenditures can easily amount to a 5 percent deduction.

DEMOGRAPHICS   Population statistics that lean on socioeconomic factors such as age, income, sex, education, occupation, and employment are the subject of the science of demographics. These are very important in planning marketing. For an entrepreneur who is seeking to locate in another area, however, studying and using demographics as a guide to where to settle can be a lifetime decision. Although research for the demographics below originated with large corporations, the findings are equally valid for small entrepreneurs. As the 1990s begin, the top-rated cities are Dallas/Ft. Worth, Atlanta, Baltimore, Portland (OR), Kansas City (MO), Pittsburgh, and Minneapolis/St. Paul. Among midsize cities, these were the major industries favorites: Salt Lake City, Memphis, Indianapolis, Scranton/Wilkes-Barre, and Buffalo. (The latter was chosen because of its adjacency to Canada.) Surveys of some factors that are especially important to small, startup entrepreneurs—family living environment, availability of municipal infrastructure, and cost of doing business—yielded these current ratings among a number of outstanding American communities:

Family Living Environment				Availability of Municipal Infrastructure	Cost of Doing Business		
	1	2	3		4	5	6
Dallas	$74,200	87	A	Good to excellent	100	98	$1,300
Atlanta	82,400	132	B	Fair	101	102	1,280
Baltimore	93,500	101	B	Good to excellent	100	117	1,740
Portland	75,800	142	A	Good	101	113	1,440
Kansas City	74,300	111	B	Excellent	101	111	1,150
Pittsburgh	64,200	49	B	Excellent	98	115	1,460
Minn./St. Paul	93,300	86	A	Excellent to good	90	121	1,730

1 = housing cost, 2 = crime index, 3 = air quality, 4 = salary, 5 = construction, 6 = local taxes.

Good sources for determining the demographics for a business are trade associations, the Census Bureau, the local library, and reference directories like those published by *Editor & Publisher* and Standard Rates and Data Service; some atlases also publish demographic tables. Since the use of demographics is essentially an attempt to plan for the future, "futurists" have developed a finely honed ability to pinpoint trends ahead (see *Future Trends for Entrepreneurs* and *Futurists*). For instance, some of the predicted trends for the year 2000 include:

- The number of Americans over 75 will double in number; more facilities for both able-bodied and dependent retirees will be necessary.
- Tax increases will be mandated by the need for more public funding for nursing homes, medical facilities, and medications.
- The surge in real estate prices will ease, since the largest market segment, the baby boomers, has already bought homes. Housing prices and mortgage rates will decline.
- Oil prices will increase again which, in turn, will affect commuting to work by car and further decentralize office construction and corporate locations.
- Car pooling will increase, under sponsorship by corporations and mandates by government.
- Current restrictions on and high prices for the use of water, electricity, and nondisposable containers will continue.
- Computerized shopping and home deliveries of goods and services will increase, aided by better time management.

City	Population (million)	Growth 1980–1990 (%)	Cost of Living Index* (Av. Housing Cost)	Other Comments
Cincinnati	1.5	4.1	98 ($74,000)	Strongly work-oriented citizenry
Houston	3.2	18.0	93 ($65,000)	Vital cultural life
Phoenix	2.0	38.2	101 ($92,000)	Moderate climate; plenty room
San Antonio	1.3	25.3	88 ($74,000)	Stable, colorful, lowest cost of living index
St. Louis	2.5	4.8	99 ($83,000)	Strong work ethic; good schools
Tampa Bay	2.0	27.1	99 ($74,000)	Tampa, St. Petersburg, Clearwater are equivalent

* U.S. average index = 100.

DIRECT MAIL An advertising medium for delivering messages through the post office, direct mail is often called third-class mail or junk mail. What makes many people consider direct mail received at home or in the businessplace as "junk" is the fact that it is usually not requested. Whenever a customer subscribes to a publication, a donor makes a contribution by mail, or a new member joins an organization, the name and address of that person goes on some kind of list. Lists of names and addresses are often published or compiled by entrepreneurs who sell them for additional income. List brokers process the lists and resell them to the thousands of publications, publishers, mail order houses, political organizations, and special-interest groups that solicit contributions, business, or participation in causes. It is difficult to prove the amount of money spent annually on direct mail (postage is the major expense) but the total probably comes close to $10 billion. To create an effective direct mail promotion for a business (or organization), three steps are needed: (1) a current mailing list, preferably of people who know or have dealt with the business before; (2) a product or service that is attractive to recipients and will get them to react favorably and quickly; and (3) an expert in direct mail packaging who can write a smashing cover letter and an irresistible brochure or illustrated enclosure. Of course, sometimes a simple, inexpensive, quick-to-read post card is as effective as a more elaborate and costly three-to-five-piece direct mail package; choice of medium depends on the results the sender wants to achieve. The traditional direct mail package should include a mailing envelope, a return envelope or card (preferably postpaid and self-addressed), a personalized cover letter, and a detailed brochure, folder, or insert. Results? A 2 to 4 percent response is good. So, if you mail 5,000 pieces and each complete direct mail package costs 50 cents delivered, the actual *per-customer* cost is between $12.50 to $25. Not cheap.

PETER F. DRUCKER, PhD His decades of teaching and his 23 books on business subjects have made Dr. Drucker an oracle of business and a guru of entrepreneurs. He works on the premise of "feeding opportunities and starving problems." Among the most important of the Druckerian pronouncements are these advisories for the next decade:

1. Innovation requires concentration. A business that splinters its focus will lose its concentration for success.

2. A company has to be big enough to do a few things very well. Drucker feels that while small businesses will go irrevocably forward, the small companies that can grow into medium-sized companies will inherit the glory during the next decade. Small

startups have no human resources to spare to work toward tomorrow—though nothing prevents them from networking, from utilizing consultants and other outside personnel, and from exploring more efficient methods of working.

3. Understanding the Big Picture is important for small entrepreneurs. Size is not always a criterion of efficiency. America's "trade imbalance" is not due as much to a real imbalance of trade as it is to bad pricing of our existing resources. For example; Japan today pays one-third less for raw materials from the United States than it did in 1980. Too much emphasis in the U.S. is placed on making resources, rather than people, productive. Our biggest advantage, however, which must be promoted, is our unique philosophy that learning continues *after* school. Dr. Drucker applauds the motivation that makes middle-aged managers leave corporate employment to set up entrepreneurial and innovative new companies.

DUN & BRADSTREET (D&B)

A national credit rating and reporting agency, Dun & Bradstreet also publishes a small-business management magazine, *D&B Reports,* and probably the best statistical surveys in virtually every category of business and industry. The D&B failure reports are unique and well-known. The D&B credit ratings are the blue-ribbon criteria of business and banking. Because these ratings are used so widely as an initial guide to a business's creditworthiness, it is important for an entrepreneur to be able to furnish D&B investigators with complete and, if possible, favorable information. Timely and accurate payment of bills is a prime necessity for entrepreneurs, especially during the startup years. Creditors are also checked by D&B investigators, and their reports on an entrepreneur's bill-paying habits eventually find their way into the published D&B ratings. The information thus gathered is disseminated by D&B to subscribers in periodic reports, special reports, and rating directories. Contact: Dun & Bradstreet Business Credit Services, 1 Diamond Hill Road, Murray Hill, NJ 07974-0027.

DYNAMICS OF ENTREPRENEURIAL SUCCESS (DOES)

Every entrepreneur should conduct a dry run or rehearsal before making a debut in a business world full of both anticipated and unexpected pitfalls. If the complex countdown is successfully completed, it's time to step back and say with righteous self-satisfaction, "That DOES it!" But until that moment, a great deal of preparation goes into the performance. The more careful the rehearsal, the better the performance—and the better the guarantee that the efforts will bring accolades of satisfaction and profits. A quick 10-point DOES checklist offers some guideposts:

1. Leadership—the owner's motivation, enthusiasm, and knowledge as the decision maker and sparkplug of the enterprise.

2. Personnel—other people who will fill in time and talent blanks as necessary.

3. Premises—the store, office, plant, or conveyance at or from which the business operates.

4. Equipment and Inventory—their location, condition, and functions.

5. Financing—adequate operating funds and 25 percent more, just in case.

6. Promotion—stationery, signs, announcements, and publicity.

7. Organization—the enterprise's legal structure, insurance coverage, accounting system, and record-keeping facilities.

8. Externals—advisors, memberships, and trade or professional affiliations.

9. Timing—the cycles, seasons, and dates when business startups are likely to succeed.

10. Projections—plans for business beyond the initial grand-opening euphoria, including how to accommodate hoped-for expansion.

Ec 1992   Twelve Western European countries plan to form one large economic family called the European Community (EC). The plan is to be implemented in 1992 and Directives are already issued or in preparation to lower artificial trade barriers, open political boundaries, phase out separate currencies, discontinue custom duties and other obstacles to joint trade, and, it is hoped, multiply prosperity. The total population of the EC market will be 320 million—potentially a $4 trillion market for American trade. United States trade deficits with Western Europe were cut from $22 billion in 1987 to $11 billion in 1988. During 1989 the trade balance with Europe continued to improve in America's favor, showing a trade surplus of $1.5 billion for the year. The Small Business Administration's (SBA) administrator, Susan Engeleiter, has encouraged small businesses to explore export options before 1992, so that they will be ready to take advantage of increased trading opportunities in 1992 when the European Community becomes operative. The SBA is working on improving its Export Revolving Line of Credit program, which provides financing for small companies developing new exports. At the same time the Department of Commerce is stepping up its "Matchmaker" program, which fields trade missions in which small American firms are taken to Europe and paired with potential customers. Each regional SBA office and most SCORE offices have international trade experts who can help local entrepreneurs explore their participation in EC 1992 and other export options. (See also *Export Revolving Line of Credit Program.*)

ECONOMIZING

A business economizes when it finds a way of doing the same or more things for less money—or in less time. (Time is a valuable asset, especially for the one-person enterprise!) While such an obvious goal appears simple to achieve, it is amazing how many entrepreneurs waste time and money performing ordinary but necessary daily tasks. Here are a few suggestions for *economizing* on time—and perhaps even saving money:

- If possible, send FAX transmissions after 11 P.M., rates are as much as 60 percent lower.
- Instead of standing on line at the post office or sending an assistant, call 1-800-STAMP-24 to order any amount of stamps needed. Charge them to a VISA or Master Card at $2.00 above the face value of the stamps.
- If business trips are necessary, stay at a budget motel for $25 to $40 instead a fancy "brand name" hotel or motel at $45 to $100. A list of 2,000 budget motels is published in a $4.95 directory by Pilot Books, 103 Cooper Street, Babylon, NY 11702.
- Develop a categorized file of "My Best Business Letters." When a letter is needed, check the file and adapt a letter, to save time.
- If the business is expanding and it's time to hire a new sales rep, think of offering extra goods or services production to Uncle Sam. (See *Government Procurement.*) Or, send $5.50 to the Government Printing Office, North Capital & H Streets NW, Washington DC 20401 for a copy of *U.S. Government and Sales Directory.*

- To remedy or prevent eye fatigue or strain from peering at the computer screen for hours, provide a pair of nonprescription, tinted glasses. (If the screen is green, use brown-tinted lenses; if it is amber, use blue-tinted lenses.)

- Tax and time savings can be effected by attending a free, IRS-sponsored seminar workshop on tax savings, record keeping, and similar topics. Call the local IRS office for the next date.

- A lease can be a business's single biggest expenditure, over 5, 10, or 15 years. Instead of analyzing a prospective location when the landlord or agent deigns to show it, make it a point to visit the location at all hours of the day or night, for a more objective picture of the premises in regard to traffic, lighting, security, sign and display needs, and so on.

Elain (ELECTRONIC LICENSE APPLICATION INFORMATION NETWORK)

For entrepreneurs considering or already in the beginning stages of the export business, ELAIN allows quick online computer acceptance of export license applications for most overseas destinations. ELAIN is handled by the Department of Commerce's Bureau of Export Administration, Office of Export Licensing, P.O. Box 273, Washington, DC 20044, phone: (202) 377-8540 or -4811. Applications may cover all commodities except supercomputers. The first step is to apply for authorization to submit applications electronically by writing to the above address, to the attention of ELAIN. The application letter should state company name, address, phone number, and name of a person to contact later. The Office of Export Licensing will send information on how to obtain company identification numbers as well as personal ID numbers for individuals mutually approved by the Office and the exporting company. The exporter will also receive instructions on how to contact the CompuServe computer network to obtain detailed filing instructions. Once exporters have the necessary authorization to begin submitting license applications electronically to ELAIN, license-related information can be entered into a personal computer and sent over telephone lines via CompuServe to the Commerce Department. Licensing decisions are electronically sent back to exporters via the same CompuServe network. To keep track of an export license application, use the System for Tracking Export License Applications (see STELA).

Electronic banking

This relatively new capacity to conduct financial transactions by computer over phone lines is destined to speed up cash flow more than any other current technology. Electronic banking takes less paper and less transit time, solving two problems that have bothered both commercial and noncommercial depositors. Businesses are already using electronic order entry systems, which enable customers to re-order merchandise and check shipping dates directly. The next steps will be the invoicing of customers via computer, and then receipt of payment electronically by wire transfer from the customer's bank to the vendor's. Some banks offer electronic banking privileges to small businesses, enabling them to have the convenience and cash management control enjoyed by larger corporations. The en-trepreneur's PC can be used to check balances, transfer funds, con-solidate cash between accounts, and pay bills. Electronic banking makes long-distance transactions as convenient as dealing with the local neighborhood bank. This opens up the entire country to finan-cial interfacing; entrepreneurs are no longer limited to dealing only with local institutions. Banking by computer should reduce the work and cost of paper invoices, payroll, and bills. Small companies that do not as yet have computer facilities to put electronic banking into practice as an in-house operation may find it cost-effective to retain a computer bookkeeping service.

ELECTRONIC RETAILING

In this new technology, "inter-active" devices are used to present a sales message and effect a sale. Traditional salespeople and pur-chasers may resent an electronic voice on the telephone, making a pitch for a new product or service, or on the screen at an airport vending kiosk or automatic bank teller machine, giving instructions for the next step. But this remarkable new option is one that en-trepreneurs need to know about. Even sales representatives of major mercantile companies are making use of computers to call up mer-chandise displays, present available color and size ranges, and con-duct virtual style shows for buyer-customers—all on a computer screen. Video selling from shelf displays or sales booths in public places like airports will be the wave of the future. Item price will be no deterrent, as everything from one-dollar food specialties to multit-housand-dollar electronic devices will be sold on the screen and charged to the customer's credit card account. Seers of remote selling even foresee fully interactive department stores that will be more complete and more sophisticated versions of home-shopping services now conducted on late-night and cable TV.

EMPLOYEE LEASING

A recent trend in personnel manage-ment is to lease employees. An outside company hires all or part of the staff for a client-company, pays their salaries and benefits, and bills the client-company weekly. The employee-leasing or staff-leasing firm administers the payroll, files tax reports, makes tax deposits, provides workers' compensation and federal and state unemployment insurance, maintains employee records, and keeps up with the various personnel laws and policies. The employee-leasing company can negotiate good benefits packages at low rates, because it employs large numbers of people. According to an SBA bulletin on employee leasing, the potential benefits of this system, especially to the smaller entrepreneur, are:

- Lower personnel costs
- More comprehensive and less expensive benefits
- Less government reporting and paperwork
- Stabilized insurance costs
- Lower employee turnover, especially among key employees
- Reduced employer liability
- More time to apply to principal revenue-producing activities

Administaff, Inc., an employee-leasing company in Maryland, phone: (800) 237-3170; (301) 974-1131, claims that the net costs of its services amount to about 2 percent. A personnel vice president of a larger leasing firm describes his company's fringe benefits as being more than 30 percent of the net salaries of the employees. Employee leasing should be especially useful in areas of high employment and low unemployment, like the Washington, DC market. A perceived disadvantage is that leased employees are hired and fired by the employee-leasing firm; the client company thus gives up these rights in favor of possible greater efficiency.

ENTREPRENEUR A nice French word, entrepreneur means contractor. It used to describe men who arranged to bring entertainment or musical presentations to the public. The modern interpretation, however, is that of a person who organizes and manages a commercial undertaking, especially one involving commercial risk. While an entrepreneur does not mind taking risks—in time, reputation, and money—a *good* entrepreneur is actually a risk-minimizer. Successful entrepreneurs have this quintet of essential characteristics:

Motivation—self-starting; secure; a strong desire to be successful.

Imagination—full of ideas, usually more than one; brimming with curiosity.

Skills—native or acquired, but soundly educated and based on a wide range of knowledgeability.

Persistence—drive mixed with optimism; willingness to try alternate approaches if results are not as desired.

Money—not the first or the last, but the necessary ingredient; the entrepreneur's own resources are often needed to get an undertaking going.

(See also *Entrepreneurial Analysis*.)

ENTREPRENEURIAL ANALYSIS

An informal survey taken in "Silicon Valley," a section of California renowned for its high-tech, fast-moving entrepreneurs, revealed the following typical characteristics that contribute toward success:

- Health: Entrepreneurs must be continually "on tap"—enthusiastic, caring, and self-disciplined.

- Independence: Successful entrepreneurs have a strong BYOB (be your own boss) drive; they choose to be responsible for their own success or failure.

- Self-Confidence: Both for the entrepreneur and as a trait that radiates outward to others, belief in oneself must be constant.

- Urgency: Success moves too fast to be put off till tomorrow.

- Awareness: Everything in the business environment must be known, observed, and directed; entrepreneurs do not have blinders on their faces.

- Realism: There is no room for wishful thinking; problems must be faced without fantasizing.

- Anti-Status: Especially at the beginning, entrepreneurs must focus single-mindedly on the development of their business, even if this means sweeping its floors at night. Status will come with success.

- Orderliness: Entrepreneurs must see order among chaos, or they will drown in the latter.

- Objectivity: Situations, relationships, and especially employees must be judged with clear objectivity, an understanding of motivations, and enough distance so as not to become subjective.

- Emotions: Entrepreneurs can only think clearly under stressful situations when emotions are kept in check.

- Risk-Taking: The ability to take calculated chances is inevitable for success, but risks can be tempered by knowledge. The more knowledge, the less the risk.

ENTREPRENEURIAL PHILOSOPHY—GENERAL

Some notable flight from America's large industries and increased competitive pressure from Japanese industrial complexes have led to an antientrepreneurial ripple among

American business pundits. Why are some well-trained, former corporate loyalists apparently deserting the alleged security of the company paycheck for the treacherous bounding main of entrepreneurship? It might be said that America's obsession with entrepreneurship is an attempt to make the best of the worst characteristics of postwar Americans: our excessive individualism and our inability to work together. A writer in the prestigious *INC.* magazine opined that "unless we do something about the tragic exodus of talented businesspeople and engineers from our major corporations, the United States will continue its downhill slide into a status as a second-rate industrial power and a Japanese colony." A dichotomy of opinions is what *makes* America. The storied "melting pot" in which a hundred races from all over the world blend together is a heterogeneous, constantly growing and moving mass of individualists, not a Japanese-style *Führervolk*. Lack of uniformity has historically given America its elasticity to bound back from adversity, to absorb gigantic upheavals, and to create endless production and material assets when the needs arise. The nature and effects of large corporate mergers, the golden parachutes that drop from the skies of economic expansions, the huge civil service and military systems that create early retirees with fat nesteggs—all combine to nurture entrepreneurship. Add to these social and economic trends Americans' inborn and rugged individualism, and the seeds are sown and fertilized for small businesses to grow and continue.

ENTREPRENEURIAL PHILOSOPHY—PERSONAL

A good way to put success on an express track is to learn to articulate personal guidelines. On the rocky road to success, each entrepreneur needs a personal philosophy to hold on to occasionally. Here are some of this writer's personal guidelines:

1. Honesty is always a good policy, even if some others do not believe in yours. *You* do and that's what counts.

2. People who are watching the clock more than their work will always be one of the hands.

3. A chicken crosses the road because its research was not complete.

4. The best way you can get credit is to give some of it away yourself.

5. A person of stature has no need for status.

6. Doing the expedient thing and the right thing are not always the same thing.

7. If your ambition propels you to start working early and quitting late, great. But more important is: *why?*

8. You cannot sink someone else's end of the boat without sinking your end.

9. If your enthusiasm for your work is evident, then others will be enthusiastic, too.

10. As an entrepreneur, remember that it is not only important to make a good living, but to know what to do with it once you've made it.

—Gustav Berle

ENTREPRENEURIAL SHOCK Entrepreneurs sometimes get jolts and disappointments when they step out of a large organization to start their own business. The shock is exacerbated among the increased numbers of former corporate executives, early retirees from the military or civil service, and big buyers and merchandise managers from department and chain stores who have decided, or are forced to decide, to go into business for themselves. In any large organization, an executive has access to sizable sums of financing, easy name recognition in the market, and an infrastructure that includes many helpers who take care of details. In the world of entrepreneurship, the executive finds that he or she becomes the chief cook and bottlewasher. Suddenly the 40-hour week is not long enough; help is hard to find and costly; half of one's time is eaten up by details—and unless these extras are accounted for in the price of the entrepreneur's product or service, the business can become highly unprofitable despite the many working hours. In businesses of their own, entrepreneurs find that no one is behind them anymore. In order to do, sell, finance, or deliver *anything,* entrepreneurs have only themselves—and not just on the first day or during the first month but every day. Harry S Truman put it bluntly: "When you're at the top, the buck stops with you." Sometimes it gets a little lonely at the top. Entry-level entrepreneurs have to become shockproof, to survive those first five crucial years.

ENTREPRENEURS OF AMERICA (EOA) Established in 1977, this business resource network serves owners of small to medium size businesses nationwide. EOA maintains a Capitol Hill lobbyist to represent entrepreneurs' concerns, publishes a quarterly newsletter, and makes financially advantageous group arrangements for a variety of small business services. If individual lobbying efforts are needed, EOA can put an owner in touch with an "insider." The organization can help new startups to incorporate by telephone, setting up a Delaware-registered company for just a little more than $100. Other EOA services include group insurance, a gold and silver charge card program, discounts on trade books, travel arrangements, investments, and low-rate credit card processing. The annual fee for joining the EOA network is $49.95 and membership can be initiated via EOA's toll-free line, phone: (800) 533-2665. The national EOA office is at 2020 Pensylvania Avenue, NW, Suite 224, Washington, DC 20006.

EQUITY FINANCING

Generally, equity financing, or selling a part of the company in order to raise capital, is done by corporations when they sell some stock, either common or preferred, to acquire more working capital. The stock that is sold dilutes the ownership a little and imposes additional obligations upon the company that sells it. The purchasers of equity may or may not take a part in the management of the corporation. Because equity financing actually gives away a portion of a business in return for money, it is not always the most desirable method of raising money—particularly for independence-minded entrepreneurs. The alternative then becomes *debt financing*. When a company borrows money without giving up a piece of the business, it does not diminish its control but this presupposes that the company is in a healthy enough condition to be able to borrow money. If its condition is not healthy or if the company cannot come up with corporate or personal collateral to secure a direct loan, then there may be no alternative to selling some of its stock. The entrepreneur is usually advised to try debt financing before resorting to equity financing. Only preferred stock that is sold with a specific payback clause can be paid back and liquidated at the option of the entrepreneur (the seller); the "sale" is actually like a loan. A good accountant can advise, based on the company's financial condition, which method is the one to pursue, but if there is a choice, borrow.

EXIMBANK

The Export-Import Bank was set up by Congress in 1934 to encourage trade with foreign countries and help reverse America's Great Depression. Today it is equally important, to help correct our international trade deficits. Eximbank's activities include the financing of exports and imports, and the granting of direct credit to foreign borrowers to help them purchase American-made goods. Eximbank also offers discount loans (it has lent about $200 billion in the years of its existence), provides export guarantees, and issues insurance against commercial and political risks abroad. It is located at 811 Vermont Avenue, NW, Washington, DC 20571, phone: (202) 566-8990 or the nationwide, toll-free hotline, (800) 424-5201, weekdays between 9 A.M. and 5 P.M. ET. Literature is available from Eximbank free of charge: an *Annual Report* describes fiscal activity and financial statements; *Certified Bank List* names the banks and other contacts that are knowledgeable about Eximbank's programs; *Trade Finance Referral List* gives specific financial contacts other than banks. One of the most valuable services of the Eximbank is its periodic Small Business Conference on Exporting, conducted jointly with the Department of Commerce and Small Business Administration. These one-day conferences show smaller firms the opportunities that exist in foreign trade and the government services that are available to help them. The conference office is in room 1278 at the Eximbank address, phone: (202) 566-8873; a library is also available in room 1373. For an in-person visit, Eximbank's advisory services are in room 1275.

Expansion

Any increase in the sales capabilities of a company as a result of more working and operating space, additional equipment, additional inventory, larger salary needs, and more promotional efforts constitutes an expansion. Reasons for expanding at a particular time may be any of a number of factors: to utilize capital generated from profits of the company and increase its size without borrowing; to meet new competition; to place a new product or service into the marketplace; to accommodate aggressive new management, such as a son or daughter or partner joining the business; or to accommodate an expanding area market. More often than not, outside capital is needed to finance expansion. A good track record and large equity to use as collateral will normally make it easier to raise capital. Lenders of expansion capital raise some cautions, however:

- Growth should be healthy and manageable, not skyrocketing. Meteoric growth scares most bankers and investors.
- Marketplace competition is no deterrent to lenders. In fact, presence of competitors can be interpreted as offering potential purchasers, should the borrower's business flop.
- Investors are impressed by an efficiency quotient that indicates an ability to effect savings.
- A requested amount that is in excess of five to eight times the cash flow makes investors uncomfortable.
- Proven management expertise is probably the best guarantee that an expansion loan is in good hands.

An entrepreneur who is uncertain about participating in an expanded company but does not want to let go of involvement in it should consider taking a smaller equity position and selling off the majority of ownership to raise expansion funds. A smaller share in a bigger company might some day turn out to be worth more than the original equity in the smaller business. (See also *Growth.*)

Export Revolving Line of Credit (ERLC) Loan Program

To assist small businesses in exporting their products and services abroad, the Small Business Administration (SBA) has established the ERLC program, through which the SBA can guarantee up to $750,000 or 85 percent of a loan. The maximum guarantee for loans up to $155,000 is 90 percent. An applicant may have other outstanding loans as long as the total does not exceed $750,000. With the Export-Import Band as co-guarantor, however, the loan limit can be increased to $1 million. The maximum maturity of an ERLC loan cannot exceed 18 months, and interest rates are subject to negotiations and maximums. The SBA does collect user fees. For maturities of 12 months or less, the fee is .0025 percent of the guaranteed portion of the loan; for maturities exceeding 12 months, the fee is 2 percent of the guaranteed portion of the loan. Other small fees may be set at the time of the loan approval. Collateral will be required, including personal guarantees, accounts receivable, inventory, assignment of contract proceeds, and bank letters of credit. All collateral must be located under the jurisdiction of United States courts. Important ingredients of ERLC loans are a cash flow projection, to show how money will be coming back in, and monthly progress reports which can serve as an early-warning system in case of discrepancies. Before applying for the ERLC loan program, discuss it with the business's private bank of account. If the bank is unable or unwilling to make the loan directly, the possibilities of a participation with SBA should be explored. (For a list of SBA field offices, see Appendix A.)

Exporting

Selling goods and services in foreign countries is a rapidly expanding phase of our economy. Exporting is getting considerable boosts from federal and state governments because of the imbalance in our international trade. Big companies favor exporting because overseas trade is often more profitable than domestic business. Official and private emphasis on exporting has especially targeted small entrepreneurs because the majority of them are doing no overseas selling at all—yet they have the capacity, if not the will and know-how, to do so. For small to modest-size enterprises to enter the export business, the first step is to resolve to do so wholeheartedly. The 17,000 small companies that are already trading internationally have literally broken down the barriers for those who will join them. Some steps that can be followed are:

- Analyze the company's capabilities to expand production or services to accommodate additional sales abroad.

- Know the export potential of a product(s) or service(s), where it would sell best, whether changes need to be made.
- Locate the foreign markets that are right for a product or service.
- Study required strategies for entry into foreign markets and the special procedures to make these feasible.
- Learn how to process exports.

Help can be obtained from the Small Business Administration (SBA), SCORE (see *SCORE*), Department of Commerce, state export agencies (36 states have overseas offices), chambers of commerce, export management and trading companies, banks that have international departments, and international trade associations.

FACSIMILE (FAX) TRANSMISSION   In this electronic method of transmitting printed material (ads, letters, orders, news releases, instructions, or illustrated materials), the page to be transmitted is inserted into the FAX machine where it is coded by an electronic scanning device, sent over phone or electronic wires, and reproduced at a destination anywhere in the world where the addressee-recipient has a FAX machine to receive it. Big businesses were the first to utilize these miraculous message carriers, but smaller entrepreneurs are now finding them to be the VCRs of the 1990s. Prices have dropped precipitously; FAX machines at the end of 1989 were available for $500, though more sophisticated ones still cost several thousand dollars. The user-industry has grown so quickly that a special directory, frequently updated, has been published to list FAX numbers. Even the famed White House hotline is no longer a red telephone but a red FAX. In 1989 nearly 1.5 million machines were sold, making FAX transmission a $2 billion industry. By 1993 it is projected that 3.2 million units will be in use in the United States. Some 25 manufacturers are offering 60 different models; four major Japanese manufacturers (Sharp,

Murata, Canon, Ricoh) collectively have captured 57 percent of the market. A small California company, Star-Signal, even makes a "Rolls Royce" FAX that sends a high-resolution, full-color image, but the current cost of the machine is $26,000. Around the corner will be plain-paper FAX, five-seconds-per-page transmissions, and a digital communications network. The FAX revolution has virtually spelled the death of telex transmission and increased the telephone companies' income by about $2.5 billion a year.

FAILURE Not achieving one's goals is not, or should not be, in the entrepreneurial vocabulary. However, statistics tell otherwise: 80 percent of small enterprises do not survive five years. Exceptions have proven to be those small businesses that start out as franchises of nationally known companies, and those that are fortunate to be part of a multibusiness incubator project. In these two groups, the statistics are reversed: 80 percent survive after five years, and only 20 percent fail. Financial setbacks are sometimes triggered by causes outside of the entrepreneur's grasp. Inflation, industry dislocations, changes in demographics, style and fashion trends, depression—all can contribute to failure, yet the individual can do little about them. In a book titled *When Smart People Fail* (New York: Simon & Schuster, 1987), Linda Gottlieb and Carole Hyatt give nine of the most common reasons for failure:

1. Poor interpersonal skills—the number-one cause.

2. Mismatch of personality, ability, style, and values.

3. Lack of commitment, often caused by fear of failure.

4. Bad luck—exactly those uncontrollable factors mentioned above.

5. Self-destructive behavior—hard to recognize or change.

6. Scattered focus—tackling too many things at one time.

7. Sex, age, and race discrimination.

8. Poor management—including inability to delegate.

9. Hanging on too long when it has become apparent that a dead horse is being propped up.

Item 10 could well be: Failure to seek advice from others who have had the experience. (See *Chamber of Commerce, SCORE,* Small Business Development Centers [SBDC].)

FAILURE PREVENTION   Learn and obey these Ten Commandments To Prevent Failure:

1. Thou shalt not tap the till for temptations.

2. Thou shalt not make big personal expenditures to show off, indulge whims, or cover up intemperate purchases.

3. Thou shalt avoid hiring relatives and friends because they are in need and thus place your business in jeopardy just to be "a nice person."

4. Thou shalt not be tempted to buy more goods than you can realistically sell at a profit, for slow-moving inventory can choke you into bankruptcy quickly.

5. Thou shalt not reinvent the wheel, but acknowledge that outside counsel can get your problems resolved despite your pride and ego.

6. Thou shalt not borrow more money than is absolutely needed, because interest and repayment schedules constrict cash flow.

7. Thou shalt not be a savior and supplier to everyone, but shall focus your business to your proper market niche and yourself to what you can do best.

8. Thou shalt not play music all by yourself, once your business requires a band.

9. Thou shalt not relax on top of the mountain, for there you will not know what is going on in the valley.

10. Thou shalt not crawl into a shell when you are needed to guide the growth of your business through staffs that are properly trained in quality and quantity and service that is composed of quality, quality, and quality.

FAMILY BUSINESS   This euphemism describes the large percentage of small enterprises known as "mom-and-pop" businesses. There are few problems in the kind of unstructured partnership typical of family-operated businesses—until the time of sale or succession. Few probates cause more rifts among otherwise close families than the inheritance of businesses. It is therefore of primary importance that the entrepreneur consider equitable means of succession, no matter what the age of the founder. In many family enterprises that have participation by one or more sons and/or daughters, those who are not directly participating in the operation will, at probate, have claims on the business—either in its day-to-day policies or in getting a monetary share out of it. The determination of the share's value, the heir's contribution or noncontribution to the business, and the role of the heir's children are only a few of the problems that will come up for discussion and determination, unless the founding entrepreneur makes appropriate Solomonic decisions during his or her lifetime. Heirs who do not share in the business operation and its ultimate gains need to be satisfied in other ways, if strife between otherwise compatible heirs is to be avoided. Methods for continuing management, appropriate inventory appraisal, accounting for past "draws" or loans against the business, and participation of second-generation family members and spouses are all factors to be weighed early. Only a third of all family-owned businesses remain family-owned past the first generation. One reason for this sad statistic is the lack of appropriate succession plans. Because there is so much emotion in family relationships, it is advisable to have outside, nonfamily counselors or members of the board of directors, as well as successors who have had at least some outside training and experience.

FARMER'S HOME ADMINISTRATION (FmHA)

This agency within the United States Department of Agriculture administers assistance programs for purchasers of homes and farms in small towns and rural areas. In recent years the agency has created outreach programs to help minorities and women who want to enter into farming and rural businesses. Another FmHA function is to provide supervised credit and management advice to farm and rural-area entrepreneurs unable to get credit from other sources at reasonable rates and terms. Loans are made to alleviate rural poverty and enhance family farms and rural communities. Three types of loans facilitated by the FmHA are:

1. *Business and industrial loans*—guarantee up to 90 percent of principal and interest on loans made by commercial lenders to establish or improve businesses and industries of benefit to people living in rural areas of fewer than 50,000 inhabitants.

2. *Farm ownership loans*—made to eligible farmers to enlarge, develop, and buy family farms, refinance them, or install farm-based recreation facilities and nonagricultural income-producing facilities.

3. *Rural community water, sewer system, and other facility loans*—specific loans to farmers and other residents in rural areas. Loans and grants apply to towns of fewer than 10,000 inhabitants.

Contact: FmHA, Department of Agriculture, 14th Street and Independence Avenue, SW, Washington, DC 20250, phone: (202) 447-4323. Check with a county agent for the address of the nearest FmHA office.

FARMERS' MARKETS   At retail locations, either within a large building or outdoors, vendors set up impermanent stands, or rent more sophisticated space, to sell foods and handicrafts. These farmers' markets vary from one-day operations on a municipal lot to highly organized, bazaar-type markets operating six and seven days a week. The DeKalb Farmers Market in Atlanta is a 116,000-square-foot building that houses more than a hundred vendors and attracts 45,000 weekly shoppers. The Lexington Market in Baltimore has been in business more than 100 years and operates all week. On the dock at Old Annapolis is a compact Farmers' Market that is a permanently tenanted business featuring gourmet foods and freshly shucked oysters and clams. In Florida a number of weekly Farmers' Markets operate al fresco each Saturday and Sunday, selling clothing, jewelry, and novelties to thousands of visitors and tourists. At Lancaster Terminal Market, Amish and Mennonite farmers provide a taste of Pennsylvania Dutch country. There are about 2,000 farmers' markets in the United States, a tremendous revival of an institution that began in the late 17th century and had almost disappeared by the 1940s. The revival of these markets provides farmers with direct retailing opportunities and offers fresh-food-minded consumers high-quality products and good prices. Other prominent locations are the Eastern Market in Detroit, an 11-acre facility famed for its Flower Day; the Dallas Farmers' Market, which has been operating since 1930; the Los Angeles Farmers' Market, an open-air attraction near the world's fanciest boutiques; and the Seattle Pike Place Market, a successful city experiment since 1907. Some others are Quincy Market, Boston; Findlay Market, Cincinnati; West Side Market, Cleveland; Public Market, Aurora (CO); El Mercado, San Antonio; and Soulard Market, St. Louis.

FEDERAL CONTRACTS   Uncle Sam is the biggest buyer of every class of merchandise and services imaginable. If an entrepreneur wants to explore doing business with the federal government, the Small Business Administration (SBA) can help in making the proper connection, getting the appropriate papers, and filing applications in the prescribed manner. Small entrepreneurs are often loath to pursue opportunities for federal contracts because they are intimidated by the amount of paperwork and the exacting specifications. Both of these are necessary in order to assure impartiality, fairness, and reasonable quality control in the expenditure of public dollars. The pot, however, holds $100 *billion,* and if a product or service is useful to one of the myriad of government branches, if it is priced competitively, and if it can be produced within government-allotted and proscribed parameters, then why not try? Here are some nuggets of advice for doing business with Uncle Sam:

- Use the local library to get reference material on federal purchasing, and look up the nearest SBA office for details.

- Many federal agencies with which an owner may wish to do business have staff members specifically charged with helping small contractors to get onto their bid lists.

- A bid price to the federal government needs to include the costs of production of manuals, test reports, packaging, and so on, in accordance with government specifications.

- A business owned by a minority member or woman may be eligible for a special "set-aside" program.

- Government contract or purchasing officers can deal only with established, proven companies which can show that they can deliver the goods or services as specified, at a competitive price.

Private consulting companies, some SCORE offices, and some books like *Free Help from Uncle Sam* (William Alarid and Gustav Berle; Santa Maria, CA: Puma Publishing Co., 1989) may be of help. (See also *Government Procurement.*)

FEDERAL TECHNOLOGY TRANSFER

Private, small businesses can obtain the results of costly technological innovations produced by federal-government-contracted scientists. This method of helping entrepreneurs was established in 1986 by the Federal Technology Transfer Act, to give the private sector access to the numerous ideas and innovations that are generated by government-sponsored laboratories around the country. Each year the government invests $60 billion in research and development, at approximately 300 facilities. Unfortunately, this largely untapped opportunity is embroiled in red tape. As with many other federally generated projects that are designed to help entrepreneurs, the vastness of the bureaucracy makes it difficult to find out what is available, whom to talk to, how to effect the legal transfer of technology, and how to pay for and protect it. One of the more helpful and effective offices is the Machine Shop of the 21st Century, a largely robotized operation developed by the National Institute of Standards and Technology (formerly the National Bureau of Standards) in Gaithersburg, Maryland, a few miles outside of Washington, DC. The Institute is the only federal laboratory with the explicit goal of serving United States industry and science through the development of a wide variety of measurement services; it also helps with energy-related technology out of its Gaithersburg complex. (Contact: National Institute of Standards and Technology, Building 202 Room 209, Gaithersburg, MD 20899, phone: (301) 975-5500. A Small Business Technology Liaison and Industrial Technology Partnership office is located at the Department of Commerce, Constitution Avenue and 14th Street, NW, Room 4816, Washington, DC 20230, phone: (202) 377-5913. A local Congressional or SCORE office may have more information and directions.

FEEDER INDUSTRIES   Small industrial companies that provide parts or services to a major manufacturer are called feeder companies. They are ideal vehicles for startup enterprises—especially spinoffs of larger corporations, which have maintained good relations with their former employer. Some major companies deliberately encourage these spinoffs because some parts can be manufactured more economically and even more efficiently in a small workshop. The larger company assures that the production of the smaller company is bought, usually by prior arrangement; it may even help to finance the smaller operation or provide raw materials. A former vice president of a gigantic aerospace corporation set up a private consulting service and furnished consultants to the large company on an as-needed basis. The net cost to the large company was lower than when these experts were on the full-time payroll—and receiving 30 percent of their salary in additional fringe benefits. The larger corporation was able to assure quick payments to the smaller company, a symbiosis that resulted in quicker services than before. It has been the experience of numerous large companies that quick payment (within 30 days) to suppliers (feeders) is a highly productive device. A reputation for quick payment assures priority treatment. One large company reported that even if it had to borrow short-term funds to make quick feeder-industry payments feasible, the results were worth the slight additional cost.

FINANCIAL PLANNERS   Members of The Institute of Certified Financial Planners (CFPs), a national nonprofit association, are accredited professionals who can help clients set realistic financial goals and make advantageous financial decisions. To obtain the services of registered CFPs, a national, toll-free hotline makes available a list of local members, phone: (800) 282-PLAN. The need for professional financial planning has become more acute as our economy and society have become more complicated. To help clients protect, accumulate, and conserve their assets, CFPs consider such factors as the current economy, the Tax Reform Act, the investment market, deregulation and its spreading effects, financial products available to investors, budgeting, insurance, cash reserves, investment and estate planning, retirement projections, and IRS tax planning. A detailed brochure on these services, "Financial Planning: A Common Sense Guide for the 1990s," is available for $2.00 from the Institute, Two Denver Highlands, 10065 E. Harvard Avenue, Suite 320, Denver, CO 80231-5965. The Institute publishes the *Journal of Financial Planning*, a newsletter ("Institute Today"), a prospective client referral program, and a client newsletter called "Asset Planning." An educational program available to international, domestic, and associate members leads to appropriate credentials and participation in the Institute's programs. Membership cost varies from $120 to $185 a year; listing in the CFP Directory adds $25.

FINANCIAL RATIOS Comparative figures called *ratio analyses* are used in making credit and investment judgments. These figures, usually gleaned from a company's financial statements, are used by investors to determine a company's value, evaluate risks, and make comparisons to prior analyses. A business owner or accountant can ascertain trends, weaknesses, and potential dangers from the analyses of these various ratios. The following types of ratios are among those that lenders and investors might employ:

- The current ratio—ratio of current assets to current liabilities.
- Debt-to-total-assets ratio—comparison of all the firm's debts to all its assets.
- Debt-to-equity ratio—calculation of the firm's fiscal soundness by dividing total liability by total equity.
- Times-interest-earned ratio—measure of long-term solvency, calculated by dividing net income before interest and income tax expense by the amount of interest expense.
- Quick or acid-test ratio—current assets less inventory, divided by the amount of current liabilities.
- Inventory-turnover ratio—how well the firm used the resources at its command; total cost of sales divided by total inventory.
- Return-on-assets ratio—net income divided by total assets.
- Net-income-to-sales ratio (also called the profit-margin ratio)— income after all expenses divided into gross sales.

Standard industry ratios are reported in Dun & Bradstreet's *Key Business Ratios*, P.O. Box 3224, Church Street Station, New York, NY 10008, and *Robert Morris Annual Report*, Philadelphia National Bank Building, Philadelphia, PA 19107.

FINANCIAL STATEMENTS From a record of total assets and liabilities, a business or individual knows what the business or individual is worth, which is important information at all times. Is the business going ahead or falling behind, expanding or standing still? Can it afford to buy more equipment or merchandise or does it need to sell some off? Can it hire an additional helper or must it buckle down and work harder? Can it launch a new advertising campaign or should it switch to promotion that is less cost-intensive? Can it issue a bonus or only promises for the future? A financial statement is a certificate of success or failure in fulfilling a business's needs. Others have needs too. The bank or other lenders from whom a business may need to borrow money will require execution of detailed and accurate financial statements of current business condition, to decide how much can be lent, how the money will be paid back, and how the loan can be used to best advantage. Financial statements include usually a balance sheet, an income statement (also referred to as an operating statement, or a profit-and-loss statement), a statement of working capital, indicating changes during the past year or years, and a conclusion that shows net worth. The more detailed the statements, the more the owner knows; and the more the potential lender is informed, the better the chance for a quick, favorable determination on the loan request. (See also *Balance Sheet, Income Statement* and *Profit-and-Loss Statement.*)

FLEXIBLE MANUFACTURING NETWORKS

Small, highly specialized manufacturing companies work cooperatively in this type of enterprise. They employ skilled workers, but pay them well above industry averages in return for higher productivity. They do not try to compete in the manufacture of traditionally mass-produced items, but specialize in technical products that are more competition-proof. Their highly trained labor force can utilize advanced technologies. By concentrating on very narrow areas, these firms usually produce top-quality parts and components, or finished products with top ratings in their category. The support system underlying a network of small firms that work together, pool their expertise, and, instead of competing, complement each other in order to compete in a larger global market, has created high employment and economic success for them. Flexible manufacturing networks have proved that they reduce the weaknesses of small businesses and build on their strengths. To take networking several steps further, these shared-support associations provide their members with numerous needed services—accounting, payroll, marketing, purchasing, transportation, daycare, and even educational facilities in local technical schools. Alone, no member could afford the variety or the quality of these services. One American observer who visited a number of such networks in northern Italy stated, "I have seen the future, and it works."

FLEXTIME EMPLOYMENT

Variable working hours are increasingly popular in areas of high employment, and this trend is causing extra emphasis in industry—especially at companies having difficulty finding workers—on special employee services such as nursery schools. For the first time, in 1988, job-holding mothers of children under the age of three—4.6

million—outnumbered those who stay home with their children; they also constituted one of the fastest growing segments of the workforce. Working mothers of children older than three are of course more numerous—15.4 million—but the number is not increasing as rapidly. Companies that grant employees some freedom in deciding the hours when they will work generally insist that everyone be on hand during a certain "core period." Employees are usually given some options on coming in before the core period or staying later, if the company performs the kind of work that allows such flextime. One survey showed that from a cross-section of companies, more than 25 percent allowed some flextime among employees, while another 5 percent were thinking of introducing it. In addition to accommodating mothers of small children, benefits to a company using variable working hours include: improved morale, reduced absenteeism, less job turnover, and increased productivity. It is feasible that, by using flextime, a company can employ more people who work fewer than 20 hours a week (which has evident tax and compensation advantages), save space by having workers take turns at workstations or machinery, and utilize physical facilities more efficiently.

FORECASTING

Polishing a crystal ball to determine what lies ahead is a necessary activity in preparing a cash flow forecast for a business plan. An entrepreneur's own experience as a business person, past trends, projections by national and trade organizations and prominent economists all are useful to take a little of the guess out of the "guestimate." The Small Business Administration's (SBA) Office of Advocacy, with the assistance of its own astute researchers and the formidable power of the government's prognosticators at its disposal, has released a report entitled "Small Business in the Year 2000" that contains the following predictions:

- The average age of the labor force will be 39.
- Wages will rise much more than productivity, necessitating increased managerial skills and better training of employees.
- The shift from an economy based on manufacturing and mining to one based on services and information will continue through 2000.
- Small businesses will experience a change from fairly stable, geographically limited markets to more volatile, international ones.
- Per-capita worker output will increase because of the twin trends of higher labor cost and relative scarcity.
- There will be continued demand for leisure-related goods and services as American workers put in fewer hours but earn more.

- Manufacturing-based and goods-producing industries will continue their decline, while service-based enterprises continue to rise.

- The fastest growing industries will be medical services, business services, computers/software, materials handling equipment, and transportation services.

- The total number of businesses by 2000 will increase to 27.2 million (from 19.3 million in 1985), which will include 21.4 million small unincorporated enterprises (up from 15.8 million in 1985).

- The number of self-employed women will more than double—up to 5.5 million in 2000 from 2.61 million in 1985.

- A backlash against big business and polluting industries will create increasing numbers of ecologically sensitive enterprises.

FOREIGN TRADE ZONE (FTZ) For small entrepreneurs who are importers or are contemplating getting into importing, the FTZs are very important. Exporters in other countries who send merchandise to the United States have at their disposal numerous trade zones where merchandise may be kept for an unlimited time, free of duty, until it is shipped out to an American destination. The FTZ charges a fee, but no customs duties are levied by the United States Customs Service until the foreign merchandise is actually transferred out of the FTZ. While imported merchandise is in a free zone, it can be stored, assembled, repackaged, sorted, graded, advertised, and even exhibited. It can be processed in the zone even if it is to be transshipped into a third country later on. There are more than 100 of these customs-privileged facilities in the United States and its offshore possessions, a list of them is available to businesses in the export–import field and those planning to handle manufactured, to-be-assembled, or repackaged goods. Contact: Foreign Trade Zones Board, Department of Commerce, 14th Street and Constitution Avenue, NW, Room 1872, Washington, DC 20230, phone: (202) 377-2862.

FRANCHISING This is the favored buzzword of 1990s entrepreneurship, principally because national survival statistics favor franchises by a wide margin. While 85 percent of small business startups succumb within the first five years, franchises have remarkable staying power, virtually reversing these statistics. Money lenders, from the Small Business Administration down to the smallest commercial banks, state development offices, and minority assistance programs, prefer to gamble on a franchise rather than an unproven, private innovation. For 25 years franchising

Franchise	Capital Requirements ($)	Franchise Fee ($)	Royalty (%)	Advertising (%)
Arby's	330,000 +	37,500	3.5	2
Bonanza	75,000 +	30,000	4.8	2
Burger King	250,000 +	40,000	3.5	4
Dunkin' Donuts	75,000	20,000 +	—	4.5
Everything Yogurt	200,000 +	12,500 +	5	—
Hardee's	470,000 +	15,000	3.5–4	5
Jazzercise	2,500	500	20	—
Kentucky Fried Chicken	400,000–500,000	10,000 +	5.5	4.5
McDonald's	270,000 +	12,500	11.5	var.
Merry Maids Service	7,000 +	17,500	7	—
Mr. Donut	50,000 +	15,000	—	4.9
Precision Tune	115,000 +	20,000	7.5	9
Sir Speedy	110,000	17,500	6	1
Taco Bell	75,000	45,000	5.5	4.5
Wendy's	340,000 +	25,000	4	var.

has been well promoted, from the $1,000 to $5,000 bookkeeping and tax services to the $150,000 to $250,000 convenience store or the $270,000 to $500,000 McDonald's. By the year 2000, according to the Washington-based Naisbitt Group, franchising volume should reach $705 billion. About 2,000 companies currently issue franchises in the United States. New franchise owners include increasing numbers of women who are entering business via this route and of capitalized entrepreneurs who have little or no business experience. To obtain a franchise business, a license must be granted by a company (the franchisor) to an individual or firm (the franchisee) to operate a business that uses the franchisor's name, product, services, promotion, selling, distribution, display methods, and company support. The license usually defines a specific, limited territory within which the franchisee may operate, participate in the franchisor's promotion programs, and use the franchisor's continuing products. Fees are based normally on an initial amount and a royalty or percentage on future purchases. Some preopening training and continuing counseling are usually involved. For more information, contact: International Franchise Association, 1350 New York Avenue, NW, Washington, DC 20005, phone: (202) 628-8000.

Within each franchise, sizable variables exist, depending on the size of the market, the timing in the life of the franchisor, and the many fringe costs involved. There are generally three basic costs: the franchise fee, royalty expense, and advertising participation. In some franchises, merchandise must be purchased directly from the franchisor or from mandated sources—and not always at the most advantageous price. Most franchises demand a range of operating capital that will ensure the franchisee's survival, especially during the crucial and vulnerable startup year.

FREE INFORMATION

Among the hundreds of free items that are available, primarily from the federal government, these are of particular interest to the entrepreneur:

4000 films—directory listing them (and small charges) available from National Audio Visual Center, Information Services DW, Washington, DC 20409.

Future information—trends are detailed in "What's Next" newsletter; to get on the mailing list, contact a Congressional Representative, U.S. House of Representatives, Washington, DC 20515.

Government publications on 250 subjects—bibliography available from Superintendent of Documents, Government Printing Office, Washington, DC 20240.

"Handicrafts Business"—pamphlet free from local SBA office.

Minority Business Locator Data Base—to locate, or to be listed in this data base of 30,000 minority-owned businesses, contact: Information Clearing House, Department of Commerce, Minority Business Development Agency, 14th Street and Constitution Avenue, Room 6708, Washington, DC 20230.

National Consumer Buying Alert—the best and worst foods to buy according to the Consumer Information Center, P.O. Box 100, Pueblo, CO 81009.

New Homemaker Information Packet—available by writing to Senators or Congressional Representatives, U.S. Senate or U.S. House of Representatives, Washington, DC 20515.

Official bitch book—111-page "Consumers' Resource Handbook," a guide to federal, state, corporate, and private consumer complaint contacts; free from Consumer Information Center, P.O. Box 100, Pueblo, CO 81009.

"Organic Growing"—200-item bibliography on organic gardening and farming from the National Agricultural Library, 10301 Baltimore Boulevard, Beltsville, MD 20705.

Productivity/quality/improvement—references and bibliographies on improving company productivity, quality, competitiveness; available from Commerce Productivity Center, Department of Commerce, 14th Street and Constitution Avenue, NW, Room 7413, Washington, DC 20230.

"Recreation and Outdoor Activities" (Catalog SB-017)—listing of all national recreation areas and all federal publications on this subject; free from Superintendent of Documents, Government Printing Office, Washington, DC 20402.

For more information, see Matthew Lesko, *Information, USA* (New York: Viking-Penguin, 1986); and William Alarid and Gustav Berle, *Free Help from Uncle Sam* (Santa Maria, CA: Puma Publishing Co., 1989).

FUTURE TRENDS FOR ENTREPRENEURS

The following seven trends, pointed out by various social scientists, could affect the way entrepreneurs do business in the next decade:

1. Companies are no longer expanding ad infinitum. They are downsizing through layoffs, attrition without replacements, golden-parachute offers to middle-management executives, and deliberate creation of smaller divisions.

2. Advancement within a company will be more limited, partially as a consequence of the downsizing trend. Lower-income opportunities will result.

    (Both trends mean that more executives will eye entrepreneurship opportunities and go into businesses of their own.)

3. The electronics industry will continue to produce more miracles in computer and laser technology, making the newest innovations obsolete.

4. Advertising and sales promotion will become more intense as competition stiffens; methods of merchandising will become more blatant and insidious, though not necessarily more effective.

5. The information age will continue to burgeon but will become more sophisticated, thus ruling out success opportunities for the smaller entrepreneur, who is unprepared to survive in the increasingly competitive and technical marketplace.

6. American society will become more introverted, like water dripped upon an oily surface; it will retrench into more compact friends-and-family circles. There will be some paranoia about crime, diseases, crazies, and strange trends and cults. There will be golden opportunities for some, dangers for many more.

7. The 1990s are expected to bring continued sales growth for three-quarters of small entrepreneurs, but profits are expected to grow at a somewhat slower pace. More than 80 percent of small entrepreneurs will not see drug and alcohol abuse as problems in their workplaces and they will not need to fear the inroads of increased competition from abroad. Their biggest concern for the 1990s will not be foreign ogres, but domestic ones— government regulations.

(Source: Reliable Corporation, Small Business Survey; Chicago [1989].) (See also *Futurists.*)

FUTURISTS

These scientists try to analyze what our lives and our economy will be like in the next or future decades. For the entrepreneur starting a new business or planning an expansion, knowing what lies ahead would be worthwhile. Futurists use statistical analyses and computerized predictions. At a recent conference entitled "Future View, the 1990s and Beyond," held in Washington, DC, the following descriptions of our future were projected:

- Increased automation, robotics, and computer applications in manufacturing.

- Average workweek of 32 hours.
- More leisure time and more activities to occupy those extra hours.
- Increased marriage rate, reduction in divorce.
- Computerized voting, income tax filing, and college entrance exams.
- Magazines available on floppy disks.
- Bets placed electronically, on sporting events like horse races.
- Greater emphasis on individual creativity in small and large corporate enterprises.
- Increased number of entrepreneurs, continued squeeze of middle management in larger corporations.
- Shift to smaller firms, with 85 percent of the labor force employed by companies with fewer than 200 people.
- A service economy employing in excess of 85 percent of the workforce; more low-paying service jobs.
- Increased home-computer use, in up to 70 percent of all homes (compared to less than 20 percent today).
- Increased number of women entering the workforce; by 2000, about 63 percent of employees female.
- Mandatory retirement age at age 70 by 2000.

(Source: World Future Society, 4916 St. Elmo Avenue, Bethesda, MD 20814.)

GOING PUBLIC The process of turning a private company into a stock company or corporation in which outsiders can buy shares shifts the firm's ownership from an individual or a few investors to a broader, usually impersonal group of many shareholders. In going public, the company becomes subject to numerous regulations and legal requirements, usually enforced by the Securities and Exchange Commission. The entrepreneur's company becomes incorporated and is permitted to issue a certain amount of shares, according to the company's state-approved charter. The purpose of all this is, of course, to raise equity for the operation and expansion of the company. Two types of shares may be issued: *common* stock entitles the purchaser to vote in the company's affairs; *preferred* stock, which is non-voting, guarantees first redemption in the event of the company's failure. To go public and sell shares to outsiders usually requires that the stock issue be underwritten by an investment banking firm, which acts as the wholesaler for the company's stock. The underwriter in turn sells the stock to retail brokers or directly to institutions, which may buy major portions of the stock. The cost of going public is quite substantial. Several thousand dollars are needed for advance fees, legal management, and printing of prospectuses, and, if and when the placement of the new stock is successful, a portion of the proceeds goes to brokerage fees. The more stock sold, the more complicated the offering process. Until institutions or a lot of individuals purchase a company's stock, nothing really has happened. To make others invest money in a company takes more than wishful thinking—it requires extensive planning, good products, proven management, and top-notch legal and accounting help.

GOVERNMENT PROCUREMENT

The descriptive information here is limited to federal government procurements reserved for small and minority businesses, which account for up to 21 million separate purchases each year, for a combined annual dollar value of more than $17 billion. There are hundreds, perhaps even thousands, of purchasing agents within the government. The rules and regulations, specifications, paperwork, and red tape are formidable, but once a company is on a government purchasing list, it can get orders forever. Some departments pay quickly; others, like the Navy Department, have a reputation for being very slow. Despite the awesome size of the customer and the amount of paperwork, the customer's representative and signatory is still a human being. The entrepreneur should get to know the voice and, if possible, the face on the other side of the transaction. As with a customer in private industry, once the government-client gains confidence in the enterprise and its product, sales will become easier and repetitive, often even without competitive bidding. The Small Business Administration has 11 procurement specialists who can help with entry into government procurement and the PASS (Procurement Automated Source System) procedures.

Numerous government publications, obtained free or for modest fees, will help to guide interested entrepreneurs through the morass of seemingly endless red tape (see below). With persistence, small businesses often find that Uncle Sam's $17 billion pot o' gold is worth working for. Remember one critical thing: don't—repeat: *don't*—deviate from specs, once they have been set and accepted. (See also *Federal Contracts.*)

Contact: the Procurement Assistance Specialist at the nearest SBA office listed below, or the Office of Procurement and Grants Management, 1441 L Street, NW, Room 219, Washington, DC 20416. There is no charge to have a business placed on the official PASS list.

Recommended Publications:

Commerce Business Daily—published each weekday by the Department of Commerce. Copies on file at GSA Business Service Centers

States/Region	Address/Phone
New England	60 Batterymarch, 10th Floor, Boston, MA 02110, (617) 223-3162
NJ, NY	26 Federal Plaza, New York, NY 10278, (212) 264-7770
Mid-Atlantic	Suite 646, West Lobby, 231 S. Asaphs Road, Bala Cynwyd, PA 19004, (215) 596-0172
Southeast	1375 Peachtree St., 5th Floor, Atlanta, GA 30367, (404) 881-7587
IL, IN, MI, MN (east), OH, WI	219 S. Dearborn St., Rm. 858, Chicago, IL 60604, (312) 886-4727
AR, LA, MI, MN (west), OK, TX	8625 King George Drive, Bldg. C, Dallas, TX 75235-3391, (214) 767-7639
IA, KS, MO, NE	911 Walnut St., 23rd Floor, Kansas City, MO 64106, (816) 374-5502
Mountain States	1405 Curtis St., 22nd Floor, Denver, CO 80202, (303) 837-5441
AZ, CA (south)	350 S. Figueroa St., 6th Floor, Los Angeles, CA 90071, (213) 688-2946
CA (north), HI, NV	Box 36044, 450 Golden Gate Ave., San Francisco, CA 94102, (415) 556-9616
Northwest and AK	4th & Vine Bldg., 2615 4th Ave., Seattle, WA 98121, (206) 442-0390

and major public libraries. Annual subscription: $81 ($160 via first-class mail). Lists all proposed civilian agency procurements over $5,000 and all Department of Defense procurements over $10,000. Contact: Superintendent of Documents, Government Printing Office, Washington, DC 20402.

Doing Business with the Federal Government —free from GSA offices.

Doing Business with the Veterans Administration —free. Contact: VA Office of Procurement and Supply, 810 Vermont Avenue, NW, Room RS 90, Washington, DC 20420.

Federal Buying Directory —names, addresses, and telephone numbers of offices in each federal agency; free. All General Services Administration (GSA) Business Service Centers in Washington, Boston, New York, Philadelphia, Atlanta, Chicago, Kansas City, Fort Worth, Denver, San Francisco, Los Angeles, and Seattle. Contact: GSA, 18th and F Streets, NW, Washington, DC 20405, phone: (202) 501-2250.

Guide to Specifications, Standards and Commercial Item Descriptions of the Federal Government —free from GSA offices.

Selling to the Department of the Treasury —free. Contact: Department of the Treasury, 15th Street and Pennsylvania Avenue, NW, Washington, DC 20220.

Selling to the Military —Department of Defense requirements. Order No. 008-000-00345-0; $6.00. Contact: Superintendent of Documents (see above).

Selling to the Postal Service —Contact: Office of Contracts, Procurement and Supply Department, U.S. Postal Service, 475 L'Enfant Plaza West, SW, Room 1010, Washington, DC 20260.

Small Business Guide to Federal Research and Development Funding Opportunities —136 pages, $6.00. Contact: Superintendent of Documents (see above).

GRANTOR RETAINED INCOME TRUST (GRIT)

A way of keeping an enterprise in the family after the owner's retirement or demise is to start to transfer ownership to children (or other heirs) during the owner's lifetime. A business owner who establishes a GRIT transfers assets into an irrevocable trust for 10 years, while retaining the income from the assets. At the end of the 10 years, the assets pass to one or more designated beneficiaries in a transfer that is subject to gift tax. Since the owner is keeping the right to the income, he or she is in effect splitting the assets into two parts; hence the gift tax is based on only a fraction of the total. Under Internal Revenue Service tables, the tax would be assessed on only 38.55 percent of the assets' value. An added advantage is that any appreciation occurring after the transfer escapes estate tax. If a GRIT is set up for 10 years and the owner does not live out this period, the trust's assets revert to the estate for tax purposes. An owner who is reluctant to give up control of a business can place a portion (less than 50 percent) of the business's value into a GRIT. Then, over subsequent years, he or she can take advantage of the $10,000 annual gift tax exclusion to pass along some or all of the balance. This $10,000 can be transferred to each recipient in case there are several heirs. (No matter how this process is explained here or in other books, a knowledgeable tax accountant or lawyer should be retained when setting up a GRIT, to unscramble the facts and limitations of the particular circumstances.)

GROSS MARGIN

Sometimes called gross profit, gross margin is the difference between sales income and the cost of the goods sold—before any expenses have been taken out. Each item and each category of merchandise has different gross margins. They can be determined by a number of factors: industry averages reported by trade associations, trade magazines, and government bureaus; competition; prestige of item or location; services that need to be expended in the item's sale; use of the item as a "leader" in trying to attract customers for other items; age or obsolescence of item; consumer demand for or popularity of item; and finally, what the traffic will bear. (See *Markup.*) To determine the gross margin needed as an average of earnings, *all* expenses of doing business must be included. To determine gross margin, an owner must anticipate: future markdowns for goods that do not sell quickly enough; "shrinkages" (theft or disappearance); returns of goods; credit losses; transportation and delivery; alterations; and on and on. The table on page 95 (top) will help in determining markup needed for gross margin requirements between 5 and 50 percent.

The average gross margins shown on page 95 were taken from an analysis, made by the Dun & Bradstreet Corporation, of more than 3 million corporations during a typical business year.

One reason for the greater profit margin of personally operated businesses is that no manager is being paid out of proceeds; the proprietor takes what's left. Lower gross margins for some categories (food markets, liquor stores, wholesalers, and so on) are made up by larger volume.

Gross Margin (%)	Markup (%)	Gross Margin (%)	Markup (%)	Gross Margin (%)	Markup (%)	Gross Margin (%)	Markup (%)
5.0	5.3	16.0	19.1	28.0	38.9	37.0	58.8
7.5	8.1	17.0	20.5	30.0	42.9	39.0	64.0
10.0	11.1	18.0	22.0	31.0	45.0	40.0	66.7
12.0	13.7	19.0	23.5	32.0	47.1	42.0	72.5
13.0	15.0	20.0	25.0	33.0	49.3	45.0	81.9
14.0	16.3	22.0	28.2	34.0	51.6	47.0	88.8
15.0	17.7	25.0	33.3	35.0	53.9	50.0	100.0

To determine the markup needed to obtain a gross margin not shown in the table, use this formula:
Gross margin + Cost of goods sold = markup.
(Note: Cost of goods sold is the difference between 100 percent and the percent of gross margin.)

Type of Business	Average Gross Margins	
	Corporations (%)	Proprietorships (%)
Agricultural production	32.26	62.45
Building materials	26.97	31.86
Business services	54.03	81.18
Construction	21.03	39.32
Drug stores	26.50	30.81
Fashion shops	40.82	40.03
Food stores	22.93	19.72
Gasoline service stations	13.91	14.92
General merchandise	35.90	21.66
Gift/Novelty shops	34.95	41.86
Liquor stores	18.42	22.68
Lodging places	55.70	85.63
Personal services	61.51	82.87
Printing	37.38	58.25
Wholesale trades	16.75	28.68

GROSS NATIONAL PRODUCT (GNP)

The GNP of a country—the total value of goods and services produced in a national economy over a specified period of time, usually a year—is regarded as the principal indicator of the status of the economy. The GNP can be expressed in total dollars or in per-capita income. Comparison of the GNP among leading industrial countries shows up some striking disparities. The USSR, for instance, has one-half the GNP of the United States; realization of this fact by the Soviet administration no doubt contributed to *perestroika* and the subsequent lessening of international political tensions.

Entrepreneurs interested in possible international trade will find GNP and per-capita income of potential foreign trading partners interesting. Listed here are a few comparative figures for guidance as of 1988:

GNP in Billions of Dollars (rounded off):

US	4,800
USSR	2,500
Japan	1,700
W. Germany	1,300
France	900
Italy	700
England	550
Canada	475
Spain	300
Poland	300
East Germany	200

GNP per capita in 1988 dollars (rounded off):

US	19,800
W. Germany	18,000
Canada	17,500
France	16,500
Japan	15,000
Italy	14,000
England	13,500
East Germany	12,500
USSR	8,800
Hungary	8,800
Spain	7,500
Poland	7,000

(Source: CIA.)

GROUP INSURANCE

The consideration of group insurance is a vital ingredient in any enterprise's budgetary planning. It provides an "umbrella" or overall insurance policy that covers members of a company, union, trade group, professional association, or other related group. With the tremendous rise in insurance rates—especially for health, disability, and automobile insurance, particularly in large metropolitan centers—and with pressures from various governments, most companies and associations make group insurance available as an option or choice of their individual members or employees. However, some companies offer group insurance as an incentive to attract workers or provide a substantial subsidy that shares the costs of the premium with the employees.

Group rates are usually considerably less than individual policies and may be easier to obtain. Disability insurance, for instance, pays about half of the employees' normal income, while health insurance varies widely, depending on the premium paid, the size of the insured group, and the company underwriting the policy. Group policies should be "shopped" for, because their costs vary widely. They form a valuable recruiting tool, however. With costs for health care becoming prohibitive, many employees consider health care coverage as important as any other factor in their decision to accept employment. Some insurance companies accept group insurance policies or individual additional enrollments only at certain times of the year. From the perspective of both the individual and the employer, interim insurance coverage, if available, is desirable. Estimated monthly costs for health policies can run from $100 to $250, depending on coverage and geographical area. A small group should explore ways of joining a larger group, for additional savings. (See also *Health Care.*)

GROWTH Many trends, whether in far-ranging international policies or in grass-roots buying decisions, affect small business growth. However, small business reports are crowing over the relatively newfound *wunderkind* of capitalism—the small business operator, who is credited for a remarkable growth trend in this segment. Even in countries behind the crumbling Iron Curtain, this trend has been noted. Documentation of the growth trend was started in 1986. The startup entrepreneur should take note of these findings:

1. Startups occur most frequently in industries close to final sales to the consumer. These include retail stores, service businesses, real estate, and insurance.

2. Economic conditions in an area affect small businesses beyond their control. For example, declines in oil production in Texas and Oklahoma affected the number of small business failures and bankruptcies. Entrepreneurs must try to guard against such uncontrollable general conditions through versatility in diversification and relocation, and by an ability to tighten up operating costs and to draw on stored-up reserves.

3. Deregulations by governments often provide opportunities for small business. Nearly one in every five new nongovernment jobs during the past decade has been in transportation and financial services (industries affected by deregulations)—double the percentage of increase in the economy as a whole.

4. New innovations, formerly restricted to large industries or shunned by a more conservative older generation, are the propellants of new small business successes. Small ventures are

now experimenting, and succeeding, with new products, new technologies, and new channels of distribution.

5. Earnings of entrepreneurial proprietorships are showing growth commensurate to their risks—a proof of long-known business theory. For several years in a row, earnings by proprietorships have increased more rapidly than wage/salary earnings. In one recent year proprietorship income rose 9.6 percent; wage-and-salary income, 5.5 percent; corporate profits, 6.8 percent. (See also *Expansion.*)

HANDICAPPED ASSISTANCE LOANS (HAL)   Loans under the HAL program are available for the establishment, acquisition, or operation of a small business concern in two categories:

HAL = 1—financial assistance to private or public nonprofit sheltered workshops or any similar organizations.

HAL = 2—financial assistance to a small business owned by a handicapped person.

To qualify for HAL, a sheltered workshop must be operated by handicapped persons at least 75 percent of the time and be recognized as such by certification of the Internal Revenue Service, the Secretary of Labor, or an appropriate state agency. When run by an individual, the workshop must be owned and operated by one or more handicapped persons. Absentee ownership does not count. The Small Business Administration (SBA) may guarantee a loan of up to $750,000 made by a private lending institution. Direct loans from the SBA (made only if the applicant is turned down by one or two private lending institutions) are limited to $150,000. Interest rates by private lenders are to be "reasonable"; direct loans are pegged at only 3 percent. However, no direct loan can be approved if a guaranteed loan is available. In either procedure, loan approval is preceded by thorough investigation. The experience, competence, and ability of the owners and operators of the small business must indicate that the business has every chance of success and that the loan can be repaid from the projected earnings of the business. Nonprofit organizations must have the capability and experience to perform successfully in producing and providing marketable goods and services. The HAL program is tied in with the Section 8(a) minority business program, which sets aside federal contract work for small, minority-owned businesses. The procedure, as with other loan applications, is for a handicapped applicant to make loan requests at two or three banks. If the applicant is turned down, as happens all too often, he or she can apply directly to the SBA under the HAL program. An example is a software company near Washington, DC, that was started 10 years ago by a Chinese immigrant who was deaf but had the advantage of a sizable and cooperative family. Three of his brothers joined in the struggle. The startup for this young company included courses at a college for the deaf. Members of the firm, from the receptionist to the president, became conversant in sign language. After acceptance into the SBA-sponsored program, it still took eight months to land the first federal subcontract, but today the company has an average of 400 employees and grosses $37 million a year. "Good management," said this entrepreneur, "depends on good communication." Evidently this businessman communicated very well. Detailed information on HAL programs may be obtained from any local SBA office. (See Appendix A.)

HEALTH CARE In any enterprise, health care planning is vital, both for the owner and the employees. Some form of subsidization must be provided—without going broke. Health care is one of the largest growth industries, a profession beset by serious labor shortages and quality control, and, on the business side, a sector of our economy that is among the leading contributors to inflation. Federal and local laws make some health care provisions mandatory, both as a preventive measure in making the workplace more secure and as a curative measure in the event of illness. Some employees will turn down an otherwise brilliant job opportunity if no health insurance or unsuitable coverage is included in the benefits package. The public's health consciousness level has been raised as the costs of providing health care have spiraled upward, and preventive health measures should be incorporated and encouraged in any entrepreneurial operating plan. Small entrepreneurs or startup businesses with fewer than 50 employees can take some actions to reduce health care costs:

1. Join or form a group (like the Council of Smaller Enterprises, formed in Cleveland) which can place a large amount of protection for 10 to 15 percent below cost.

2. Do some research among companies of a similar size, which have had health care plans in force for at least three years.

3. Explore a "cafeteria plan" in which employees can pick and choose what type of coverage they want; some choose none because they are automatically covered by a spouse's policy.

4. Look into HMO (health maintenance organization) or PPO (preferred provider organization) plans to see whether managed care may be economically advantageous.

5. Involve employees in frank health discussions and cost-containment communication—and share the costs.

6. Form and administer an independent plan, but be advised that this requires a company of some size, a ceiling on what and how much can be covered, and knowledgeable administration.

HISPANIC-OWNED SMALL BUSINESSES

In 1988 the Small Business Administration (SBA) provided 695 loans, totaling more than $103.5 million, to Hispanic-owned small businesses in the United States and Puerto Rico. Through its Section 8(a) program, the SBA awards contracts to eligible socially and economically disadvantaged firms. During 1988, more than 1,100 contracts, valued at more than $876 million, were assigned to Hispanic-owned companies. Nearly 800 Hispanic-owned firms are in the Section 8(a) program portfolio, and more than 6,800 are in the PASS (Procurement Automated Source System) program. The number of small businesses owned by Hispanics is estimated as close to 400,000. (See *United States Hispanic Chamber of Commerce.*) The vast majority of Hispanic-owned firms are operated as single proprietorships (233,476 or 94.1 percent in the 1980 Census). Corporations numbered only 2.1 percent but accounted for more than 33 percent of the gross receipts. The highest gross receipts were recorded by automotive dealers and service stations. California and Texas had the highest number of Hispanic-owned firms. Projected figures indicate that Hispanic-owned firms have grown 60 percent since the 1980 Census. Miami/Hialeah is unofficially the leading center of Hispanic ownership. (See also *Asian Americans, Native Americans, and Other Minorities.*)

HOME DELIVERY BUSINESS

Some enterprises deliver products or services to the homes of their customers. Trend-spotters have noted that these enterprises have been proliferating for the past decade. Since the days of "the

Fuller Brush man," the Avon and Mary Kay representatives, and the plethora of neighborhood party-sales for Tupperware and similar products, home delivery businesses have become American institutions. The Domino Pizza chain has gone into franchising in a gigantic way and delivered 230 *million* pizzas to homes and offices during 1988. Mom-and-pop grocery stores have become computerized and now take orders and deliver. Shoppers Express in the East coordinates orders with local supermarkets. Grocery Express in California fills orders from its own warehouses, except for gourmet and specialty foods, which are drawn from smaller, local stores in the system. As more and more homeowners come online with personal computers, the shopping-by-electronics business will expand as well. The baby-boom generation, which typically has two substantial incomes per household and too little time for housekeeping necessities, is identified with the growth of this luxury industry. Elderly and handicapped people who are homebound, single parents, professionals working at home, and college students all add to the market for home delivery products and services. In Los Angeles a new magazine, *L.A. Delivers*, has scored a big success; it features only businesses in the home delivery mode. Home delivery enterprises are becoming a dollar-versus-time tradeoff and they will be expanding during the current decade.

HOME EQUITY

The value an owner has in a home can serve as collateral for a business loan, but home equity is a risky way to raise capital: Should the business not succeed, the home can be endangered. Still, home equity should be considered as collateral because it is readily available, no co-signer other than a spouse is needed, and it can be obtained quickly and inexpensively. If a new business or an expanding business is a pretty sure bet, or if a big deal is pending that is sure to materialize in a relatively short while, then taking out a short-term equity loan at prevailing rates (currently 10.5 to 12 percent) is an option. An equity loan on a home is not advisable if the business is on the downgrade or if the business is a partnership or corporation. The amount that can be borrowed on a home is usually 75 percent of its clear value—that is, 75 percent of the current, appraised value less any mortgage balance. For example, on a $100,000 home with a $50,000 mortgage, the equity amounts to $50,000. Seventy-five percent, the amount of the equity loan value, is $37,500. At about 11 percent interest, payments will be $343.75 a month in interest plus any lender charges, which can run from $500 to $1,500. Equity loans are variable; rates often drop considerably from one year to the next. If the difference is substantial, the bank charges are low, and the equity is high, it may be profitable to pay off the old loan and take out a new loan at the lower rate. Refinancing a home is another way of raising cash, providing the closing costs do not eat up the advantage of this process.

HOME OFFICE

Millions of home-based businesses operate from a kitchen table, a spare room, a basement or garage. They are consultants, service enterprises, artists and artisans, manufacturers' representatives, mini-daycare moms, and professional and medical support services. Some find their way into national statistics when they apply for tax numbers, take out loans, employ people, or register with associations. All too often, these home-based businesses are started with insufficient planning and organization. The entrepreneur may find, after a few months, that the enterprise is not profitable, there are objections from neighbors, a spouse or children are uncooperative, or, simply, the bridge or golf game has priority. The mini-enterprises then join those in the "going out of business" category, the 85 percent of small businesses that disappear before a five-year life. Anyone who is serious about a home-based business should follow seven basic principles, which are valid for any other enterprise:

1. Set both business and personal goals and put them down on paper.

2. Set up a plan to fulfill these goals—what is needed to achieve them.

3. Be realistic about being the chief cook and bottle-washer; assume that all goals won't be done on time; set up priorities.

4. Organize assigned tasks so that they can be done together and more efficiently, especially the many daily errands outside the home and the business calls that must be made in person.

5. Set up regular routines, for efficiency, economy of time, and less confusion.

6. Be flexible. The world will not come to an end if a goal is missed or changed. *You* are in charge of yourself.

7. Evaluate results and plans at least monthly.

For more information, see P. Edwards and S. Edwards, *Working from Home* (Los Angeles: Jeremy P. Tarcher, 1989).

HOMEWORKERS

A growing number of people perform independent labor for companies or general contractors, producing knitwear, artwork, handicrafts, jewelry, assembled parts, keyboarded computer disks, and so on. The advantages to the contractor or employer of having this type of casual labor done outside of the premises of the plant or office have substantially encouraged the importation of items completed, as they once were, generations ago, in American homes. However, primarily because of pressure from unions, this contractual cottage industry production is now subject to numerous restrictions and regulations.

From the entrepreneurial perspective, having employees work from their homes is a mixed blessing; there *are* pitfalls. While home-workers save space and make it possible to attract either better- or lower-paid personnel, there are at least a half-dozen caveats to take into consideration:

1. Managing workers from a distance, supervising their production, or determining how much time they actually put in is difficult.

2. Team spirit, esprit de corps, is lessened.

3. There may be liability for a worker who is injured at home while, allegedly, performing work for the enterprise.

4. Reliable telephone, FAX, and/or computer link-ups are needed.

5. There may be jealousies between workers in the office or plant and the "lucky ones" who can work from home.

6. Clients may need assurance that there is no security threat by having workers take work home or process work away from the office.

One more, for good measure: Do executives feel any less like executives while working at home, where no subordinates make them feel important?

Entrepreneurs who employ homeworkers must know the material in the *Homeworker Handbook* (Department of Labor, Employment Standards Administration, Wage and Hour Division; OMB No. 1215-0013, Form WH-75). The *Handbook* outlines the activities that must be included in "hours worked" and in projecting expenses and selling costs. These considerations include:

(a) setting up and putting away machines and materials,

(b) adjusting, threading, cleaning, oiling, or repairing machines,

(c) actual production of the articles,

(d) inspection of the articles,

(e) repairing or re-work,

(f) sorting and packing or unpacking materials,

(g) training to produce new designs or new items,

(h) rest periods of short duration (up to 20 minutes),

(i) traveling to and from the distribution point to pick up and/or deliver the homeworker's own work or the work of other home-workers (where the travel includes time spent in personal activities, such as shopping or going to the post office, this personal travel time need not be included in counting the hours worked),

(j) waiting at the distribution point to pick up work or deliver completed work and have it inspected,

(k) any other activity required to produce the article, or otherwise required by the employer to be performed.

The following notice to employers and homeworkers was issued by the Department of Labor:

1. Under the Fair Labor Standards Act, homeworkers are entitled to the same protections of the law as other employees. Any violations committed with respect to homeworkers are subject to the penalties set forth in the law and in Regulations, 29 CFR Parts 530 and 579.

2. Homeworkers must be paid at a rate of not less than the minimum wage provided in the Act for all hours worked unless a lower rate is permitted under a special certificate for an individual homeworker in accordance with Regulations, 29 CFR Part 525.

3. Homeworkers must be paid overtime pay at a rate of not less than one and one-half times their regular rates of pay for all hours of work after 40 in a workweek.

4. Deductions from wages for damaged goods, cost of tools or materials (yarn, thread, packing materials, etc.), cost of machines or other equipment, etc., are not permitted and workers may not themselves pay such costs without reimbursement where this reduces the wages received to less than the minimum wage or cuts into required overtime pay.

5. No one under 16 years of age is permitted to perform industrial homework as defined in Regulations, 29 CFR Part 530.

6. The work record entered in this handbook must be only for the employee named on the front page.

7. Records of hours worked and earnings of homeworkers must be kept by the employer in accordance with section 516.31 of Regulations, 29 CFR Part 516.

8. No homework may be performed on Government manufacturing or supply contracts subject to the Walsh–Healey Public Contracts Act.

HOUSE AGENCY   This is an advertising "agency" established within a company and handling only the advertising of that particular company. A house agency may have a different name or even a different address, but its overhead is defrayed by the company-client and all commissions earned from various media in which the company advertises revert back to the company. While many media frown upon such in-house arrangements, as do independent advertising agencies, the creation of house agencies goes on. There are pros and cons with this kind of arrangement. On the surface, it sounds good: advertising placed in local and national media immediately earns 15 percent commission. Some of this rebate goes to pay for the in-house advertising staff and overhead, which generally cost less than the 15 percent. The output of the in-house agency can be controlled closely with the one-client monopoly. The agency is at the company's beck and call and is always available. Its loyalty is absolute; no confidential information about the business is likely to leak out. All forms of advertising, sales promotion, and public relations can be handled by this in-house group, without paying extra fees to outside firms for noncommissionable services. This is especially advantageous if the company does extensive cooperative advertising with retail customers. However, not everything is so ideal. The biggest drawback of an in-house agency is its parochialism: outside viewpoints, ideas, creativity, and exposure are lacking. It's like running a company with only family members. If this shortcoming is remedied and steps are taken to assure creative light to enter from the outside, then this method might be worth investigating—*if* the company's ad budget is substantial enough.

IMMIGRANTS   Americans-to-be, people who come to the United States from foreign countries, usually legitimately through the official immigration process as permanent residents or as political refugees under special dispensation, should be included in any volume on entrepreneurial ventures. While there are sizable humanitarian reasons for allowing hundreds of thousands of foreigners to enter the country as residents, workers, business operators, and, of course, taxpayers, the steady addition to our heterogeneous melting pot is a sound socioeconomic gesture. Consider these two examples: during a recent year, 13 of 17 valedictorians at Boston high-school graduation ceremonies were foreign-born and had learned English as an acquired language; on the other coast, 60,000 Southeast Asian immigrants, many highly skilled and motivated, have become the mainstay of the burgeoning assembly and hi-tech industry in Los Angeles and Orange County, California. In areas such as Miami, the newly arrived Cubans and Central Americans have created an entirely new and vibrant economy. According to the president of an old Miami bank, "Cuban-Americans have become entrepreneurs par excellence . . . creating 25,000 businesses in the past two decades." Richard B. Freeman, a professor of economics at Harvard University, has stated that immigrants "produce more than they consume, and that benefits everyone." America's entrepreneurial history, and indeed its future, may depend on keeping our gates open—polls notwithstanding. Had the Indians been polled in 1620, we undoubtedly would not be here to read this page.

INCOME STATEMENT A company's income statement is a financial statement that shows operating results, such as net income, loss, and depreciation for a specific period of time. Other terms for the income statement are *earnings report, operating statement,* and *profit-and-loss statement.* (See also *Profit-and-Loss Statement.*)

INCUBATORS These growth environments for small business startups represent a relatively new (1984) concept in nurturing new businesses and have shown remarkable success. The Small Business Administration (SBA) uses "survival figures" as a criterion of entrepreneurial frailties. For most small businesses the survival rate after five years is about 15 percent; for franchises, it stands at 80 percent or higher. The same success ratio holds true for small businesses that are part of an incubator system. More than 300 incubators now operate in 40 states but, because of the lasting success of this type of business startup, 1,000 incubators will soon be in existence. Many universities sponsor technology-oriented startups; of these, 47 percent are publicly sponsored and 53 percent are privately sponsored by venture and seed capital investors, corporations, and real estate partnerships. The sponsors usually seek a share in the business and a high return. At academically related incubators, university staff members and students participate in the incubators' research, marketing, and income. Some incubators are hybrids in combination with government sponsors and enjoy the advantage of access to sizable government funding. For more information, contact: National Business Incubation Association, One President Street, Athens, Ohio 45701 (phone: (614) 593-4331); the Association has a complete, up-to-date directory of incubator facilities (membership is $125). Or, contact: Small Business Administration, Office of Private Sector Initiatives, 1441 L Street, NW (Room 317), Washington, DC 20416. Incubator programs have also been established by the National Rural Electric Cooperative Association (Washington, DC). The table on page 108 shows the types of incubators, the services provided, and the advantages to entrepreneurs of participating in an incubator. Following are the addresses of nine major state incubator associations:

California Business Incubator
Network
c/o San Pedro Venture Center
1951 N. Gaffey Street
San Pedro, CA 90731
(213) 855-8393

Illinois Small Business Incubation
Association
c/o The Decatur Industrial
Incubator
2121 U.S. Route 51 South
Decatur, IL 62521
(217) 423-2832

Michigan Business Incubator
Association
c/o Jackson Business Development
Center
414 N. Jackson Street
Jackson, MI 49201
(517) 787-0442

North Carolina Business Incubator
Association
c/o University Business Center,
Inc.
5736 N. Tyron Street
Charlotte, NC 28213
(704) 597-9851

Ohio Business Incubator
Association
c/o The Business & Technology
Center
1445 Summit Street
Columbus, OH 43201
(614) 294-0206

Oklahoma Business Incubator
Association
c/o Rural Enterprises Incubator
120 Waldron Drive
Durant, OK 74701
(405) 924-5094

Pennsylvania Incubator Network
Association
c/o Meadville Redevelopment
Authority
628 Arch Street
Meadville, PA 16335
(814) 336-4290 or 724-2975

Texas Business Incubator
Association
c/o Business Resource Center
4601 N. 19th Street
Waco, TX 76708
(817) 754-8898

Wisconsin Business Incubator
Association
c/o Meadville Redevelopment
Authority
5317 West Burnham Street
West Allis, WI 53219
(414) 643-8720

HOW INCUBATORS REALLY WORK

Types of Incubator	Services Usually Provided by Central Facility	Incubator's Advantages to Startup Entrepreneur
Commercial hi-tech company	Central phone system	Affordable space
	Staffed reception area	Flexible space
Research and development	Reference library	Flexible leases
	Mailroom	Less startup capital needed
Service business	Federal Express and/or UPS	
Light manufacturing		Time-saving because of available services
Wholesalers	Shipping and receiving	
Retailers	FAX transmission	
Mail-order	Typing and secretarial	Availability of consultants
Import/export	Data and word processing	Availability of high-level academic assistance
Nonprofit organization	Photocopying	
	Notary public	
	Translation service	Networking among other incubator entrepreneurs
	Mass mailing service	
	Conference room	Encouragement to produce necessary "tools":
	Child daycare center	
	Coffee shop	
	Accounting services	Business plan
	Business and financial planning	Market analysis
	Legal services	Cash flow statement
	Tax and financial services	Realistic projections
	Loan and banking services	Inventory control
	Seminars and workshops	
	SBA and SCORE availability	
	Chamber of Commerce	

INDUSTRIAL FABRICS ASSOCIATION INTERNATIONAL (IFAI)

This is the world's largest textile organization. Started in 1912, it now has an international membership of over 1,800 and its annual trade show and convention attracts nearly 5,000 attendees and more than 200 exhibitors. IFAI publishes three magazines: *Industrial Fabrics Products Review,* for the vertical industrial fabrics trade;

Geotechnical Fabrics Report, for civil engineers and others who need this industry segment; and *Fabrics & Architecture,* which promotes the use of industrial fabrics in commercial and industrial construction, renovation, and restoration. Entrepreneurs will be interested in this organization and will want to use its expertise and contacts in the following fields: furniture fabrics, casual or outdoor fabrics, tent and awning materials, marine fabrics, transportation covers, ribbons and nonelastic narrow fabrics, geotextiles and geomembranes used by civil engineers, tent renters, and those in associated industries (fiber and yarn producers, coaters, laminators, dyers, and finishers). IFAI is a good source for satisfying special fabric needs, for locating suppliers, and for solving problems in this field. Membership runs from $250 to $2,000, depending on the size of the company. Contact: IFAI, 345 Cedar Street, Suite 450, St. Paul, MN 55101 (phone: 1-(800) 225-4324 or (612) 222-2508.

INGENUITY   A form of cleverness or inventiveness, ingenuity is related to necessity and therefore to the mother of invention. Classic examples are easy to find. Two apple growers sell their Washington State and Oregon fruit by direct mail at somewhat better markups than the corner produce stands. One season, after prominent mail order ads had been placed in national prestige magazines, a sudden hailstorm hit the mountain slopes where their new crop was ripening. Most apples received very noticeable pockmarks and the crestfallen growers thought their season was ruined. They underestimated their ingenious adwriter. Little copy gems were printed up and enclosed with each mail order shipment. The paper slips pointed out that these were, indeed, genuine mountain-grown apples—attested by the small pockmarks which were caused by typical mountain hailstorms and which in no way marred the flavor of these highly superior apples. The season, the crop, and the company's profits were saved and merchandising history were made. In Norman, Oklahoma, a solar panel installer faced hard times when subsidies for solar panels diminished. He created lighted billboards powered by solar panels and is now selling them to licensees and realtors all over the country at $350 apiece. A scientist from Texas developed a contraceptive inoculation for humans, but found that it would sterilize patients. However, she correctly figured that this result would be ideal for nonsurgical spaying of pets. Zonagen will soon be available to veterinarians and the big bucks necessary to market the product will come from the Perot venture capitalists. Ingenuity made these near-disasters into bonanzas. (See also *Innovation.*)

INNOVATION   Finding a new way of doing things, a new process for a product, is the lifeblood of the entrepreneur and the spark that sets a company apart from the crowd. Each year

600,000 innovators take the plunge into a business of their own. Five years down the road, 100,000 of them will still be in business. Some of the others may give up, but the true innovators, even if they fail once, will dust themselves off and start all over again. Here are a half-dozen examples:

- Leo Gerstenzang saw his wife trying to clean their baby's ears with toothpicks and cotton. He invented Q-Tips.

- Otto Diffenbach was toying with the cellophane from a pack of cigarettes. He twisted it around and noticed that it made a tube. He developed the plastic drinking straw.

- King Gillette was inspired by the then-new soda-bottle cap: he thought of other disposable products that were needed. He invented the disposable razor and blade.

- Ole Evinrude, a Swede who lived on a lake, had to row across it to the store where he bought his provisions. Ice cream, which he dearly loved, was soup by the time he got back. He invented an outboard motor that got him home more quickly.

- Ralph Schneider was embarrassed one night; he had forgotten his wallet when he took his wife out to dinner. He thought of a credit card that would allow him to do without cash—and developed the Diners Club.

- Charles Strite worked in a factory. He ate lunch occasionally in the in-plant cafeteria. Most of the time his toast came overdone and often it was burnt. He invented an automatic toaster.

The path to entrepreneurship and riches was the same for all these innovators. They used their heads to get ahead.

INSURANCE   Protection against various forms of risk is a necessary part of business operation and needs to be included as a fixed expense in any budget projection. All insurance comes under one of three major headings: liability, life and health, and property. In buying insurance, several precautions should be observed:

1. Shop around to find an agent with whom a comfortable relationship is possible, who represents a good company (or companies), and who is able to give good advice at the best price.

2. Know the enterprise's exact insurance needs and resist any arm-twisting tactics; buy insurance that is needed and can be afforded—no more.

3. Determine how much deductible the business can afford without being endangered.

4. Check whether a complete package is available at a more favorable price or whether comparable coverage is available through a trade or professional association, at a lower group rate.

5. Make a note on a calendar to review all policies at stated intervals, to be sure of adequate coverage.

Under the three major headings, there are so many different kinds of insurance to consider in our lawsuit-happy society that it would be advisable to make up an insurance business plan. Here is a brief checklist of types of coverage or policies to explore:

- Liability—general liability, automotive liability, and product liability.
- Workers' compensation—if the company has any employees besides the owner.
- Life and health—on owner(s), partners, employees.
- Property—comprehensive, all-risk, inside-outside coverage that includes (where necessary) fire, theft, flood, crime, vandalism, and inland marine.
- Business interruption—to cover losses that result from any property damage or personal injury or incapacitation.
- Partnership and/or keyperson compensation.
- Glass insurance.
- Credit and bonding.
- Transportation insurance—for goods in transit.

INTERNAL REVENUE SERVICE (IRS) The tax collection agency of the United States government is a division of the Treasury Department, employs in excess of 82,000 people, and in various taxation ways siphons off $1 trillion from the more than $4 trillion annual gross national income of the United States. IRS offices are located throughout the country; major offices are listed in Appendix A. The IRS maintains special services for the elderly within its Taxpayer Service Division, 1111 Constitution Avenue, NW, Washington, DC 20224, phone: (202) 566-4904; services for the hearing impaired are at the same address (Room 7324). The Office of Planning and Research can be contacted for information on a wide range of statistics, phone: (202) 376-0216 or on individual returns, phone: (202) 376-0155. Dozens of manuals and films on every conceivable tax problem are available, often at no charge, at local IRS field offices or in the Freedom of Information Reading Room, 1111 Constitution Avenue, Washington, DC. Some are for sale, at prices ranging from less than $5 to over $100. To appear before the IRS, the representative for a taxpayer must be a CPA or an attorney or must pass a special examination administered through the Office of the Director of Practice (phone: (202) 535-6787). Most entrepreneurs know that todays tax laws benefit freelancers and self-employed individuals like consultants. However, accurate records on small, professionally run businesses are more important than ever. One of the few small business benefits in the Internal Revenue Code is the Section 179 deduction or "special depreciation" writeoff that allows up to $10,000 a year to be written off for office furniture, equipment, and other qualified fixed assets. Under the writeoff provision, small entrepreneurs can invest in a computerized accounting system, for instance, and use Section 179 to help reduce the after-tax costs of the system. The bane of entrepreneurs is an invitation to have their books and tax returns audited by a friendly emissary of the Internal Revenue Service. Even though hardly more than one percent of filing companies are actually audited, inquiries about discrepancies are received by far greater numbers. Corporations are generally audited in greater numbers than simple proprietorships. "Red flag" categories of deductions, such as entertainment and travel expenses, should be treated with caution and always backed by proof of expenditure and iron-clad reasons. A manual prepared by the IRS for its staff lists the following among the items government auditors look for:

- Large or unusual inventory changes
- Asset sales without corresponding gain-and-loss schedules
- Dubious bad debts
- Expenses that are far higher than the averages for similar businesses
- Any deviation from the "norms and standards"
- International deals and foreign tax credits
- Lack of detailed schedules in a consolidated return
- New incorporation of an established business, especially when it reports good will and accelerated depreciation
- Starting of a last-in, first-out inventory accounting system
- Large income from passive investments such as rents, royalties, and investments
- Large or negative cash balances
- Investment income that was omitted in the returns
- Premature writeoffs
- Unreported interest from accounts receivable
- Loans to and from stockholders

- Stock issued for services rendered
- Inadequate or incomplete Schedule M (reconciliations)

Some philosophical changes that have occurred in the IRS will expand auditing procedures, beginning in 1990. The first group targeted for auditing attention will be direct sellers—door-to-door salespeople, house-party sellers, and independent contractors (including small subcontractors who work for larger construction firms). Next will be waiters and waitresses and other individuals who receive tips, sellers of primary residences (they have 24 months to reinvest their proceeds), and dependents who show up on more than one taxpayer's returns.

INTERNATIONAL TRADE ADMINISTRATION (ITA)

This division of the Department of Commerce administers a number of vital programs for American entrepreneurs interested in selling goods and services abroad, including the Electronic License Application Information Network and the System for Tracking Export License Applications. (See *ELAIN* and *STELA.*)

The Commercial Information Management System (CIMS) offers custom-tailored market research information on foreign business and economic climate, regulations, tariff barriers, competition, distribution, promotions, standards, foreign contacts and their addresses, contact numbers, and specialties. Once an international trader has obtained research data from CIMS, the next stop should be the Export Trading Company (ETC) Affairs Office which helps in finding actual overseas opportunities by promoting and encouraging contacts between American producers and potential overseas clients.

Commercial News USA, a magazine published by the ITA, circulates to about 100,000 foreign agents, distributors, government officials, and end users. Each issue contains up to 200 American products and services, with descriptive literature and black-and-white photos. Companies participating in this international promotion medium experience 30 to 40 inquiries from a single insertion. The average dollar return is in excess of $10,000. There is a charge for each insert. For all programs and services above, contact: ITA, Department of Commerce, 14th Street and Constitution Avenue, NW, Washington, DC 20230. Attendance at an ITA Export Seminar is recommended. For the next available one, call (202) 377-0300.

INTRAPRENEURS

Entrepreneurs who work within a larger corporation represent a trend that sprang up in the early 1980s among major corporations as a means of retaining some of the brighter, more innovative executives and at the same time producing new products and methods for the benefit of the company. Limited, more or less independent units were set up within the larger organizations and were allowed to concentrate on a single product or process. The hope was, of course, that these intrapreneurships would not only lead to major new product lines, but would help to develop management techniques that could be applied to the companies' traditional operations. In practice, intrapreneurship has not worked out as well as was hoped. The sponsoring companies discovered at least six problems:

1. The special attention given to the intrapreneurs caused resentment among the other employees.

2. Intrapreneurial ventures often lacked the commitment and dedication found in truly independent groups whose own money was invested and at risk.

3. Some of the intrapreneurs decided that there was too much pressure and insecurity in these special cadres and returned to their regular jobs.

4. Some projects at the beginning were too heavily funded, and intrapreneurs lacked the push and drive needed to achieve results.

5. There was corporate interference from top management; money had been invested in these projects and the executives were pushing for results.

6. Many corporate analysts found that inventiveness and innovations were not strengths in their organization and that the money invested in intrapreneurship could produce equal or greater returns if concentrated on the company's regular lines.

INVENTORY CONTROL The accounting system used to maintain current records of all merchandise on hand should reveal a number of things needed to operate the business efficiently and profitably: How many items of each category are in stock; the value of the inventory; the items that need reorders; what products are selling well or not at all; the efforts needed for promotion, price changes, or more advantageous display of the slow-selling items; what is popular and what is not; where profit is coming from; whether any "inventory shrinkage" (stealing) exists. To achieve all this, any one of at least six basic techniques of inventory control can be used: inventory sheets (forms), cash register key-in, color coding, rotating system, computerization, and on-hand/on-order index cards. Any method that gives the right answers—provides the information needed—is the "correct" method. Obviously, the inventory method used by a supermarket or large variety store with thousands of items and a high turnover will be quite different from the method for an exclusive fashion, gift, or jewelry boutique, or for an automobile or major appliance dealer. Inventory has to be taken at least once a year, to satisfy IRS requirements. In practice, however, a business should know daily where its merchandise is. No successful entrepreneur could survive long if someone is stealing the business blind, or if the merchandise bought does not sell, or if the neighborhood dubs it the "just out" store.

ITCH   "A restless desire or longing" is one of the dictionary's definitions of an itch. It is the feeling an entrepreneur experiences when he or she is about to burst forth with a new business idea and to implement it by actually doing something about it. To be or become an entrepreneur, one might say, "You gotta have the ITCH," with this interpretation of the acronym:

I   Idea or innovation, which is the seed that nurtures a new business

T   Talent that every entrepreneur must have, abetted by the propellant called motivation

C   Calculated risk or capital, some of which is always needed (usually more rather than less)

H   Hard work, the fuel that runs entrepreneurship and without which even the best ideas evaporate into idle dreams

Anyone who truly has the ITCH has the stuff entrepreneurs are made of. If the *itch* is honestly there, the *scratch* is sure to follow.

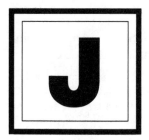

JOB MARKET   At the outset or eventually as they grow, enterprises need to hire help. Availability of labor is a crucial factor in choosing a location. Beyond a perennial hard-core sector of our population that seems to be virtually unemployable, the

available labor pool in many areas is shrinking. Standards have been lowered, training sessions have been instituted, grants and tax rebates have been offered for each job creation, and incentives have been offered that were unthinkable in the 1930s. Washington, DC is a high-employment area where $15,000 semiskilled jobs are going for $20,000–$25,000. It is not unusual to plow through 30 to 40 pages of help-wanted ads in the Sunday edition of the *Washington Post*. One of the phenomena spawned by high employment is the temporary employee; another is the return to work of elderly, formerly retired men and women. A new and innovative source of employees is the employment contractor, who hires all employees, pays their deductions and benefits, and sends one unified bill to the client-company at the end of each week. Another serious problem in the job market of the 1990s is a growing mismatch between the emerging jobs, which will call for increasingly higher levels of skills, and the people available to fill the vacancies. The number of workers entering the United States job market has fallen to the lowest levels observed in four decades. The newcomers will increasingly be women, disadvantaged minority workers, and non-English-speaking immigrants. The existing public school system does not lend much encouragement, particularly in the large metro areas. Rapid technological changes and a more competitive global economy put additional strains on current employees. The employee need in the next decade will be greatest in business, health, social and other services, and wholesale and retail trades. Hispanics will show the greatest employment growth (75 percent); Asian Americans will be next (74 percent); then blacks (26 percent). Whites will stay virtually stable.

JOB TRAINING   Two out of every three workers get their first jobs in small firms. Many of these employees require training—a situation that is increasingly a fact of business life. The government has made some provision to subsidize the training process under the Job Training Partnership Act, aimed at economically disadvantaged youth and adults and dislocated workers, and the Work Incentive (WIN) program. The Tax Reduction and Simplification Act of 1977 also offered new-job tax credits. Entrepreneur-employers should check out the available options with the local office of the Labor Department. Other job incentive programs are under discussion in Congress. Labor Department surveys have profiled on-the-job training participants as:

- Male rather than female
- Married rather than unmarried or divorced
- White rather than nonwhite
- Veterans rather than nonveterans

- College-educated rather than high school dropouts
- Full-time rather than part-time workers
- Salaried rather than hourly employees
- Better paid rather than low-paid workers

Small firms are not only the first employers of most of the work-force, they are the most flexible. More than large firms, they hire younger and older workers, women, part-time workers, and less skilled workers. Small firms were the first to hire most of the baby-boom generation; they have been primary employers of women entering the workforce for the first time. The workers who find their first jobs in small firms are a diverse group, but they include many of those least prepared by prior education, experience, or economic background to meet the changing demands of the workplace in the 1990s. They will require some form of training, and it should be part of the business plan of small, labor-intensive enterprises, to provide it.

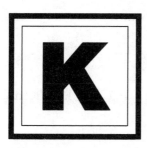

KEOGH PLAN A "Keogh" is a tax-deferred pension plan for full-time or part-time self-employed entrepreneurs. If there are other employees, they must be included in any company pension plan IF they work at least 1,000 hours a year and have been with the company for a minimum of two years. Part-time employees who work less than an average of 20 hours a week or who are employed for only a short while need not be included. Up to $30,000 per year can be sheltered, but if there are other employees, the same *percentage* of their income must be contributed to a Keogh plan as is put into the owner's shelter. Contributions to a Keogh can vary up to 15 percent. If $50,000 is drawn out of a business as personal income, up to $7,500 a year can be contributed to the Keogh. Eligible income is figured on gross income; it is available whether the business is a proprietorship, partnership, or corporation. Obviously, an owner looking to draw out the allowable maximum of $30,000 will have to show a gross income of $200,000 a year. All paperwork for the plan must be completed by December 31 of each year, though the actual money need not be paid into the fund until tax-filing time—April 15 of the following year. Form 5500C must be filed along with the declaration. After age 59 1/2, Keogh plan savings can be withdrawn as a lump sum and taxed using five-year forward averaging. This is one advantage of Keogh plans over IRA plans—the latter do not have five-year forward averaging available.

KIAM CREDO   This entry will be new to most readers; even the innovator of the Kiam Credo may not recognize his pronouncements by that title. But Victor K. Kiam II is the entrepreneur's entrepreneur. He is the man who liked Remington electric shavers so much, he bought the company and turned it around from a loser into a very profitable company. So when Kiam tells us the 10 steps to success as an entrepreneur, they are worth repeating:

1. Have confidence in yourself. Be confident enough to assume calculated risks and be responsible for your actions.
2. Have your eyes always open for opportunities. Keep an open mind as well.
3. Commit yourself to your business. If you enjoy the business you have chosen, give it your all.
4. Have a game plan. Put down both short-range and long-term goals in a business plan.
5. Be prepared to make sacrifices. Be willing to put some personal activities on the back burner.
6. Have the courage of your convictions. Once you make a well-researched determination, go for it.
7. Lead by example. Your own energy and enthusiasm should lead others on toward success.
8. Don't be afraid to excel. This is the nature of entrepreneurs, to be a little different, to stand out from the crowd.
9. Weigh your risks-vs-rewards ratio. If your proposition is too negative, leave it alone and start something else; calculated risks are OK; foolish risks are just that.
10. Evaluate your motivation. Entrepreneurship requires high energy levels, a large measure of emotional investment. That's why a successful enterprise requires motivation other than mere financial returns.

For more of Kiam's wisdoms, see *Going For It! How to Succeed as an Entrepreneur* (New York: Morrow, 1986).

KISS (KEEP IT SIMPLE—AND SELL) Selling anything—in the retail store, to the retail store, off a truck, door-to-door, to small groups or large audiences, in front of a television camera or over a makeshift table at a flea market—is an art. It takes intimate knowledge of the merchandise or service: not only the physical facts but the advantages over the competition and, most of all, the benefits and advantages to the purchaser. Teaching how to sell has become a huge profession, simply because selling is a skill that can be highly profitable, is not limited by age or gender, and can be carried to any location the salesperson chooses to go. Innumerable books, audio cassettes, and videotapes have been published that purport to inspire and teach selling. They are available at tape stores, book stores, through mail order offers, and at countrywide seminars. Here is just a short selection:

KISS: Selling Techniques that Really Work, by Fred Herman with Earl Nightingale. $54.95*

Nice Guys Finish Rich: The Secrets of a Supersalesman, by Jim Hansberger. $59.95*

Sell Your Way to the Top, Pearls of Wisdom from the Master, By Zig Ziglar. $59.95*

No Bull Selling: Winning Sales Strategy from America's Super Salesman, by Hank Trisler. $59.95*

Non-Manipulative Selling, Building Sales Through Trust, by Dr. Tony Alessandra and Phil Wexler. $59.95*

Changing the Game: The New Way to Sell, by Larry Wilson. $59.95*

The One-Minute Salesperson, by Dr. Spencer Johnson and Larry Wilson (2 cassettes). $19.95

The Psychology of Selling: The Art of Closing Sales, by Brian Tracy. $69.95*

How to Master the Art of Selling Anything, by Tom Hopkins (12 audiocassettes plus workbook). $180.00

* Each package contains 6 audio cassettes.

L.A. XPORT This project of the City of Los Angeles extends credit to small firms, to increase exports from the city. Supported and encouraged by the federal Eximbank, this system allows an approved local company to borrow 90 percent of its foreign receivables. This is the kind of transaction private-sector lenders are reluctant to finance. Los Angeles accepted Eximbank's proposal (six cities were offered the package), which includes backing a loan with a guarantee and receiving credit insurance. In addition, the city was able to obtain financing from a local bank, because of its clout with the institution. L.A. Xport is a reversal of the usual scenario in which banks avoid doing business with small exporters in favor of larger companies or purely domestic deals. Eximbank's guarantee program enables a local bank to engage in international business without the usual overseas risks. In 1988, as a result of the Los Angeles experience, 102 export loans amounting to nearly $96 million were approved and guaranteed by Eximbank. The average transaction size indicated was about $276,000. Los Angeles has also established an administrative agency called CEDO (City Economic Development Office) which provides technical services, such as analyzing and structuring deals. Similar programs are being structured in such diverse areas as Tucson, Baltimore, Portland, and the Port of New York–New Jersey. This service to small exporters does not come without cost, because Eximbank expects its services to be self-liquidating. The loan or line of credit costs 1.75 percent over prime; a 1/2 percent fee is paid to the local authority and a 1 percent fee to Eximbank for federal credit insurance.

LABOR FORCE The composition of available employees can be of interest to entrepreneurs expanding an established business and to those entering a new business, particularly if theirs is a labor-intensive enterprise. In the next decade the average age of workers will increase to 36.3 years of age (in 1980 it was 30 years). While the overall population will have grown only 11 percent between 1980 and 2000, the segment 45 to 54 years old will increase by 39 percent. During these same years certain industries will create more job demands than others. More training will be required and more competition for good employees will result. The following are the projections of new salaried jobs in 2000:

Eating/drinking establishments	2,471,000
Health/medical offices	1,375,000
Construction/renovation	890,000
Nursing/personal care	852,000
Personnel services	832,000
Education	784,000
Machinery and equipment wholesalers	614,000
Computers/data processing	613,000
Food markets	598,000
Hotels/lodging places	574,000

The above factors in turn can influence employees' productivity, longevity of employment, importance of benefits to be anticipated, flexibility, and type of training required. By 2000, women will comprise 47 percent of the labor force. The growth of the labor force will be drawn from the following groups—a fact of importance to recruiters and trainers:

Residential women	52.6%
Residential men	24.0
Immigrant men	12.8
Immigrant women	10.6

From an ethnic viewpoint, the following growth is expected:

White women	34.8%
Hispanics	28.7
Blacks	17.4
Asians	11.4
White men	8.5

LAWYERS AND LEGAL COSTS

Persons admitted to practice law in a specific jurisdiction and to perform representation functions for clients in civil or criminal actions are lawyers or attorneys. The terms solicitor and barrister are equivalent English designations. Lawyers are necessary to help organize a business and to draw up agreements, contracts, and leases—or at least to check them to make sure that the entrepreneur's neck is not sticking out too far. Lawyers are also able to look ahead, to anticipate any legal, leasing, or contractual problems that might be encountered in the future conduct of a business. In many court cases or appearances before the IRS, lawyers are the only ones allowed to participate. Since lawyers are only human and thus fallible, wise entrepreneurs acquaint themselves with some basic concepts of business law. There are popular books that even laypeople can understand, in most neighborhood libraries. There are also law clinics where advice may be obtained, consumer advocates in various government bureaus and at the Better Business Bureau, alternative dispute resolutions and arbitration proceedings—all of which can conserve already limited business funds. At the base of all entrepreneurial efforts is one truism regarding lawyers: Legal fees are a necessary business expense but paying more than is needed is foolishness. The more an owner knows about the law and the more complete the preparation of a "case," the less the cost in time and money. Here are some steps to take when engaging legal service of any kind:

- Know the charges up front—flat fee, hourly, or contingent fee.
- Try to settle or arbitrate cases rather than litigate them.
- *Prepare*, and don't be afraid to suggest cost-saving steps.
- Don't chit-chat on the phone; the law-clock ticks on. See the legal eagle during business hours and *be prepared*.

LEADERSHIP A leader has a quality that makes that one person or product stand out among many others. Entrepreneurs, by the very nature of their thinking and ambition, by their restlessness and intrepidity, their curiosity and persistence, assume leadership—or, failing this, they succumb and rejoin the faceless followers. On January 2, 1915, there appeared in the *Saturday Evening Post* an advertisement for the Cadillac Motor Company. It said little about the product, but volumes about the quality that made Cadillac the envy of the automotive world. The message, entitled "The Penalty of Leadership," is still valid:

In every field of human endeavor, he that is first must perpetually live in the white light of publicity. Whether the leadership be vested in a man or in a manufactured product, emulation and envy are ever at work. In art, in literature, in music, in industry, the reward and the punishment are always the same. The reward is widespread recognition; the punishment, fierce denial and detraction. When a man's work becomes a standard for the whole world, it also becomes a target for the shafts of the envious few. If his work be merely mediocre, he will be left severely alone—if he achieves a masterpiece, it will set a million tongues a-wagging. Jealousy does not protrude its forked tongue at the artist who produces a commonplace painting. Whatsoever you write, or paint, or play, or sing, or build, no one will strive to surpass or to slander you, unless your work be stamped with the seal of genius. Long, long after a great work or a good work has been done, those who are disappointed or envious continue to cry out that it cannot be done. Spiteful little voices in the domain of art were raised against our own Whistler as a mountebank, long after the big world had acclaimed him its greatest artistic genius. Multitudes flocked to Bayreuth to worship at the musical shrine of Wagner, while the little group of those whom he had dethroned and displaced argued angrily that he was no musician at all. The little world continued to protest that Fulton could never build a steamboat, while the big world flocked to the river banks to see his boat steam by. The leader is assailed because he is a leader, and the effort to equal him is merely added proof of that leadership. Failing to equal, or to excel, the follower seeks to depreciate and to destroy—but only confirms once more the superiority of that which he strives to supplant.

There is nothing new in this. It is as old as the world and as old as the human passions—envy, fear, greed, ambition, and the desire to surpass. And it all avails nothing. If the leader truly leads, he remains—the leader. Master-poet, master-painter, master-workman, each in his turn is assailed, and each holds his laurels through the ages. That which is good or great makes itself known, no matter how loud the clamor of denial. That which deserves to live—lives.

LEGAL BUSINESS ORGANIZATION

There are three major categories of business organization: proprietorships, partnerships, and corporations; the latter can be divided into general corporations and S corporations. Most of the small business organizations in the United States are proprietorships—70 percent to be exact—while 20 percent are corporations and 10 percent are partnerships. However, corporations earn 90 percent of the money; proprietorships, 6 percent; and partnerships, 4 percent. Profits, too, are dominated by corporations, which earn 75 percent of reported profits; proprietorships earn the other 25 percent, and partnerships report a slight loss. (See also *Corporation, Partnership, Proprietorship.*)

LETTER OF CREDIT

A request from an exporter to a bank for a loan on a business transaction is a request for a letter of credit. When the bank guarantees payment of a debt, it is substituting its own credit for that of the applicant: the bank will pay for the transaction if the applicant fails to make the agreed payment. In this way, the bank makes a loan to the local entrepreneur and charges a fee or interest for the generally short term of the transaction. The seller has little risk in such a transaction. Most sellers are far away and may be operating under different legal, political, and business practices. With a letter of credit issued by a reputable international bank, both parties are assured and protected—goods will be properly shipped and received, and payment will be rendered as promised. As an example, a book distributor in the United States wants to buy an assortment of dictionaries produced in West Germany. The price is agreed upon; terms of shipment, standards of quality, and quantity are spelled out; and all these provisions are included in the letter of credit. The American book distributor arranges with an international bank to issue a letter of credit for the total amount of the German books plus shipping expenses, to be released to the German company when the books are landed in satisfactory condition here in America. The German publisher is notified of this letter of credit, giving assurance that payment for the books will automatically be released once the conditions of the sale are met. A similar procedure can be used for a domestic transaction, but its most frequent use is in international trade.

LOANS See *Bank Loans.*

LOBBYING The act (or art) of persuading legislators to enact or pass laws that are favorable to the lobbyist or client, or conversely, to defeat those laws that are unfavorable to the interests of the lobbyist or client, occupies hosts of people in state capitals and in Washington, DC. Most trade associations, of any size, that maintain offices in Washington have one or more people on staff who act as lobbyists. All state legislatures are also targets for lobbyists, especially states in which an industry or trade association has vital interests. In New York, an average of 23,000 laws are introduced annually in the Albany legislature. Only 5 percent or less ever become law, which illustrates the difficulty of proposing legislation to a representative. To be effective in lobbying a proposal to a Senator, Representative, or state legislator, the following checklist will be helpful:

- Make the presentation in writing on letterhead stationery, in an original letter. Ask for an appointment and be prepared for a personal follow-up.
- Give a clear description of the problem or proposal, both its pros and cons, and what has already been tried, to achieve results.
- Propose a resolution of the problem and how the legislator could be of assistance.
- Begin the initial lobbying approach early in the session.
- Make appointments by phone with the legislator or aides about a month in advance, then confirm the call in writing.
- After a meeting with the legislator or aide, leave a written summary of the proposal for further reference.
- Recognize that no matter how important the lobbying interest or the proposal is, the legislator represents many constituents. State in writing how the proposal will benefit the legislator's district and constituents.

- Be prepared with a compromise, for that is the nature of legislative procedure; have an alternate idea in reserve.

For further information, see: "Lobbying Reports," 2626 Pennsylvania Avenue, NW, Washington, DC 20037; subscription: $137 a year; *The Lobbying Handbook,* Cornell University, 146 State Street, Albany, NY 12207.

Loss Leader

In merchandising, this term is used to indicate an item that is sold at or below cost in order to attract customers into the store. The term could also be applied to services. Consider three examples. A supermarket introduces a series of children's books. The first one is sold for 99 cents; the later books in the series or set are sold at the regular price of $4.95. A new neighborhood dry cleaner offers to clean a pair of pants or a skirt for 99 cents even though the regular charge is $2.95. The idea is, of course, that once customers become acquainted with the store and like its services, they will continue to come in and bring items for dry cleaning at regular prices. A supermarket features a half-dozen items at half-price each week. The store knows that the average weekly purchase is $25 per customer and that customers buy an average of two items on the special half-price list per week. The items cost normally 99 cents but are sold for 48 cents. The wholesale cost of the items is 66 cents each but the manufacturer has allowed a special discount on a number of cases of the item, so that the supermarket paid only 56 cents instead of 66 cents. Still, selling the items at 48 cents means an 8-cent loss on each of two items (the average purchase). Therefore it costs the store 16 cents to bring a customer into its premises where, on an average, the shopper will spend $25. Translated into percentages, the supermarket has thus invested 16 cents or 6.4 percent in promotion expense. The "loss leader" is actually "magnet merchandising" that can be applied to local or national merchandising, to single stores or services, and to shopping centers. It can be the most effective sales promotion tool in an entrepreneur's arsenal.

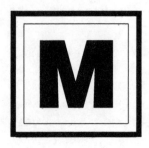

MAGAZINES They come in several shapes and sizes, cover collectively all types of reader appeal and demographics, and make the determination of which ones are right for ad placement a mind-boggling task. There are around 5,000 trade or business magazines, covering 165 separate trades and professions. For the consumer market, advertisers can choose from among nearly 2,500 domestic, international, and farm magazines. Top publications, like the *Reader's Digest,* have circulations over 16 million and advertising rates of over $100,000 for a single, four-color page. On the other hand, smaller regional or limited-audience magazines price an ad at a few hundred dollars; classifieds are far less. Magazine ads are best for direct sales offers—mail order ads that sell merchandise or information through the mail or through an 800-number. They are also ideal for post-advertising merchandising—aids such as reprints of the ad, enlarged and mounted copies, demographic statistics, and marketing data that will be useful. Since magazines pay a 15 percent commission to recognized advertising agencies, there is usually an advantage to placing magazine ads through an agency. (For the entrepreneur's company to earn this discount, it has to establish a "house agency," and this is pretty tricky; see *House Agency.*) The bible of the media trade is the Standard Rates and Data Service. This multivolume catalog, published monthly for most editions, tells all that owners need to know about advertising rates, magazine circulation, local demography, and more. A major library or an ad agency would most likely have a copy.

MAIL ORDER This is a marketing method of bringing goods from seller to buyer. Goods may be advertised in any one of several paid media—direct mail, newspapers, magazines, radio, or television (the latter is referred to as "telemarketing"). The method of delivering mail-order goods is usually through the United States Postal Service. However, direct delivery is sometimes used in local areas, and private carriers like United Parcel Service offer traceable deliveries worldwide. Advertising goods via mail order is quite expensive because of postage. Two other factors add to the costs: (1) the low percentage of orders received in relation to the advertising coverage ($^1/_2$ to 4 percent is normal), and (2) the high rate of returned goods. Mail-order merchandisers must be sure to take these two costs into consideration when buying or manufacturing mail-order goods and when pricing them. In normal store-marketing, a 50 to 100 percent markup is sufficient; mail-order pricing should allow for two to four times the cost of goods in order to arrive at a profit-producing selling price. Only highly efficient mail-order operations that do a big volume of business (like Sears or L.L. Bean) or department and specialty stores that have high in-person sales can afford to sell mail-order goods at normal markup—usually "keystone" or double-the-cost prices. The venerable L.L. Bean Co. which, like most reputable mail-order merchandisers, sells goods on a 100 percent satisfaction guarantee, has a return-of-goods ratio of 14 percent, which costs the company $18 million annually in shipping and handling costs alone. Fit, not defects, is the problem when fashion goods are sold via mail order. Accurate, honest mail-order advertising copy and better training of shipping personnel can reduce this overhead cost. A company's best bet is to keep good records of customers' addresses. Repeat customers are the best and most profitable mail-order clients.

MAILING LISTS

Records of customers and prospects, often numbering thousands of names and including their complete addresses, are used for advertising solicitations and surveys and for any contact that demands an answer from the recipient. Because the best mailing lists are those of a business's own customers or clients, it is vital to maintain an accurate and up-to-date record of individuals and companies that buy from the business. There are many ways of collecting and building a mailing list. When customers buy goods or services, when they make inquiries, when they visit the business establishment and register their presence, when they write in or request a catalog, a sample, or a promotion piece, when they visit a trade show exhibit and leave a business card, or when they join an organization—these are all opportunities for collecting names and prospects for future direct mail solicitations. Mailing lists can be bought or rented from any of hundreds of professional mailing list companies or brokers or from publications to which the business subscribes. Invariably, the name and address of anyone who joins an organization, gets a listed telephone number, files for a license or permit, subscribes to a magazine or book club, or places an order with a mail-order merchandise company winds up on a mailing list that can be purchased. The cost of the list depends on its size and exclusivity. A list of names and addresses culled from a city directory or telephone book might cost only $30 per thousand names, whereas a list of executives of major companies or a list of subscribers to elite magazines would cost upward of $50 per thousand. With postage costs scheduled to increase soon, having a "clean" and up-to-date list that is continually revised is very important.

Manufacturing Technology Centers

This program is operated by the National Institute of Standards and Technology (formerly the National Bureau of Standards), an agency of the Department of Commerce, Building 220, Room A319, Gaithersburg, MD 20899, phone: (301) 975-5020. It promotes the transfer of technical knowledge to American businesses, to enhance the productivity and competitiveness of small American businesses in the domestic and international marketplace. Manufacturing Technology Centers are nonprofit shops and laboratories that develop new techniques in research and manufacturing and make their innovations, techniques, and methods available at cost to American entrepreneurs. The centers' robotics shop is a research facility that invites visits from prospective clients. The National Institute provides planning and operating funds to the centers, along with exchanges of modern technologies. Advanced manufacturing techniques and successful methods for fostering their use at one center are then passed on to centers and businesses throughout the nation. This level of high-tech networking would be impossible to attain on an individual basis. Entrepreneurs who take advantage of these centers can save a great deal of their own funds that would otherwise be earmarked for research and development. (See also *Federal Technology Transfer.*)

Manufacturing technology centers are operated by the engineering schools of many universities. A list of some of the major ones follows:

University or Institution	Phone
Clemson University, Clemson, SC	(803) 656-3291
Drexel University, Philadelphia, PA	(215) 895-1541
Georgia Institute of Technology, Atlanta	(404) 894-4133 or -6101
ITT Research Institute, Chicago, IL	(312) 567-4800
North Carolina State University, Raleigh	(919) 737-3262
Northwestern University, Evanston, IL	(312) 491-5066
Ohio State University, Columbus	(614) 292-6814 and 292-2980
Oklahoma State University, Stillwater	(405) 624-6055
Purdue University, West Lafayette, IN	(317) 494-7434
Rensselaer Polytechnic Institute, Troy, NY	(518) 276-6021
Stanford University, Stanford, CA	(415) 723-9038
University of Maryland, College Park	(301) 454-4526
University of Michigan, Ann Arbor	(313) 764-6565
University of Rhode Island, Kingston	(401) 792-2531
University of Wisconsin, Madison	(608) 262-0921
Worcester Polytechnic Institute, Worcester, MA	(617) 793-5335

MARKET/MARKETING   The entrepreneurial interpretation is that a market is a large group of people who have the present or potential ability and desire to purchase a product or service. A product that is in demand or is desired is said to have marketability. The process by which a product or service is promoted for sale is called *marketing*. The components of marketing are the four Ps:

Product: Select and develop the right product or service.

Price: Determine the selling price at which the public will acquire the product and the seller can make a profit.

Place: Analyze and design the distribution channels.

Promotion: Generate or enhance the demand for the product or service.

Based on a 1988 survey of Yellow Pages listings, the following metropolitan markets, listed in descending order, were the fastest growing in the United States (all but four are below the Mason–Dixon Line):

1. Baltimore, MD
2. Charleston, SC
3. West Palm Beach/Boca Raton/Delray Beach, FL
4. Orlando, FL
5. Norfolk/Virginia Beach/Newport News, VA
6. Raleigh/Durham, NC
7. Knoxville, TN
8. Miami, FL
9. New Haven/Meriden, CT
10. Washington, DC
11. Allentown/Bethlehem, PA
12. Greenville/Spartanburg, SC
13. Boston, MA
14. Las Vegas, NV
15. Atlanta, GA

MARKETING PLAN   This is also called an action plan or action program, or a marketing strategy. It can be applied to a single product or to an entire company. The simplest way to develop such a plan for a company, a product, or a service is to set down answers to these questions, as they apply to special needs:

Definition of the business:

- What is the product or service?
- What is the planned geographic marketing area?
- Who is the competition?
- How do they promote their product or service?
- How do we promote our product or service?

Definition of the customers or clients:

- What is the current customer base—age, sex, income, home?
- How do customers learn about the product or service?
- What are the current shopping/buying patterns of the customers?
- What do existing customers like best about the product?
- Who else has a need for the product? Where are they?

Definition of the marketing plan and budget:

- What past methods of marketing have been used?
- Which were the most effective and cost-effective?
- What was the cost per unit? Per customer?
- What new method might work for additional customers?
- What percentage of profits can be allocated to this program?
- How can these new ideas be tested? Their results measured?

List the business's marketing tools and outlets, their pros and cons, their costs, and who will implement them. Include advertising, co-op promotion, customer exploitation, direct mail, mail order, point-of-purchase, merchandising tie-ins, contests, demos, and publicity.

MARKUP   In merchandising, markup is the increase a retailer adds to an item over and above its original cost or wholesale price. The markup is supposed to take care of all expenses involved in handling the item, plus some profit. This gain is called the gross profit. When all expenses are deducted from the selling price, the remaining amount is the net profit. For example:

Selling price of item		$16.50
Less: Cost of item	$10.00	
Total operational overhead (35%)	3.50	
Allowance for returns, losses (5%)	.50	
Commission to salesperson (5%)	.50	14.50
Desired net profit on investment (20%)		$ 2.00
Markup		$ 6.50

In determining markup, analyze whether there are any other expenses, obvious or unforeseen, that will have to be figured into the final selling price. How about markdowns? If all items cannot be sold at the regular price, will their price have to be reduced at the end of the season, to get at least some money out of them? If 20 percent of the items are not sold at full markup, then the reduction has to be added to the initial markup. Suppose 80 percent of the items are sold at the beginning of the season for $16.50; 20 percent are left over. These will be reduced to $10. If 10 units were being sold originally, two units must be sold at $6.50 below the "normal" selling price. Planned income is reduced by $2 \times \$6.50 = \$13$. In order to anticipate this end-of-season markdown, spread the $13 "loss" over the eight items that are sold at full price: $13 \div 8 = \$1.62\frac{1}{2}$. Go back to the original calculations and add this $1.62\frac{1}{2}$ to the original selling price: $\$16.50 + \$1.62\frac{1}{2} = \$18.12\frac{1}{2}$ (or $18.13). This then should be the gross price in order to come out at the end of the season with the desired profit.

MATURE AMERICANS

The rapid pace maintained by the aging population in the United States has created an entirely new demography. Entrepreneurs need no longer be in their twenties and thirties. More and more "retirees" get their second wind by starting second careers after age 50 or 60. Armand Hammer, the 90-years-young oil tycoon, started a new "career" to push for research leading to a cancer cure. This group, the Mature Americans, must be known as a source of both customers (with lots of expendable money) and entrepreneurs in commercial, professional, and volunteer enterprises. Eighty percent of these people own their own homes, often free and clear, and if and when they sell them, they will receive a big lump sum to invest in other real estate, extensive travel, luxury cars, or even independent businesses. Longer life spans mean that today 25 percent of all Americans are 50 or older and 70 percent reach age 65. The over-55 age group is growing at twice the rate of the general population. Here is the current demography for Mature Americans:

- 50–60 age group—at 33 million, the largest and most affluent segment.
- 65–74 age group—17 million and growing in affluence.
- 75–84 age group—9 million senior citizens who spend the highest portion of their income on health care and charity.
- 85 and up group—the most rapidly expanding elder group; 3 million strong today and expected to double in the coming decade.

The total number of Mature Americans is expected to be 35 million by 2000 and double that in the next generation (2040).

MEDIA KIT A collection of data prepared by newspapers, magazines, TV or radio stations, billboard and bus card companies can serve as a sales tool. Media salespeople use it when they make their pitch to a prospective advertiser and they invariably leave the kit with the advertiser (or send it, if the request comes from out-of-town where no personal representation is feasible) or present it to the advertising agencies representing prospective advertisers. Advertising and publicity are vital to the progress and success of an enterprise. Media kits should be accumulated from media that might be worth considering for those needs. This is the information that should be studied and that is usually included in a media kit:

- Editorial or general content of the publication or type of programming, as well as an editorial calendar
- List of important advertisers who have used the medium
- Comparison of readership, listenership, or exposure with other advertising media in that category
- Demographic information on the viewers, readers, or listeners
- Circulation, based on audits or verified distribution statements
- Industry and market data pertinent to a particular medium
- Advertiser and reader/listener testimonials
- Awards won
- Special issues or programming or locations
- Merchandising and promotion aids available
- Costs for one-time or multiple use and costs per thousand
- Deadlines, mechanical or production data, contracts, discounts

MEETINGS Often regarded as the bane of an executive's existence, meetings have been joked about and maligned and are usually detested by restless entrepreneurs who would rather go ahead and DO something and take a chance on making a mistake. In a popular old meeting story about the creation of the earth, God, faced with the creation of a beast of burden and transportation in arid desert areas, had already created the horse but found it inadequate for long-range desert use. He turned the problem over to His committee of angels. After considerable hassling, the angel committee announced its solution—the camel. Some entrepreneurs insist that a weekly meeting with peers, advisors, and/or employees saves time in the long run. Well-organized, planned meetings do have many advantages. They expose ideas conceived by one person to the opinions and experiences of others, who, because they have a more dispassionate view than the creator of the idea, can see its problems more objectively. If a committee is assigned to carry out a task, such as selling an idea or product, arriving at a consensus during a meeting will help to move the project forward—the psychology of "going with the gang" makes action more feasible than in one-on-one persuasion. A business meeting that will achieve the sharing of information and responsibility has four basic needs:

1. Create a formal meeting schedule, a written agenda.
2. Keep discussion open, candid, but impersonal.
3. Continue discussions until a consensus for action results.
4. Assign concrete responsibility for all actions to be taken.

MERCHANDISING This term is used mostly by department stores and retail stores; manufacturers seem to prefer *marketing*. The American Marketing Association defines merchandising as "the planning involved in marketing the right merchandise or service at the right price, at the right place, at the right time, and in the right quantities." It is any promotional sales activity involving the sales force, retailers, wholesalers, or dealers, and includes advertising, point-of-purchase displays, guarantee seals, special sales, and in-store promotions. Merchandising is therefore a very complex procedure that involves every phase of selling and its supports, all kinds of people, and an endless variety of props and promotional possibilities. It requires ingenuity and experience, crystal-balling, and just plain gut reaction. Any technique, device, medium—or trick—that can create sales is merchandising. In retail, chain, and department stores the top sales executive is known as the merchandise manager. He or she has usually come up through the ranks, starting as a buyer for a department or group of departments and becoming the undisputed boss, responsible only to the general manager or owner. Because millions of dollars often ride on the merchandise manager's techniques and decisions, the job, while highly paid, is also highly vulnerable. Former merchandise managers sometimes step out into the world of entrepreneurship and buy or start up a business. While their experience is invaluable, their shortcoming is their familiarity with departmentalization of responsibilities. As entrepreneurs, unless they are heavily financed and have lots of money to hire the people they are used to dealing with, they have trouble running the whole show. Merchandising is maximizing business. That's the bottom line.

MERCHANTS' ASSOCIATIONS   Shopping centers under central ownership and management, as well as many neighborhood commercial sections, organize themselves into merchants' associations. In most shopping centers, membership is not voluntary; it is mandated as part of the tenant's lease. Members of a merchants' association pay dues usually in proportion to their size and/or volume. The larger stores, high-volume stores, professional services, and highly advertised stores tend to pay less because most of them spend money for their own promotions and even provide some of their own services (such as internal security), or they operate on a huge volume of business and high traffic count (supermarkets; discount and variety stores). Prestigious stores can often make special deals with mall developers who are anxious to attract well-known stores into the center; as primary or anchor tenants they will attract smaller satellite stores—and customers. Mall developers can take their lease contracts to banks and request more favorable construction and operating loans, often running into millions of dollars. Associations provide many services efficiently and economically. These can include cooperative advertising, joint promotions and special events, security and maintenance services, refuse collection, signage, and continual leasing and management services necessary for efficient operation and optimum occupancy. Smaller merchants would do well to join in the merchants' association management and to participate in its cooperative advertising, promotions, and networking.

MINIMUM WAGE   The lowest hourly wage permitted to employees of the federal government or allowed in a union contract for an employee performing a particular job is called the minimum wage. Periodic increases in minimum wage levels are always fraught with emotional and partisan (i.e., political) overtones. Advocates of minimum wage increases argue that a higher minimum is vital so that American workers on the bottom of the economic scale can support their families. Other government spokespersons argue that when the current $4.25-per-hour minimum wage is raised to $4.65 (effective April 1991), it will result in the loss of 650,000 job opportunities. President Bush has proposed a compromise that is designed to strike a balance between the needs of employees and the ability of America's entrepreneurs to create new goods, services, and jobs. One of these proposals includes a six-month training period at a lower pay rate for workers who then gradually work up to the higher minimum wage. Since the last minimum wage increase took place in 1981, it is likely that today's entrepreneur must count on paying more for basic labor in the future. It is vital, therefore, to anticipate the wage increase in the projected pricing structure of goods and services and in an enterprise's long-term financial projections. Under the present minimum wage law, some retail service businesses with sales under $362,500 a year are exempt from the minimum, as are auto service stations with annual sales under $250,000. Companies exempt regardless of sales include: laundries, dry cleaners, and construction firms. In the final analysis, a shortage or excess of labor supply will determine the "minimum" wage over the legally mandated level.

MINORITIES   See *Asian Americans, Native Americans, and Other Minorities, Black Entrepreneurship, Black-Owned Businesses, Women in Business,* and Appendix B.

MIT ENTERPRISE FORUM   A highly selective small business panel that examines an equally selective number of startup and expansion-minded enterprises for investment possibilities, the MIT Forum is made up of professors, heads of high-tech companies, professionals, and entrepreneurs who themselves attended MIT. They serve on the Forum without charge—and get a charge out of listening to some of the brightest and most innovative applicants. The Forum renders straight-from-the-shoulder advice, comments, and counter-proposals, and, if warranted, makes recommendations for financing. The companies selected for an MIT Forum presentation pay $200 to cover minor costs and are required to submit a business plan at least a month ahead of the scheduled appearance before the panel. The programs have been presented about 10 times a year since 1978; each session examines two proposals. Applications are at least double the number that are accepted. The Forum has about 500 MIT alumni to draw from and makes sure that at least one expert in the business area of the applicant is on the panel. Forum presentations are open to the public and 100–150 persons attend each one, both to learn from these experts and to get ideas about what to do in their own enterprises. A lateral benefit of an MIT Forum interview is that a member of the audience may be an important banker or specialist and may then make efforts to become involved with the presenter-company. The MIT Forum conducts an annual workshop for technology-based small businesses and publishes the *"Forum Reporter,"* a subscription newsletter. For additional information about the program, contact: Paul E. Johnson, MIT Enterprise Forum, Massachusetts Institute of Technology, 201 Vassar Street, Room W59-219, Cambridge, MA 02139, phone: (617) 253-8240. Forums have been established in 15 other cities throughout the country. An analysis of MIT Forum applicants is revelatory of the type of entrepreneurs who, according to the MIT group, appear to be most successful:

New jobs created collectively (Massachusetts)	100,000
Job creation worldwide	250,000
Cumulative company sales	$25 billion
Advanced university degrees	73%
Doctorates or higher	33%
Company started:	
While in school	16%
Within 5 years	34%
Within 6–10 years	23%
After 20 years	2%
Parents were entrepreneurs	over 50%
Parents were immigrants	high percentage

MOM-AND-POP BUSINESSES

Generally, these small enterprises are run by a husband-and-wife team. Some have been immensely successful; others have led to divorces. Among the big successes are Tootsie Roll Industries of Chicago, a candy company doing $170 million a year and run by Melvin and Ellen Gordon for more than 20 years. A somewhat smaller firm, Mothers Work, Inc. of Philadelphia, owned and operated by Rebecca and Dan Matthias of Philadelphia, manufactures $8 million worth of maternity clothes a year. Mrs. Fields Cookies is a $180-million-a-year success story, the product of Debbi and Randy Fields of Park City, Utah, who now own 700 cookie franchise shops around the world. It is estimated that there are 1.5 million mom-and-pop businesses in the United States and their phenomenal growth is increasing among the baby-boom generation. The latter, 80 million strong, are clearly entrepreneurial-minded. Today's wives are better educated than earlier generations were and they are more able to pull their own weight in a business enterprise. Today, women represent about 46 percent of all college business majors in bachelor's degree programs, 31 percent in master's degree programs, and nearly 22 percent in PhD programs. The vital ingredient in a mom-and-pop business is the personal relationship between the partners, in business as well as in private life. For some couples, sharing of common interests and aspirations, of successes and failures, strengthens the bonds of matrimony— if they are solid to begin with. If their talents are complementary, if both are enthused about the business, if they have worked well together on previous projects, and if they enjoy each other's company even during stressful moments when mutual support is vital, then the 1990s version of the mom-and-pop enterprise has a better-than-ever chance of success. (See also *Coentrepreneurs.*)

NATIONAL ASSOCIATION OF CONVENIENCE STORES (NACS)

More than 67,500 convenience stores are represented by the NACS, which was founded in 1961 and marks its 30th annual meeting in 1991. The industry chalks up in excess of $60 billion in annual sales with a $1.3 billion profit. Its regional seminars, in-depth research, and numerous printed and electronic training tools make the $200 annual dues requirement a worthwhile investment. The field is dominated by the Southland Corporation's 7-11 Stores, with nearly 8,000 stores and an annual volume in excess of $8 billion. On the volume average of about $1 million per store, the corporation or its franchisee nets about $40,000 annually. Gasoline sales amount to close to $2 billion or nearly 25 percent of total volume. A southern chain, National Convenience Stores, which operates Stop 'n Go as well as ShopNGo markets, grosses about $1 billion in its more than 1,000 units. Even though there are about 67,500 convenience stores in the United States, their total percentage of grocery sales is only a little over 7 percent. Why do customers patronize convenience stores, even though their prices are generally 10 to 15 percent higher? A NACS study revealed the following reasons:

	%
Store location	84.4
Fast checkout	75.3
Store cleanliness	74.9
Available parking	72.8
Accessible from street	69.4
Open 24 hours	68.9
Employee attitude	68.6
Merchandise quality	67.3
Gas availability	63.0

The most frequently purchased items are milk (74.4%), ice (58.5%), dairy products (50.3%), fast-food items (37.9%), and candy (36.7%).

NATIONAL ASSOCIATION OF HOME BUILDERS (NAHB)

America's largest home builders' membership organization, the NAHB has over 155,000 members in 800 state and local builders' associations. Chapters range from

10 to 2,500 members. The parent NAHB organization is at 15th and M Streets, NW, Washington, DC 20005, phone: (202) 822-0200 or the national service hotline: (800) 368-5242. At the headquarters office, the National Housing Center has 275 staff members available for members' benefit. The NAHB Bookstore claims the largest assortment of home-building-related books and publications in the country and maintains an information system to answer virtually any question on the industry. The annual housing and building trade show is the largest of its kind in the United States. More than 170 seminars are presented, as well as economic forecasts by outstanding economists. For presidential and congressional elections, the organization raises about $2 million for its political action committee, in addition to maintaining a year-round state legislative and Congressional lobbying effort. International study tours, student chapter networks, job training programs, certifications on several levels, and programs for remodelers, residential marketers, apartment managers, and senior housing management specialists are some of the activities available from the NAHB. A legal research service that is maintained by an in-house staff is open to members. Monitoring of land development problems and architectural and design methods are other available functions. The NAHB publishes *Builder* magazine, *Nation's Building News, RAM Digest,* and nearly a dozen other publications.

NATIONAL ASSOCIATION OF THE REMODELING INDUSTRY (NARI)

This national trade association represents all segments of the professional remodeling service industry—remodelers who specialize in windows, doors, sidings, roofing, kitchen and bathroom products, and specialties. For more than 50 years NARI has promoted a code of ethics that would tend to elevate this industry in the consumer market. An entrepreneur entering the remodeling field as a manufacturer, distributor, or direct applicator would be well advised to explore NARI affiliation. Dues for individuals are $125 a year; those for larger manufacturers and suppliers can run up to $3,750. NARI conducts an active government affairs program, supported by an "Action Alert" newsletter, and holds an annual exposition at which new products are displayed. A continuing-education program enables members to acquire certification, which can be translated into definite business advantages. Increasing customer satisfaction and improving members' image are the functions of a Remodelcare program conducted jointly with the Council of Better Business Bureaus. Other services include *Focus,* a monthly newspaper, group insurance plans, and nationwide consumer promotion campaigns to promote and improve the industry. NARI is located at 1901 North Moore Street, Suite 808, Arlington, VA 22209, phone: (703) 276-7600.

NATIONAL BURGLAR AND FIRE ALARM ASSOCIATION (NBFA)

The national voice of the 14,000 companies in this phase of the security business, the NBFA spearheads the more than 50 local alarm associations in Washington as a lobbying representative with Congress. The NBFA also provides liaison with other trade associations like Underwriters Laboratories and the Association of Police Chiefs. Each year the association trains more than 1,500 installers, provides a national insurance liability program, and publishes a monthly newsletter and pertinent trade bulletins. At a national convention (in 1990, in Anaheim, CA) the latest industry innovations are exhibited; four trade shows are held each year in various locations. Entrepreneurs planning to enter the alarm industry may want to consider the formal courses offered by the NBFA: an entry-level course (10 weeks, 350 hours), or advanced technician courses for in-depth training. Dues range from $150 for individuals to more than $1,000 for manufacturers. For information, contact: NBFA, 7101 Wisconsin Avenue, Suite 1390, Bethesda, MD 20814-4805, phone: (301) 907-3202.

NATIONAL BUSINESS INCUBATION ASSOCIATION (NBIA)

The NBIA is the key organization representing the fast-growing business incubator industry. Incubators, an important avenue for startup entrepreneurs, especially in the area of technology, provide considerable leverage for the beginning business independent. Most of all, the incubator-entrepreneur has a measurably improved chance of survival. The NBIA evaluates the nation's incubators and their progress, develops detailed data bases on both American and Canadian incubators, conducts an annual conference, publishes a quarterly newsletter, "NBIA Review," and devises NBIA training institutes for developers, managers, and participants. Membership dues are $125 for individuals and $250 for organizations. Three studies available from the NBIA, each costing $25, are: "Planning and Implementing Incubators and Enterprise Support Networks," "The Business Incubator Industry in 1987," and "Small Business Incubators and Enterprise Development." Produced by Dr. David N. Allen and colleagues, the studies present findings from surveys of dozens of incubator operations and hundreds of incubator participants. Dinah Adkins, executive director, is at NBIA headquarters, One President Street, Athens, Ohio 45701, phone: (614) 593-4331. (See also *Incubators.*)

NATIONAL DECORATING PRODUCTS ASSOCIATION (NDPA)

This association of independent decorating products retailers includes those who handle paint, wallcoverings, carpeting and other floor coverings, window coverings, and sundry decorating services.

The industry encompasses more than 20,000 stores with a total volume of almost $11 billion in 1987. Projections, according to a University of Chicago study, point to a 1992 gross of $16.8 billion. Income shares for the five major categories of the industry are shown as:

1987 Totals		1992 Projection
$4.1 billion	Paint	$5.90 billion
2.59	Wallcoverings	4.10
1.36	Window coverings	2.60
1.10	Floor coverings	2.20
1.30	Sundries	1.90

While home-center stores, department stores, and variety/discount stores rely primarily on self-service, the decorating-center stores, purveying wallpaper, paint, and floor coverings, are heavy on personal services. According to the above survey, most buyers preferred the service type of store. Decorating centers receive a 50 percent market share of paint sales, 70 percent of wallcovering sales, 47 percent of drapery sales, between 57 and 79 percent of other window covering sales, 44 percent of carpet sales, and 21 to 36 percent of other floor covering sales. The NDPA holds a national trade expo each November and a number of regional shows in the Spring. It publishes *Decorating Retailer* magazine, a 20,000-entry directory, and numerous other training and informational materials, and runs a co-op advertising program and model decorating center at the Decorating Products Industry Building, 1050 North Lindbergh Boulevard, St. Louis, MO 63132-2994.

NATIONAL FEDERATION OF INDEPENDENT BUSINESS (NFIB)

The NFIB is the nation's largest advocacy organization, representing more than 500,000 small and independent business owners. It is a melting pot of commercial enterprise: high-tech manufacturers, family farmers, neighborhood retailers, and service companies. Founded in 1943, NFIB was created to give small and independent businesses a voice in governmental decision making. The organization is unique in that it polls its membership to determine NFIB policies, rather than having committees or board officers speak and decide unilaterally for its members. Dues start at $50 and are capped at $1,000, which tends to keep members' voices on relatively even levels. In fact, 73 percent of its members have fewer than 10 employees, 63 percent have annual gross income of under $350,000, and 84 percent are under $1 million. NFIB's total membership employs about 6 million people and reports annual gross sales of about $42.6 billion. Of its members, 28 percent are in retailing, 26 percent in services, 13 percent in manufacturing, 12 percent in construction, 6 percent each in agriculture, financial services, and wholesale, and 3 percent in communication and transportation. The politically conscious small entrepreneur will especially enjoy the NFIB's brochure, "How Congress Voted." Offices are maintained in all 50 state capitals; the national NFIB office is at 600 Maryland Avenue, NW, Suite 700, Washington, DC 20024, phone: (202) 554-9000; and a West Coast office is at 150 West 20th Avenue, San Mateo, CA 94403, phone: (415) 341-7441.

NATIONAL OFFICE PRODUCTS ASSOCIATION (NOPA)

Founded in 1904, the NOPA is an 8,500-member association of those who make, distribute, and sell office supplies, furniture, equipment, machines, and computers. It is the only major group bringing together all manufacturers, wholesalers, retailers, and sales representatives in this field. Services developed by large associations like NOPA can be invaluable to and afforded by any individual entrepreneur; here are some descriptions of their benefits. "The Dealer Operating Results Survey helps me judge my progress against that of similar firms," stated member Peter J. Elsenbach of Portland, OR. "I do not believe a dealer can be as successful without joining NOPA," stated Wallace Pellerin, a store owner in Austin, TX. Kenneth Rahberg of Topeka, KS, a stationery store proprietor, added, "To any new business, I would highly recommend immediately joining NOPA. The help they will receive will be the wisest expense money they will ever spend in any one year." The annual NOPA Convention and Exhibit, held at McCormick Place in Chicago, attracts more than 800 exhibitors at 3,000 booths, and more than 25,000 attendees, including over 17,000 retailers. Several annual surveys are taken and the information gathered is disseminated. Manufacturing members can utilize a 10,000-store mailing list. Directories of manufacturers and representatives are published, as well as handbooks on various operating programs, videos on operating problems, training packages, an ad clipbook, and a bi-weekly *Industry Report*. Two-day meetings are held each Spring in each of the association's 12 districts. NOPA maintains its headquarters at 301 North Fairfax Street, Alexandria, VA 22314-2696, phone: (703) 549-9040.

NATIONAL RETAIL HARDWARE ASSOCIATION (NRHA)

For entrepreneurs wanting to go into any phase of the hardware business, the NRHA will be a useful contact. Hardlines retailers today operate in an increasingly competitive environment. Variety stores, discount stores, home furnishings novelty chains, and even department stores carry overlapping lines. The programs and services of trade organizations such as the NRHA can provide leverage to the independent business operator that can make a real difference in customer loyalty and survival. The thousands of members of the NRHA are divided into 18 regional hardware associations. General trade and educational meetings are held annually; dozens of books, pamphlets, and video cassettes are available at sharp member discounts; and interior design and layout ideas are suggested. Training materials cover such topics as employee education, pricing errors, inventory shrinkage, damaged merchandise, management, and energy and store resources conservation. Available training programs cover the handling of hazardous materials, how to sell plumbing, telephone skills, shoplifting, residential estimating, and how to perform almost any home improvement task and sell it. The NRHA is located in the Hardware Industry Center, a national facility that is worth visiting. Contact: NRHA, 770 North High School Road, Indianapolis, IN 46214-3798, phone: (317) 248-1261.

NATIONAL SHOE RETAILERS ASSOCIATION (NSRA)

The 77-year-old NSRA represents a large number of the 24,000 independent shoe retailers. Membership in this organization offers a number of practical and numerous potential advantages; among the first is a group rate with the VISA/MasterCharge program, ranging from 1.42 to 2.87 percent, depending on volume and charge amount. In this one item, members can more than recoup the $100 to $1,000 membership expenses. Other valued benefits include an information service that can call up any resource or other contact needed; a confidential consulting service to respond to business problems; a number of merchandising and training aids available at discounts; a group-rate insurance program; and specialized workshops. A national shoe fair is held each year in February, usually in New York, though shoe travellers' and footwear association "markets" (buying shows) are held throughout the year and are announced in the monthly *NSRA News*. Valuable reports for the entry-level and progressive shoe entrepreneur are the "Shoe Store Operations Survey" (comparative data on various types of retail stores) and the Trend Committee Reports (merchandising trends in various shoe lines). The latest reported net sales average for independent shoe stores was $457,576; leased departments reported an average of $215,545. Net profit for these types of operations were 5.56 and 4.73 percent, respectively. Women's shoe stores reported average net profit of 5.00 percent; men's, 1.91 percent; children's, 6.42 percent; and family stores, 4.73 percent. Contact: NSRA, 9861 Broken Land Parkway, Columbia, MD 21046, phone: (301) 381-8282.

NETWORKING

Making use of professional and business contacts can be as simple as a restaurant owner's invitation to an entrepreneur to display a business card, or a weekly Rotary or service club luncheon where business cards are exchanged.

The Tyson Entrepreneurs' Club meets informally once a week at a local hotel in Tyson's Corner, VA, and enjoys a buffet breakfast while each member takes a turn telling the others what *new* business he or she has called on during the past week and what the business might be looking to buy. The North Tier Venture Group in Allentown, PA, meets six times a year to eat lunch, hear a pertinent speaker, and get to meet each other. Each attendee gets two minutes to tell the others about his or her business and about opportunities that may exist for all or some of the group. The relatively recent and innovative Incubator Club is a perfect networking opportunity. Startup businesses should network not only their own talents and products, but their contacts with university professors and graduate students. The success of so many new immigrants from Southeast Asia is a result of ethnic networking—established Asian-American businesses provide a *hui* to finance startup enterprises and provide entrepreneurial guidance to the newer arrivals. Says attorney Sanford Piltch, a member of the North Tier Group, "Networking provides an awareness of options. Two entrepreneurs with parallel or complementary ideas may get together, or they may end up talking to a market analyst who helps them re-focus a business plan."

NEW BUSINESS LOANS   See *Bank Loans, Startup Advice, Startup Checklist, Startup Costs, Startup Loans.*

NEW BUSINESS TRENDS   What's hot and what's not for the 1990s? Much depends on the experience of the entrepreneur, yet almost 85 percent of the people who go into a business of their own start or buy a business that is *not* based on their experience. The owners of most of the innovations of the new decade were venturing into completely new types of businesses. Here is just a selection of likely trends in the years ahead:

- Specialty stores in limited space in high-traffic malls—sock stores, stuffed animal zoos, all-white fashions, teen gadgetry, specialty or ethnic foods.

- Personnel leasing—the agency pays all fringes, salaries, and benefits and handles all paperwork.

- Popular seminars and professional training—widespread effort to close the education gap.

- Telemarketing—expanded selling via the TV screen, including meals and specialty foods.

- Shop-by-phone—especially for groceries, and in particular in large, urban apartment houses.

- Daycare and private school operations—for preschool tots, latch-key kids, and elderly persons who require some custodial care; some are subsidized by and run in conjunction with corporations.

- Mobile maintenance shops—come to the customer's home to handle everything from auto emergencies to minor home repairs and installations.

- Nanny schools and placement services—where domestic and immigrant women can be trained and placed in the growing number of homes with working mothers.

- Ecological merchandising—products, packaging, and services that are beneficial to our planet, will not pollute, and are environment-friendly.

- Health-conscious eating out—emphasis on foods low in cholesterol, high in nutritional values.

- Teen-directed merchandising—*everything*, from clothes, video games, tapes, foods, toys, and novelties to entertainment, to siphon some of the $2,500-per-kid annual expenditure plus unknown millions in earned but undeclared income.

NEWSPAPERS These basic local media for advertising and publicity have varied schedules: daily newspapers come out every day, in the morning or afternoon, and on Sunday; business "dailies" publish Monday through Friday, in the morning. Weekly newspapers come out mostly on Wednesday or Thursday, to catch the increased weekend retail business. Since newspapers are sold for 10 cents to 50 cents, which is well below the cost of producing a complete newspaper ($1.00 to $2.00 per copy!), advertising must make up the vast difference. Many weekly newspapers are free and thus depend 100 percent on advertising revenue. Newspapers are produced quickly and printed overnight on inexpensive paper. This makes their use for ads and news very flexible, but it also means that the paper does not last long in the home or office. The life span of an ad or news story in a newspaper is brief at best. Some metropolitan newspapers are so big that the small advertiser can easily be overlooked in the medium's 100 to 200 pages. For the small entrepreneur, a large newspaper might not be the best choice; being a minnow in an ocean does not get much attention. But in every area of the country newspapers exist that will meet the needs of local and small entrepreneurs. If a big daily offers great circulation all over the area, but most of it is irrelevant for local needs, a local or suburban newspaper with more targeted circulation and far lower prices is a better choice. There are also parochial newspapers (Catholic, Jewish, Protestant denominations) and specialized ethnic and association newspapers; their costs are usually much higher, but they target ads and news to specific audiences. All newspapers have contracts which allow substantial discounts on ad rates. They can also help in the preparation of ads, usually at no cost. (See also *Advertising Media Selection.*)

NONPROFITS   A nonprofit association or even a nonprofit corporation is allowed to operate without paying taxes. Most nonprofit organizations are in a socially desirable business—charities, hospitals, and educational institutions. Organizations that are thus qualified can solicit contributions from the public that are tax-deductible to the donor. Nonprofits can be incorporated but their stockholders or trustees do not share in any profits or losses. Some major corporations have established foundations through which contributions are channeled. These contributions, including the expenses incurred for managing them, are not taxable. Small entrepreneurs who are in for-profit businesses have long objected to the vast number of nonprofits that enjoy tax-exempt status and subsidized mailing privileges—particularly those in open competition with entrepreneurs who pay taxes. Another unfair advantage, claim entrepreneurs, is that nonprofits promote a public image that causes the public to buy from them, believing that they are thus making a donation to a worthy cause. Many universities, especially in their bookstores, and huge international nonprofit corporations like National Geographic, sell products that are in direct competition with private enterprise. Scientific testing done by university laboratories, mailing houses that solicit greeting card sales and are owned by charitable or veterans' organizations, bus tours promoted by elderly-citizen or church associations—these are some of the business-related activities nurtured by nonprofits. More than one million nonprofits exist nationwide. Their annual revenues exceed $300 billion and they employ 10 percent of the workforce. The House Ways and Means Committee is considering changes in the Unrelated Business Income Tax, but it is doubtful that the nonprofits' "halo effect" will ever be removed in favor of tax equalization.

NONTRADITIONAL RETAILING   There are a number of types of retailers in this category; home demonstration sales, door-to-door direct selling, and club sales are some of the established ones. In some unsettled markets, like Miami, "gypsy retailers" are prolific. They sell from temporarily leased stores that happen to be vacant and hold "grand opening sales" one month and "going out of business sales" the next. Flea marketeers can be found everywhere, especially in urban areas where inexpensive selling space is available or long stretches of good weather make outdoor selling practical. In some cities with large minority and/or immigrant populations, "curbside capitalists" provide a smorgasbord of merchandise for quick turnover at low prices. New York City's midtown street corners are home to often illegal quick-buck artists who sell "genuine" Rolex knock-offs for $40 or $50. Washington, DC has many similar vendors; their principal investment is a shared panel truck, a four-by-seven-foot stand, and a variety of merchandise, plus an easily obtained sales license from the city. Underdeveloped countries have long seen this type of entrepreneurial activity. Some, like Trinidad and Jamaica, forcefully removed the uncontrolled, tax-dodging vendors from their narrow urban streets and built or provided under-roof bazaars—against the vociferous protests of the itinerant capitalists. Many American cities are imitating the nation's capital, which requires a $1,000 deposit fee from its nearly 2,500 curbside vendors. Earnings are reported to vary between $30 and $200 a day. With the vagaries of the weather, yo-yo sales success, and blatant thievery, the life of the "curbside capitalists" is not an easy one, but the call of independence continues its siren melody.

OBSOLESCENCE   A reduction in value, or even total uselessness, can develop in a property, an item of merchandise, and even a personal skill. There are numerous causes for obsolescence and they are not always the fault of the owner. Deterioration may be caused by age; by scientific and technological advances; by economic changes such as inflation, income reduction among customer groups, and changes in the nature of a neighborhood from residential to industrial, or white-collar to blue-collar; by competitive pressures from lower-priced goods and services or from imported goods; by changes in styles and fashions; or by popularity shifts that are often inexplicable. Career obsolescence is also a very real factor. The advance of scientific, educational, and technological knowledge (particularly the use of computers) has left many highly educated and motivated older entrepreneurs and workers behind the times. Thinking can be subject to obsolescence. Because economic and technological demands change so rapidly, continual updating is required for all product and service enterprises. Antiobsolescence training must include: reeducation, retraining, reading of publications and books, attendance at seminars, shifting to new and advanced areas in the field, and use of outside consultants who have updated expertise. Entrepreneurs and employers must watch for obsolescence in the marketplace and correct it quickly. Adjustments may involve: salary analysis as younger people bring in not only few skills and learning, but willingness to work at lower salaries; closing the generation gaps between older and newer employees through internal training and public relations programs; elimination of alienation among age groups; judging potential obsolescence within the industry and making changes before it becomes too late and too costly.

Overhead   A business's fixed costs are its overhead and they include all the expenses incurred in running the enterprise whether it sells anything or not. On the business's income statement, the overhead is usually listed as "General and administrative costs" and may include fixed (and even somewhat variable) costs such as legal and accounting fees, salaries, utilities, rent or mortgage payments, advertising, and other selling costs. An accepted rule of thumb is the 5 percent rule: If an item accounts for more than 5 percent of the overhead, it should have its own category on the financial statement. If too much is thrown into "Miscellaneous," control over expenditures is lost and the company may run afoul of the tax authorities. If overhead is climbing faster than gross profit—such as might occur during slow periods or downsizing of the business, when fixed overhead remains static while sales are decreasing—then it is time to manipulate variable overhead and take another look at the fixed items for any feasible adjustments. At the beginning of a business, it is best to keep commitments (leases of property, equipment, and rolling stock) short-term, even if long-term commitments are lower in costs. During startups, entrepreneurs might be better off to have materials produced on the outside, rather than manufacturing them in-house and making long-term commitments to suppliers and workers. The same cautions apply to personnel. Investigate whether part-time employees will do, during the tooling-up years; consider leasing a staff, especially to obtain nonsales and nonproductive personnel. Ask an accountant and ask the employees for ideas on keeping overhead down, because if overhead gets over an owner's head, it can drown a business in no time.

PAPERWORK   A chief complaint of most small entrepreneurs is the profusion of paperwork that a business generates—and what to do with it afterward. Computers were supposed to be the panacea, but they generate their own unwieldy printouts and files. Besides, suppose the computer develops a glitch; suppose the diskettes get ruined . . . . Many companies have backup systems because they don't entirely trust the computer, so they are back beyond square one. How can the amount of paperwork be minimized? Answer these questions candidly: What is the fundamental purpose of this paper? Will anyone ever want to see it again? What is the goal of this form? How long must it be kept? (See *Record Retention.*) Suggested guidelines can be the following:

1. Question the tradition. Just because the company has always done something a certain way, does that mean it cannot be done in another way—perhaps more efficiently?

2. Analyze the problem before reaching for a solution. Discuss it not only with yourself, but with others in the company or the family. Should the form be redesigned? Is it really needed?

3. Ask the right question, to get the right answer. Is this effort possibly duplicated elsewhere?

4. Keep things simple. If the person who now handles this paper goes on vacation, gets sick, or leaves, can a replacement pick up the task easily?

5. People are the key to any paperwork. They have to understand what the purpose of the paperwork is. When a form is proposed or designed, it will be more effective if the people who are going to be using it have a hand in designing it.

6. Control the system. Devising a great paper control system and then walking from it makes no sense. A system won't remain effective unless somebody keeps track of it.

7. Don't rest on laurels. Systems are made and systems can go awry. They need periodic reviews.

PARTNERSHIP   When two or more individuals join together their expertise and money to form a business, acquire a business, or expand an existing business, a partnership is created. The members of a partnership share in its profits, assets, management, responsibilities, and liabilities in accordance with the partnership agreement, which should be drawn up at the beginning of the association. A partnership theoretically offers access to more personal and financial resources, greater stability, and increased assets. However, as in a marriage, problems can crop up, long after the partnership has been formed. Unlike a marriage, a partnership can be controlled from the outset by objectively analyzing all the potential problems and trying to incorporate them into an agreement drawn up by an attorney. The agreement must include such normally mundane items as management responsibilities, remuneration, profit sharing, participation of family members, choices of employees and services, determination of resources, provisions for emergencies and dissolution of the partnership, borrowing policies, credit, expansion, advertising and public relations methods, and the more specialized requirements of doing business in a particular field. According to figures released by Dun & Bradstreet, partnerships have lower average profit margins than proprietorships or corporations. Should loans or guarantees be required, all active partners would most likely have to sign the obligations personally. Still, there are many advantages to a partnership, some realistic and others psychological: greater talents and connections are available; multiplied assets are at the business's disposal; more free time can be arranged for each partner. Two heads *are* better than one, and many entrepreneurs like the idea of being able to consult and to share. It is then less lonely at the top.

PATENTS   When a product or process has been registered with the United States Patent Office, the patent applicant is granted the right to exclude others from the making or selling of the invention for a specified time. The owner gains a legitimate monopoly. While the Patent Office is conducting a patent search, to make sure that a product or process has not previously been patented, interim protection of a *patent pending* applies. This statement is permitted after a patent has been filed, even before the Patent Office makes a final determination of patentability under the law. A patent infringement is an act of trespass upon the rights secured by a patent. The test of infringement is whether the device being contested does substantially the same work in the same way and accomplishes the same results as the device that has already been patented. Many inventors are concerned that someone will steal their idea before it can be patented. The best protection is to market it as quickly as possible and with a lot of fanfare, but this often takes more effort and money than most small entrepreneurs can manage. An alternate, two-year protection costs just $6.00: file a Disclosure Documents Program form with the Patent Office. Write to the U.S. Patent Office, Department of Commerce, 14th Street and Constitution Avenue, NW, Washington, DC 20231, and ask for the booklet "Disclosure Document Program." Inventors can conduct their own patent search at the Search Room of the Scientific Library of the Patent and Trademark Office, Crystal Plaza, 2021 Jefferson Davis Highway, Arlington, VA. The library stocks patents filed since 1836. Major libraries in virtually all states have online access to this library through its computerized program.

PERSUASION

To influence others to believe in ideas or offerings, or to get people to buy products or services takes persuasion. The medium can be a letter, an advertisement, an announcement, a face-to-face talk, or a speech. However, if an audience is hostile to a product or idea, or is totally disinterested, no amount of persuasion will move them to act favorably, so getting a message to the right audience is an entrepreneur's initial step. But once the right product or service is determined and the audience that would be receptive to it is identified, how can the audience be *persuaded* to react favorably? How can they be made to want the service or buy the product? There is a 50-year-old formula that was taught when entrepreneur was still a foreign word—the formula of AIDCA: Attention, Interest, Desire, Conviction, Action. These are the psychological steps to persuading prospects to react favorably to an offering, no matter what the medium:

Attention: Ask a question; make a startling statement; focus on the prospects' interest; use a dramatic illustration or sound.

Interest: Define a proposition logically and show how it fits into the audience's interests, how it benefits them.

Desire: Expand on the benefits—how they have profited others or made life better for them; make the audience *want* what is being offered.

Conviction: Support claims with proof—test reports, visualization, testimonials, statistics, profit figures.

Action: Ask for the order. Nothing has happened until the sale is consummated. Get the reader, listener, or audience to *do* what it is they have been asked to do.

That's persuasion!

PETROLEUM MARKETERS ASSOCIATION OF AMERICA (PMAA) This is America's association for the more than 10,000 independent purveyors of oil products, including gas stations, convenience stores with gas pumps, quick-lube stations, deliverers of heating oils to 16 million American homes, truck stops, car washes, and agricultural suppliers of fuel. Service stations number nearly 50,000 individual units, and about 18,000 convenience grocery stores have gas pumps available. Collectively, these two categories of members account for 55 percent of the gasoline sold in the United States and 75 percent of the home heating oils. PMAA marketers sold 92 billion gallons of refined products in 1987. They employ 242,000 full- and part-time employees and own bulk storage facilities with a capacity of 1.7 billion gallons. Founded in 1909, PMAA publishes numerous booklets and videos on underground tank storage problems, safety regulations, and accident handling; a manual of employee benefits; and a complete and comprehensive directory (available for $50). Forty-three state associations belong to the national umbrella group. Entrepreneurs planning to enter this field by opening a new business, adding automotive services to an existing business, or acquiring an existing business in the petroleum field, can obtain more information and direction from PMAA at 1120 Vermont Avenue, NW, Suite 1130, Washington, DC 20005, phone: (202) 331-1198.

PITFALLS Stumbling blocks, caveats, or problems are inevitable for any entrepreneur. Their numbers are no doubt endless, but the major pitfalls that need to be considered by anyone going into a startup business involve the following:

1. *Dependence:* Some entrepreneurs leave behind a relatively sheltered existence in civil service, the military, or a large corporation, where everything is departmentalized and different people are assigned separate tasks. Other people called managers make all these activities dovetail and the results achieved are the efforts of many minds and hands. Entrepreneurs may be fulfilling all the departmentalized tasks—and more. The buck stops with them; there is no passalong person to make it less lonely at the top.

2. *Business plan:* A business must have one. Whether for the owner as a guide to projected operations, or for a bank or loan official, a "roadmap" or blueprint of plans and projections is vital. If it seems overwhelming, a good accountant or lawyer may help.

3. *Banker:* In all likelihood the business will need one. If the business needs a loan, go to the bank's headquarters *prepared.* Bring

along a solid business plan. The banker is being asked to become a partner.

4. *Expertise:* Successful entrepreneurs have a good business sense, but they cannot do everything and be everywhere. Family, friends, teachers, associates, trade organizations, SBA, SCORE, anyone who is a resource for a new enterprise can be enlisted for help. Lawyers, CPAs, bankers, and insurance agents can become best friends.

5. *Advisors:* Lean on the people who lend their expertise. Approach those who show genuine interest, who can be trusted, and who can contribute and not distract. No one is an island, not even an entrepreneur.

PRESTIGE Translate this word as "image" or "public relations." It is the respect for a person or company or product that results from a good reputation and past achievements. Why is the term included here? Professor Richard A. D'Aveni of the Amos Tuck School of Business Administration at Dartmouth College, explained prestige this way: "Prestige provides the illusion of competence and control, and is sometimes a proxy for actual skill." He found in a survey of 57 bankrupt companies that some survived bankruptcy, while others succumbed. Those that survived had corporate and product prestige; some of them even renegotiated loans at lower interest rates. The survivors discovered that creditors do not, for the most part, want a company to go under. A bankrupt company ceases to be a customer, and suppliers—whether manufacturers or bankers—want and need viable customers. They will bend over backward to help a company survive, provided that they believe that the company in trouble has a chance. Having a reputation for honesty, credibility, and a solid economic base in the marketplace helps an enterprise when the chips are down. For an entrepreneur to create the kind of image that builds prestige, sound public relations must be practiced from the very beginning. (See *Public Relations.*) Prestige starts with the product or service, but it is reinforced by every representative who speaks for the company, every piece of paper or statement that is issued in the name of the company, the people with whom the owner is seen, and the companies the owner keeps. Prestige is an intangible asset, but when the going gets tough, it could be the ingredient that saves an enterprise.

PRINTING INDUSTRIES OF AMERICA, INC. Thirty-two separate printing industry associations are represented by this national council, a first-class operation located at 1730 North Lynn Street, Arlington, VA 22209. The PIA Book Store maintained at this location stocks a couple of hundred titles on the printing industry and general business subjects, as well as supporting electronic material. These may be ordered by mail, or phone: (703) 841-8138. Members receive substantial discounts. A valuable item for acquisition is a 15-item set of financial ratios that shows complete financial operating costs for every phase of the printing industry. Members can receive a large number of free newsletters on such topics as makeready, marketing, and association activities; for-sale publications cover color separation, layout grids, type specimens, computer composition, newsletter publishing, quality control, management, and trade customs, among other topics. More than a dozen meetings are held each year in various parts of the country and Graph Expo, a major convention and exposition, is held annually, usually in a metro area like New York. There are 70,000 commercial printers and 11,000 silkscreen printers in the United States. A fairly new but growing segment (10,000) of the printing industry is the "quick printers," most of which are franchises.

PROCUREMENT   See *Government Procurement.*

PROFESSIONAL PHOTOGRAPHERS OF AMERICA

This organization is typical of the countless membership associations available in virtually every profession, craft, service, or enterprise. The advantages of membership in a well-organized association are as much pragmatic as psychological. Members can learn from the association's newsletter, magazine, or literature, as well as from its trade shows and meetings. At and between meetings members can network their skills and needs. For example, suppose a photographer who is a member of this association gets an assignment that would require such extensive time traveling that the fulfillment of the assignment would be unprofitable. By consulting the membership directory, the photographer can locate a member of professional standing in the distant location and arrange for cooperation in satisfying an important customer. The use of the association's logo on stationery, displays, vehicles, IDs, and lapel pins can be a mark of prestige and confidence. Seminars that are held by the association, either separately or in conjunction with periodic trade shows, are valuable learning tools that can be applied in practical ways to the enhancement of the individual enterprise. Completion of courses or attendance at seminars can earn members certificates, special designations, and awards that add prestige when displayed on an office or studio wall. The cost of membership, about $150 for this particular association, is usually regarded as a good investment. Contact: Professional Photographers of America, 1090 Executive Way, Des Plaines, IL 60018, phone: (708) 299-8161.

PROFIT-AND-LOSS-STATEMENT   This financial statement shows detailed earnings, generally for the previous year, for an established business, or for a full projected year, if part of a business plan. The "P and L Statement" is a summary of business income and expenses during a specific accounting period. It lists the total amount of sales, minus expenses and costs, and shows whether the business made or lost money during the period covered by the statement.

(See also *Financial Statements* and *Income Statement.*)

PROFIT SHARING   Under profit-sharing plans, employees get a share of the company's profits, according to their longevity or performance. Some companies issue profit-sharing awards at the end of the calendar year, combining them with a Christmas bonus; others issue them at the conclusion of the fiscal year. The amount can be arbitrary, or it can be calculated on each person's salary, using the same percentage as the corporate profits for the period. The CEO of a Virginia company doles out profit-sharing checks each month. He claims that the little time it takes to disburse more frequent rewards creates a harder-working group of employees who need less supervision and tend to minimize their absences—in his company, the average is two days a year. "Even when profit shares go down one month, the rewards come often enough for employees to remember the 'big one' last month—and they'll work harder next month to get the profit shares back up there." Some companies use profit sharing as a means to keep employees longer—they start employees on the plan after their third or sixth or twelfth month. Another reported advantage is that employees police each other, knowing that their rewards are affected by the inattention or inefficiency of another employee. Among larger companies, 65 percent of officers get bonuses of one sort or another but only 26 percent are on a profit-sharing plan. This figure doubles among companies that exceed $5 million in annual volume. The amount of profit sharing is discretionary in 62 percent of U.S. companies; 17 percent employ a fixed formula and 16 percent set a formula annually.

PROPRIETORSHIP   This simplest form of business may consist of just one person who will assume complete liability for all actions of the business. Seventy percent of all American businesses are proprietorships. This form of business organization appeals to rugged individualists because it is easy to get into and to get out of. The proprietor has all the obligations but takes all the profits that might accrue. Single owners have the most freedom of action, the maximum authority, a number of tax advantages, and social security. The principal disadvantage is the total liability of the proprietor, both as the owner and as an employer who has people on a payroll or acting on his or her behalf. Should the owner die, the business may be ended—and is, in many cases. Growth of the business is limited by the capacities of its solitary owner. Financing is limited to the credit line of the owner. When the proprietor is tired, ill, or needs a vacation, there is no one to take care of the business during an absence—unless other family members or employees take over for a while. Another danger, though quite inadvertent, is that personal affairs too often get mixed up with business, which can affect precious time, merchandise, cash flow, and the checkbook. If the business operates under a pseudonym for the owner (i.e., a fictitious person's name), that fact usually needs to be announced in a legal notice in the local newspaper (check with the municipal or county courthouse). One more caveat: The owner's personal assets, such as property, are vulnerable in the event the business goes bankrupt and owes a lot of bills. Anything the proprietor owns can be attached by creditors.

PUBLIC RELATIONS

The image that an owner and a business present to the public can help the business grow faster. Abraham Lincoln was the first president to define the concept of public relations, when he stated in 1858: "With public sentiment, nothing can fail; without it, nothing can succeed. Consequently, he who molds public sentiment goes deeper than he who enacts statutes or pronounces decisions." Good public relations can make sure that the best foot that is put forward has well shined shoes. When customers and contacts think well of a company, its sales job is easier. The good image will continue even when the company stops advertising, or when reverses hit its profit curve, or when competition crowds it in the market. Public relations is often subtle. It is not simple to put one's finger on exactly what it does; it is anything at all that makes an impression on customers or clients: the format of advertising, a logo, stationery, an exterior sign, the ways in which bills are sent out, the behavior of sales representatives, or clerks, or delivery people, the way the owner and the staff dress, the markings on and cleanliness of trucks or uniforms, the exchange or make-good policy, the way telephones are answered, the professionals with whom the company is associated (law firm, accountant, banker, insurance carrier), the organizations to which the owner belongs, how often and how well the company is mentioned in the press. Public relations is communications, publicity, marketing, opinion research, and more. It is a highly skilled, professional tool that every entrepreneur can and should put to good use. (See Peter G. Miller, *Media Marketing*, New York: Harper & Row, 1987; 200 pp.)

PUBLICITY   News about a business that appears in some public
medium like a newspaper or magazine, or is mentioned during a radio broadcast or telecast is wonderful advertising—and it is free. Publicity, however, has two drawbacks: the company cannot control its wording, and there are no guarantees on its appearance or timing. A news release may have been supplied but its final format and timing are entirely up to the editor or program director, columnist, or commentator. How can a company be sure to get the best possible opportunity for publicity? And why is publicity so desirable? Taking the latter question first, publicity is highly desirable because of the credibility of the printed or electronic medium that mentions the business. By association, the business becomes credible. When someone else says something nice about an owner, a product, or a service, the message is not a paid-for, obviously self-serving ad; instead, a supposedly neutral and respected outsider is lauding or calling attention to the company and what it sells. The impact of publicity can be greater than more costly advertising in a larger space. That's why it is so desirable. How can an owner be sure to get into the media? As a start, when advertising is placed, an attempt should be made to try and get some free publicity into that medium. With trade magazines and small-town newspapers this kind of *quid pro quo* is understood and always rendered. With larger media it is more difficult because of the historic division between the editorial and the advertising departments—but it is not impossible. Liaison with publicists has to be professional and consistent. News releases have to be handled correctly; the event or purpose has to be relevant and newsworthy; the timing has to be appropriate; the format has to be neat and professional. If necessary, get help from a public relations expert or friendly editor. Getting to know the editor or program director personally can be of great help. A sample news release is shown on page 157.

SCORE®   Service Corps of Retired Executives
Association

Sponsored by U.S. Small Business Administration

For Immediate Release to: [name of newspaper or station]

SCORE Contact: [name of spokesperson and phone]

Date:

Subject: World's Largest Small Business Counseling
         Association Marks 25th Anniversary in
         October 1989

SCORE, the Service Corps of Retired Executives, will
mark its Silver Anniversary during the first week of
October with the televised counseling of its
2,500,000th client.

The event will take place on October 7, 1989, at 10
a.m. at the Omni Hotel in Baltimore, MD and will be
attended by a representative from The White House,
Governor Donald Schaefer of Maryland, and Mayor Kurt
Schmoke of Baltimore. SBA and SCORE officials and
more than 200 representatives from around the country
will be in attendance.

Baltimore, the host city for the event being observed
by the more than 12,000 volunteer members of SCORE,
was one of the several cities in which SCORE began
its small business counseling activities in 1964.
Thousands of men and women entrepreneurs in all 50
states have received individual assistance, while
many others (116,000 in 1988 alone) attended SCORE
workshops in one of the more than 750 locations which
SCORE volunteers serve.

SCORE volunteers come from private, corporate,
government, and military ranks. They serve without
pay to help American entrepreneurs become independent
businesspeople or assist those already in business to
expand their operations. The U.S. Small Business
Administration helps to finance administrative costs
with $2.5 million annually.

QUALITY CONTROL Quality is a characteristic measure of excellence. It is a standard which every entrepreneur should try to achieve. Quality control is the process of assuring that products are made to consistently high standards. Inspection of goods at various points in their manufacture by either a person or a machine is usually an important part of the quality control process. Phillip Crosby, the guru of quality control, has been preaching that "doing it right the first time" is the most economical way of production. Proper motivation of all workers involved in a manufacturing or servicing process, and appropriate incentives for errorless production are the twin bases of quality control—even before post-production inspection. Small entrepreneurs have a better chance of quality control because of their proximity to their products and services. Large companies will find it more difficult to control the output of hundreds or thousands of employees. Motorola, a company that practices a high degree of quality control, is a repeat winner of the Commerce Department's annual quality standards award. Motorola deals with 6,000 suppliers and by assuring that these suppliers adhered to certain quality standards Motorola improved its end-products. If the suppliers refuse to make the effort, they are likely to lose the account of this big manufacturer. IBM, Ford Motor Company, General Motors, Texas Instruments, Pitney-Bowes, Xerox, and other major manufacturers have started quality control programs and are in the process of curtailing purchases from suppliers that do not introduce quality controls. Their policy is a lesson for small and startup entrepreneurs who are looking to the future: quality control is likely to be even more important than cost control.

RADIO   There are about 8,500 AM and FM radio stations in the United States. Some of the smallest towns have at least one station and big cities may have a dozen or more. Fragmentation of audiences has both advantages and disadvantages for the entrepreneur. Fortunately, radio stations develop a "format" that is designed to attract a certain audience. By matching this audience with a company's needs much waste coverage can be eliminated. By determining whether the audience might be listening during traffic hours (when car radio listenership is at a peak), during news broadcasts, or during the daytime at home, the entrepreneur can reach prospects by placing radio announcements during times that have the most targeted listeners. This entry on *Radio* would take about two minutes to read aloud; use it to gauge the proper length of a radio message that would fit a standard 10-, 20-, 30-, or 60-second spot. (The message-length units are priced proportionately.) Radio advertising is most effective when it is repetitive. Commercial announcements are usually sold in packages of 10, 20, 30, or more, broadcast between certain hours over a given time period of days or weeks. The more announcements contracted, the lower the rate. (This is especially applicable to co-op advertising from several suppliers; a radio station rep can explain the best way to pay the least.) The most effective radio announcements are those that are repeated several times; that utilize the voice of a station announcer who is well known; that fit into the program format (the listener is, after all, tuned in for entertainment, not for advertising); and that offer a message that is memorable and to the point.

REAL ESTATE   This term means property—which might include land, residential, commercial, or industrial buildings, and condominiums—and all the activities concerned with ownership and transfers of the physical property. Certain commercial areas like New York, Washington, Central and South Florida, California, and some resort properties are said to be "hot," and speculation in such properties has made many millionaires. One investor was able to obtain title to over 160 acres of agriculturally zoned property on the outskirts of a major eastern city. Thirteen years later, he was finally able to get commercial and residential zoning. He divided the property and sold it as follows: $10 million for a 50-acre shopping mall; 10 acres for light commercial buildings and 100 acres for 1,200 townhomes, totaling $19 million. The $29 million he received cost him $3.2 million but it took about 20 years for the property to be built out. Still, a $25.8 million appreciation, less the legal costs over the 20-year period, gave this speculator a gain of better than a million dollars per year. No wonder many entrepreneurs consider real estate a quick-rich field: buy, fix, rent, sell or hope for zoning that will bring a road out of the city right past the property, and anyone has it made. There's a lot more to it: Real estate speculation is risky, it takes time, and not every entrepreneur has the patience or can afford the wait. A Seattle resident worked and invested for 35 years. He started with a $2,500 house, fixed it up, rented it, and kept on going. It took 20 years before he could look at his assets and say he had gained a really sizable sum. But when he retired at age 60, he was a real estate millionaire. Read his advice carefully. It's especially valuable because it's from someone who did it—*worked at* making a fortune in real estate:

- Look for a property that is under the market price. Even if the first offer seems ridiculously low, try it anyway. A buyer never knows what motivates a seller to accept an offer; it may be the only one received.

- Never buy the most expensive house in a neighborhood; a house and property can always be improved in time. Many people buy *neighborhoods* and will not be interested unless a house is the best on the block. Proximity to roadways, schools, and shopping is sometimes more weighty.

- Buy a house that has a special selling point—a large corner lot, or a wooded lot, or handy access to shopping or recreation, or a school that has the best reputation in the area.

- Buy a house that has a full basement (unless it is in a high-watertable area like Florida or next to a body of water). A basement doubles the house space, saves on fuel, and keeps the rest of the house drier.

- Hire rental agents to collect rents. For an owner with a full-time job or a business to run, rent collection is a life-complicating chore.

- Get repairs done by a professional, unless the family business is home improvement, or the owner has special skills or takes special pleasures in working on a house or grounds.

- Make accurate estimates of the income needed to cover *all* overhead, but keep the rent reasonable enough to attract good tenants who will stay a long time and even add to the improvement of the property. They might even become future purchasers (saving the owner 6 to 7 percent in realty commission).

RECORD RETENTION   Owners should keep papers referring to business transactions for specified periods of time that vary with the papers' potential use in the future. Obviously, contracts, leases, and warranties must be retained for as long as the business occupies the premises, uses the equipment, or maintains the relationships to which the papers pertain. Tax references must be kept for as long as the law allows taxpayer liability or possible audit by taxing authorities, although even annual tax returns should be kept for as long as the business is in operation. The Code of Federal Regulations contains a "Guide to Record Retention." Here is a brief list of the retentions recommended, subject to local or regional adjustment and to the advice of an attorney or accountant.

Retain Indefinitely:
- Audit reports and financial statements
- Canceled checks for taxes, capital purchases, important contracts
- Capital stock and bond records
- Cash books
- Contracts and leases that are current
- Copyrights, patents, trademark registrations
- Corporation charter, minute books, bylaws
- Correspondence on legal and tax matters
- Deeds, mortgages, easements, other property records
- General ledgers and journals
- Insurance records
- Property appraisals
- Tax returns, including supporting records and workpapers

Retain Seven to Eight Years:
- Miscellaneous canceled checks
- Vouchers for payments to vendors, employees, and so on
- Inventory records
- Payroll records and time sheets
- Expense reports
- Payables/receivables ledgers
- Old contracts and leases
- Purchase orders

- Invoices and sales records
- Plant cost ledgers

Retain Six Years:

- Monthly trial balances
- Employee withholding statements
- Employee disability benefits records

Retain Three Years:

- Personnel files on departed employees
- Bank reconciliations
- Petty cash vouchers
- Expired insurance policies (no cash value)

Retain Two Years:

- General correspondence
- Requisitions

RECYCLING   Old materials like paper, plastic, and metals can be reused by sorting and compressing them and selling them to dealers of recycling materials. This alternative to wasting them helps to clean up our environment. The recycling of plastics into pellets for packing and other applications, or of metals into reusable production, requires considerable investment in machinery, property, and marketing. The recycling of papers and cardboard is simpler. Every business generates commercially usable loads of paper. Despite computer use, the amount of papers and packing board generated is staggering, and turning trash into cash can be a profitable and beneficial sideline. American businesses were paid a billion dollars in 1988 for turning their paper waste products into recycled waste. The American Paper Institute estimates that the more than 26 million tons of waste paper recycled in 1988 represented only 30 percent of the paper waste products generated by American business. Each ton of recycled material saves about 3.3 cubic yards of landfill space. There are more than 2,000 waste paper dealers across the country to help in this ecological transformation. Some entrepreneurs have saved several hundred dollars a month in hauling costs; others have actually made money by contracting their paper waste to a recycler instead of a trash-hauling company. Among the papers that can be saved for recycling are: typing, writing, scratch, and photocopy papers (white only); tabulating and index cards; and computer printout paper. Carbon paper, envelopes, blueprints, film, photos, tapes, newspapers, books or magazines, styro cups, and wax papers are not suitable.

RED TAPE   The name of this symbol of government procrastination and confusing language in laws and regulations originates from the red ribbons with which lawyers used to tie their bundles of documents. "Red tape" appeared in the writings of Irving, Dickens, and Carlyle. In *David Copperfield* Dickens used a description that many corporate managers can identify with: "Skewered through and through with office-pens, and bound hand and foot with red tape." Why are government pronouncements the leading contender in the red tape derby? Perhaps writers of government laws and gobbledygook were former insurance policy writers. One of the most outstanding unnamed associations of red tape professionals is the group that writes Internal Revenue Service regulations. Entrepreneurs are vitally affected by this problem. Having overcome the many hurdles of initial startup, financing, organizing, bookkeeping, promotion, and marketing, entrepreneurs then face a hodgepodge of tax laws that few of them have either the time or the background to unravel. Compliance with all of them has literally driven some entrepreneurs out of business. One accounting expert stated, "Small companies don't have the staff that can devote the man hours necessary to review, interpret, and comply with regulations. . . . While most laws are designed to protect people and provide order, [the tax codes] are causing chaos among small businesses." An antidiscrimination clause in the 1986 Tax *Reform* (Congress's name for it, anyway) Act was referred to as Section 89. In the Spring of 1989 the "completely unclear . . . frankly a mess" clause caused Rep. John LaFalce (D-NY) to introduce legislation to repeal this provision. Winston Churchill's polemics for basic English appear to have been lost on government regulation writers, and that is a shame, considering the thousands of bright and talented people whose salaries come from taxes paid by the people they represent.

RELATIVES (ROLE MODELS)   Family members can be partners or investors in a small enterprise or can act as role models during the entrepreneur's developing years. Every survey and analysis of entrepreneurs seems to indicate that family members as role models are highly important. One survey undertaken by the Department of Commerce indicated the following percentages of entrepreneurs who had close relatives who owned a business or were self-employed:

Nonminority males	38.5%
Asians	32.8
Hispanics	27.6
Blacks	21.1

When entrepreneurial relatives serve as role models in family environments, children learn from an early age what behavior and attitudes are appropriate for a business owner. The children are given motivation and a psychological headstart toward future business ownership and are more likely to follow in their relatives' footsteps than those who lack such a tradition. Two other related surveys by the Department of Commerce revealed these pertinent statistics:

Training and experience in family businesses:

Nonminority males	18.7%
Asians	11.9
Hispanics	10.4
Blacks	7.3

Start-up capital provided by family and friends:

	Family	Friends
Asians	11.8/6.4%	18.2%
Hispanics	9.5/3.4	12.9
Nonminority males	7.3/2.3	9.5
Blacks	5.2/2.5	7.7

* Department of Commerce, Bureau of the Census, Report CBO82-1, Washington, DC: Government Printing Office, August 1987.

RETAIL PRICING Stores put a "regular price" on merchandise; manufacturers attach to their merchandise a "suggested retail price." Since the rise of the discount store, the term "regular price" has become clouded. Some retailers and mail order merchandisers have resorted to artificially high "regular prices" so that they can call the announced price a "sale price"—even though the item was never sold at the "regular price." This subterfuge is usually done in answer to competition from discount stores, which sometimes quote artificially high "regular" or "former" or "retail" comparative prices, in order to make *their* "regular" or "discount" price appear more attractive. Conditioned by an ever increasing number of sales promotions, American consumers have become more skeptical than ever about what merchants claim to be "regular prices." Customers have learned to wait for markdowns, particular at traditional department stores and prestige merchants, and are usually rewarded for their patience and alertness. All too often, customers return merchandise they had bought at regular prices; then, seeing the identical item advertised or on display at a lower price, they return their purchase for refund or exchange at the reduced sale price. This consumer awareness is gradually leading to a polarization of retailing—a clear-cut division between discount stores that offer merchandise without frills at "everyday low prices," and quality stores that sell merchandise at higher or "regular" prices along with numerous services required by customers of high-end retailers. Jewelry and furniture are two lines of merchandise typically discounted from questionably high "original" prices.

RETAILING Retailers sell goods directly to the general public. Retailing could involve selling either merchandise or services in stores ("over the counter"), in warehouses, at no-frills indoor/outdoor markets, through vending machines, at catalog stores, during in-home demonstrations, or via mail order. On pages 166–167, 45 categories of retail enterprises are profiled with some general statistics and overviews. The most prolific retail businesses are restaurants; there are at least 125,000. Fast-food restaurants come next, with about 110,000 establishments, followed, surprisingly, by clothing stores, numbering nearly 100,000. Among "fast-food" eateries, pizza restaurants are the most prolific. Nearly 40,000 of them exist nationwide and about 10 percent of them operate under the Domino Pizza sign. The largest dollar volume is rung up by supermarkets. About 30,000 of them do an annual business well over $200 billion—with an average of $11 million per store. Even department stores, the former number-one category in American retailing, average only $10 million each, for an industry total of about half that of supermarkets. One of the most notable trends in retailing is toward franchise operations. (See *Franchising.*) While an exact figure is hard to pin down, it is estimated that currently more than a half-million retail establishments are franchised and their income is approximately $650 billion a year. (See table, pp. 166–167.)

RETIREMENT For entrepreneurs, the word "retirement" often means a second career. Some innovators "retire" from their primary work at a relatively early age. People in the military or civil service, or corporate employees who are retired early because of mergers or retrenchment, find themselves at age 50 or 55 with a sizable nestegg and a long-suppressed itch to go into business. They might take an "interim" position, sometimes called "bridge employment," for as long as 10 more years, but 20 percent of these early retirees will return to work in their original specialty. The rest may switch into something they "really want to do," become consultants in their specialty, or set up a small business. A married couple may join in a mom-and-pop business that is based on the hobby of one of the partners. Most Americans, even at 60 to 70 years of age, are too energetic to be considered aged. Income-producing activity is a natural outlet for their energies. Having gotten used to a life style that is predicated on a high income, many of these retirees find that they have to work to bring in income as a supplement to social security

RETAIL CATEGORIES IN THE UNITED STATES

Category	Approximate Industry Total ($ million)	Approximate Number of Establishments	Gross Average Income per Unit
Appliance stores	$ 6,000	10,000	$ 600,000
At-home shopping services	3,000 +	NA	NA
Auto dealers—new vehicles	200,000	80,000	2,500,000
Auto dealers—preowned vehicles	8,000	12,000	665,000
Auto repair shops	25,000	180,000	139,000
Bars and taverns	9,000	60,000 +	150,000
Beauty salons	16,000	200,000	80,000
Book stores	4,000	10,000	400,000
Card shops	4,000	NA	NA
Clothing stores	50,000	100,000	500,000
Computers and software	10,000	5,000 +	2,000,000
Convenience stores	20,000 +	45,000	445,000
Daycare centers	1,500	30,000	50,000
Department stores	100,000	10,000	10,000,000
Discount (variety) stores	9,000	10,000	900,000
Donut shops	1,400	4,000	330,000
Drug stores	40,000	50,000	800,000
Employment agencies	10,000	10,000	1,000,000
Fabric shops	2,700	9,000	300,000
Fast-food eateries	60,000	110,000	555,000
Florists	4,500	22,000	180,000
Franchises (all categories)	650,000	500,000 +	1,118,000
Furniture stores	20,000	25,000	800,000
Gas stations	100,000	120,000	833,000

Category	Approximate Industry Total ($ million)	Approximate Number of Establishments	Gross Average Income per Unit
Gift shops	5,000	25,000	200,000
Hardware stores	10,000	20,000	500,000
Ice cream shops	1,600	10,000 +	160,000
Jewelry stores	10,000	25,000	400,000
Laundry/dry cleaning	10,000	45,000	220,000
Liquor stores	18,000	35,000	500,000
Mail order companies	85,000	10,000	8,500,000
Music stores	4,000	9,000	440,000
Optical stores	2,000	11,000	182,000
Photo shops/photographers	2,000	4,000	500,000
Photocopy shops	1,600	3,500	450,000
Radio-TV stores	12,000	20,000	600,000
Records and tapes	2,500	5,000	500,000
Restaurants	50,000	125,000	400,000
Rug/carpet stores	6,000	11,000	500,000 +
Shoes stores	12,000	35,000	340,000
Sporting goods	8,000	22,000	365,000
Supermarkets	210,000	30,000	11,000,000
Toy and hobby shops	4,000	7,800	500,000
Travel agencies	5,000	32,000	156,000
Video stores	7,500	30,000	250,000

Figures are compiled from Department of Commerce, trade association, and Dun & Bradstreet sources and are rounded off and estimated.

and/or savings and pensions. In planning enough income for retirement, entrepreneurs need to take into consideration a modest inflation factor. Financial needs of retirees might be lower than they were during their working years, but inflation still affects stationary income. If $20,000 a year is needed to live comfortably, a person aged 60 should calculate on having 20 years ahead. At a modest 4 percent annual inflation, over 20 years $567,000 will be needed. Social Security may account for only 30 percent of this, so sharpen a pencil and start figuring.

RURAL DEVELOPMENT INITIATIVE This program for small business owners in rural areas is sponsored by the Small Business Administration (SBA). In 1988 it was called "Access"; in 1989, "Alliance." Its purpose is to inform small agricultural and other businesses in rural areas of the several advisory and management services available through the SBA and its constituent organizations. It also facilitates small business loans to enterprises in rural areas. During 1988, about $865 million in small business loans were approved for rural small businesses; an additional $55 million in loans came from Certified Development Companies in the form of SBA-backed loans. A guide available from SBA field offices is entitled "Working Together: A Guide to State and Federal Resources for Rural Economic Development." Other rural assistance has been rendered during numerous disaster situations, when the SBA granted emergency funds to keep agricultural enterprises and small business support companies going. Two outstanding examples are the economic and management assistance rendered to whole communities by SCORE (Service Corps of Retired Executives) at Strawberry Point, IA, and Hopkinton, MA, which were affected by natural disasters. The SBDC (Small Business Development Center) also renders free assistance through the universities in which they are located, particularly in rural areas. SBA, SBDC, and SCORE offices located in or near rural areas have specialists who may be contacted for counsel and information. To get the location of the nearest ones, contact: the national Answer Desk, 1-(800) 368-5855 toll-free.

RURAL ENTREPRENEURIAL ASSISTANCE LOANS (REAL) Under this program, small start-up entrepreneurs become attached to larger, existing companies. A secondary purpose is to keep high school graduates from leaving their home area by showing them local entrepreneurial opportunities. The program started in South Dakota and has spread to eight adjoining states. It is the nation's first program of this kind and is certainly not for those with lofty ideas of instant riches. REAL Enterprises offers an 80 percent guaranteed loan of up to $2,500. The young entrepreneur has to come up with about $500 of personal savings. REAL then turns matchmaker and tries to put the startup together with those who have more experience or with an established business, or to help the young newcomer into a business of his or her own. The goal must be borne in mind—to reverse the trend of young people leaving for greener fields instead of building their own communities, by pointing out opportunities and thus countering the worldwide trend of rural flight to already overburdened cities. The SBA has a Youth Entrepreneurship program which can help high school grads to explore the road to independent business. SCORE offers counsel to individuals and conducts business startup workshops in some areas. (See *SCORE.*)

S CORPORATION   An entrepreneur who is starting out in business or who finds a present corporation too cumbersome should consider the S corporation. It retains the corporate characteristics of limited liability and transferability of interests, but will never be subject to personal holding company or accumulated earnings penalty tax. If the owner sells or liquidates the company, an S corporation setup might avoid the double taxation that regular corporations face. Another advantage is that, instead of paying corporate tax rates, it pays no federal tax at all. Instead, it passes all of its income to its shareholders or owners. Corporate tax rates range up to 34 percent; the top individual tax rate is 28 percent. A regular (C) corporation can be converted to an S corporation with some judicious planning; an accountant can advise on the circumstances under which S corporation earnings may still be taxable. Being an owner or investor in an S corporation has other advantages: The owner/investor can deduct costs of benefits such as group, life, accident, or health insurance. Losses that exceed a shareholder's basis in stocks and loans cannot be currently deducted. If the S corporation engages in rental activities, it is considered passive activity and its losses are "suspended" until passive income (rental income) is generated. Entrepreneurs contemplating any change should do it before the end of the calendar year and should discuss its ramifications with a tax professional.

SAFETY (INDUSTRIAL)

Provisions must be made to eliminate accidents in the workplace. For any growing entrepreneurs, but especially for those in construction, manufacturing, or any vehicle-intensive business, employees' safety is a vital operating factor. It affects insurance costs, time waste, inefficient operation, and sometimes legal costs and a company's reputation. The faster a company grows, the more the possibility of accidents rises. Many entrepreneurs have found that posters, bulletin boards, and notices in newsletters and pay envelopes urging safety precautions have little positive effect. The federal government, under the Occupational Safety and Health Act (OSHA), sets safety standards, provides display material, and sends inspectors into industrial and commercial premises to assure compliance with the law. Still, accidents happen, the time of valuable employees is lost, and income suffers. To foster employee awareness, one company decided to offer awards to employees who had no accidents over a period of time. The cost of the program, worked out with the cooperation of the employees, was around $5,000 for the year. The savings in insurance premiums alone amounted to $40,000 during the second year. Thus $35,000 in net profits were saved, in addition to countless workhours, and greater employee efficiency and happiness resulted. Reported accidents for 1987 were 20; in 1988, when the reward system went into operation, there were 4 accidents. Six employees shared $5,000 in prize money. Accident awareness was the answer.

SALES LETTERS

Even in this electronic age, the use of sales letters is going up and up. The 25-cent postage stamp has not reduced the daily avalanche of mail. When all the costs that go into a sales letter—stationery, postage, typing or printing, photocopying, addressing, handling—are totaled up, it is easy to understand that each first-class letter mailed to a customer, client, or prospect is conservatively estimated to cost 50 cents to a dollar. While the pertinence and accuracy of the address are paramount, the quality of the letter spells the difference between action and inaction, results or failure, profit or expense. The most important parts of any sales letter are the lead-in, the first paragraph, the postscript, and the closing. The initial opening should include a two- or three-line opening paragraph and use of *You*. Start out with the top benefit of the proposition or message. Ask a question; quote from a testimonial; use a news opening; use flattery; imply exclusivity; employ story or anecdotal openings; invite curiosity, perhaps with an astounding statistic; force the reader to become mentally involved with the offer; and so on. (See the AIDCA formula, under *Persuasion.*) Here are additional tips from the sales letter pros:

1. Think of the major objections that the recipient might have and answer them.
2. Ask for only one decision; never give readers a choice.
3. Don't plant new ideas in old minds—find ideas that are already in readers' minds and latch on to them.
4. Use eye-attention getters like italics, capital letters, indentations, a second color, quotes.
5. Describe the product or offer imaginatively—let prospects see, feel, and smell it.
6. Watch that fine line between genuine enthusiasm and artificial sensationalism.
7. Be absolutely sure that *you* love the proposition.
8. Know when to close and be sure to tell readers exactly what they are to do, to *act*.

SALES PROMOTION

This function of the selling process includes any activity—except paid advertising—that helps to promote the movement of merchandise or services from a business to its customers or clients. Sales promotion can include signs, sales training, painted trucks, imprinted gimmicks such as lapel buttons and pencils, reprints of ads, contests, displays, direct mail, painted balloons, fashion shows and other exhibits, and some publicity (usually regarded as a public relations function). Sales promotion takes more work and ingenuity, but can be considerably more economical than paid advertising in public media. Often it is more direct—point-of-purchase material can promote merchandise right at the counter or shelf location—and its impact and results can be measured more directly than advertising's. There is no end to the means of sales promotion. A century ago P.T. Barnum pasted colorful posters on walls, prior to moving his circus into a town. Fifty years later the Burma Shaving Cream Company put up rhyming signs on tens of thousands of roadsides and had all America quoting them. For decades, sales promoters have gotten famous people to sign testimonials in order to induce readers to buy their products and services as "recommended" by the familiar faces or signatories. Red Buttons helped sell 30,000 condos at Century Villages throughout south Florida. Remember that a pertinent and credible sales promotion tool placed close to the product or service to be sold can do the best job. Getting attention is easy, but if the promotion does only that, the whole effort fails. (For 100 more ideas see Gustav Berle, *The*

Do-It-Yourself Business Book [New York: John Wiley & Sons, 1989], pp. 73–87.)

SALESMANSHIP

Persuading people who can afford to pay for products or services—convincing them that they should buy what is being offered for sale—is an art. The world is full of master salespeople—men and women. They never fade away—they just make instructional tapes and give seminars. Skill of salesmanship—composed of equal thirds of know-how about the product or service being offered, nerve, and perseverance—is the most needed ingredient in keeping virtually any enterprise moving into a profitable orbit. Joe Girard bills himself as the world's greatest salesman according to the *Guinness Book of World Records*—and according to his own book, *How to Sell Anything to Anybody* (New York: Simon & Schuster, 1985). These are summaries of the ingredients for successful selling that Girard described:

- Put a smile in your voice by smiling when you talk, especially on the telephone. It does come across.
- Practice smiling, chuckling, and laughing. It is infectious. Makes you feel better, too.
- Never forget that your purpose is to make a sale that is of benefit to both of you.
- Remember that each customer knows 250 people, just as you know 250 people. One satisfied customer means you may have created 250 prospects; one angry customer means that you could have lost 250 prospects.
- Know everything you can about your customer and focus on those points in your sales talk—before you press home the fact that you are trying to trade your product or service for his or her money.
- Keep in touch with your customers by personalized mail—using a different color, size, and style each time—and don't send it out at a time when heavy bills are arriving.
- Use "birddogs"—customers and friends who recommend other customers—and show your gratitude by a gift (cash or some token of appreciation). One-third of Girard's business comes through this channel.
- Avoid talking about depressing topics. Be positive and optimistic; share your positive thoughts; send out good vibes.

SBA LOAN GUARANTEE

Much is written in the public press about the SBA playing Santa Claus by handing out millions of dollars to would-be entrepreneurs. Dreams die hard, because at one time the SBA did funnel public money to people who claimed to be "businesspeople" and, in the euphoria of "equalization," millions of public dollars were squandered. This is no longer the case. The early loan money—all paid into the SBA's generous coffers by taxpayers—has virtually dried up. Now the SBA makes direct loans only in the direst of cases. Instead, it *guarantees* loans to select banks, who in turn make loans to serious and deserving applicants. The maximum amount of a small business loan guarantee has been set at $750,000 as of 1988. This SBA guarantee is available to small businesses that cannot otherwise obtain credit on reasonable terms. The SBA will guarantee a maximum of 90 percent of loans up to $155,000 and 85 percent of loans over that amount. The typical SBA-guaranteed loan has a variable interest rate that is two percentage points over the New York prime rate and has a maturity of about nine years.

SCORE (SERVICE CORPS OF RETIRED EXECUTIVES)

Every entrepreneur, whether planning to go into a business or already in business, should know about SCORE. It is an association of about 12,000 men (about 90 percent) and women (10 percent), most of whom are retired from a wide variety of businesses and professions. They have banded together in about 385 chapters, located in every state, and they receive subsidies of about $2.5 million from the Small Business Administration and a few large corporations that fund special projects. All SCORE members are volunteers and do not get paid fees or salaries. The funding goes only for travel expenses, operating costs, and some literature. SCORE members give counseling only upon request; they are not and should not be considered consultants, though the differentiation is sometimes difficult. They conduct workshops in many areas, for groups of 10, 20, and more. Most of the workshops are for startups, though some are held to address problems in financing, taxation, inventory control, and so on. While SCORE members are often matched to applicants' specific needs, this goal is more theoretical than practical. Due to the vast variety of working backgrounds, the brevity of counseling sessions, and the very nature of volunteerism, the effectiveness of SCORE counseling is not always objective; however, the service is free, nonobligatory, and confidential. Workshops require a contribution ranging from $5 to a top of $25. SCORE offices are located within SBA offices in federal buildings, within chambers of commerce, and at community colleges. Look in the blue pages of the phone book, under Small Business Administration, or phone: 1-(800) 368-5855 for a computerized, toll-free answer.

SEED MONEY

Startup entrepreneurs use seed cash or seed money to get their businesses off the ground. This venture capital is the first contribution toward the financing or capital requirements of a startup business. A loan from a friend or family member may be subordinated or exchanged for preferred stock that will be paid off early and with guaranteed interest attached. Rarely does seed money come from a lending institution or government agency. The vast majority of startup enterprises are funded with the startup's own funds. According to one survey conducted by *INC.* magazine, 56 percent of startup entrepreneurs began with their own seed money, 41 percent received bank loans, and only 2 percent obtained venture capital. Of those who used their own resources, 40 percent got loans by mortgaging their personal assets, primarily real estate. Because so many businesses start up with very small amounts of seed money, these statistics are rarely reflected in surveys or news columns. Among more than 600,000 new enterprises formed in an average year, the average startup capitalization is $1,500. This low figure indicates that many kitchen-table and garage businesses are born annually and that a high percentage of small service enterprises require little or no outside capitalization. But, one item must be considered in estimating or projecting seed money requirements—the money needed by the entrepreneur to meet his or her personal needs until the new business develops sufficiently to generate an income for its proprietor.

Selling   See *KISS*.

Selling a Business

There are several ways to evaluate the worth of a business, but the bottom line is, of course, *demand*. How do sellers, who must establish a value for their businesses, or buyers, who must evaluate someone else's business, arrive at a rational bargaining point? There are five methods for stating the value of a company:

1. Liquidation value—the amount that could be realized if all assets, such as inventory, equipment, and furnishings, were sold separately.

2. Going concern value—the amount that could be realized if the business entity were sold as a whole.

3. Market value—the price at which buyers and sellers trade similar businesses in an open marketplace, adjusted for specific or local differentials.

4. Intrinsic value (also called cash flow or present value)—a value independent of market forces, but based on assets, earnings, dividends, assured prospects, management, and so on.

5. Book value—taking the figures from the company's record books, as depreciated at time of sale or amortized according to

generally accepted accounting principles or current tax legislation. This method involves some problems for sellers, especially if they have depreciated the assets too much in order to gain prior tax advantages.

Regardless of which method is used, buying or selling is usually subject to negotiations—giving on some point, taking on another; it combines supply and demand, psychology, and how anxious one is to get out or get in.

The disposition of a business must be as carefully planned as the acquisition. Small businesses are often more difficult to sell than large corporations. The purchaser of a small enterprise may buy a business with only a small down payment, paying the balance out of income over a period of years. All too often, problems arise that transform the long-term sale into a short-term fiasco. The seller may have no other security or recourse than to take back his or her formerly owned business and try to rebuild it—if indeed it can be resuscitated. In selling a small business, it is as important to have good contractual agreements as it is to have good chemistry between seller and buyer. No matter how good the lawyer who draws up the sales contract, two considerations should be taken into account: What does the seller want out of the sale? And, what can the buyer realistically afford and still keep the business acquisition functioning? The seller should set down all the factors that he or she wants out of a sale and have an attorney incorporate them into a sales agreement. Leave out demands that ask for the moon; no flights to it have been scheduled for a long time.

Here are some of the points to be considered:

- How long should the seller of the business be involved in the day-to-day operation of the business?
- How long should the seller be available for consultation?
- How long should a noncompete clause be in effect?
- How much nonreturnable down payment should be rendered?
- How should installment payments be made and what provisions for collection should be required in case of delayed payments?
- What security can be offered against nonpayment or default? What happens to the money already paid in and to all the records of the business in case of a default and recourse?
- What insulation from liabilities is in effect? Starting when?

These are just a few points to be raised. A lawyer will supply more.

SEMINARS

Seminars are workshops in which one or several experts address a group of interested people on a subject—business or entrepreneurship, for example. Following the seminar, the speaker(s) opens the floor to questions and tries to answer them, or encourages discussion from the attendees. Usually some literature pertinent to the subject is passed out. Seminars can last a couple of hours or a couple of days. They may be free, as when they are sponsored by a company that hopes to sell the attendees some of its products or services, or require a small registration fee, but they can cost several hundred dollars when conducted in a fancy hotel by a high-powered expert—and more, when they are multiday events. Libraries, especially in larger cities and suburban communities, conduct some seminars, drawing on local experts who contribute their time. SCORE (Service Corps of Retired Executives) seminars or workshops cost between $5 and $25 and last from two to six hours. Their most frequent topic is business startup and they are geared to those who are exploring entry into the business world. Separate workshops may discuss taxes, financing, accounting, home businesses, or franchising. Because of their low cost, they are a worthwhile first step into entrepreneurship. (See *SCORE; Small Business Development Centers* [SBDC].)

SENSITIVITY TRAINING

The method used for sensitivity training—an unstructured group of individuals exchanging thoughts and feelings face-to-face—is valid for both laboratory/classroom or personal/on-the-job training of people who will be in close business contact with employees, customers/clients, or the general public. Sensitivity training helps give insight into how and why others feel the way they do on issues of mutual concern. In recent years sensitivities that had never been considered important suddenly became exposed. Male executives had to accept women in equivalent or higher positions; both white-collar and blue-collar workers found increased numbers of minority and non-English-speaking employees in their ranks. While the sensitivities involved have indubitably been present from earliest memory, people in dominant positions have chosen to ignore the feelings of those of lesser status, whether in socioeconomic contacts or on a business organization chart. A typical example came up in a business counseling session in which an elderly volunteer executive, a former ebullient sales manager, was advising a young woman who sought his counsel about an enterprise she was about to enter. At the conclusion of the session, the elderly counselor put his arm around the young woman in a benign and fatherly gesture and wished her good luck. The woman-client became upset over this display and launched a complaint procedure with the volunteer's organization, carrying it all the way to the top. This in turn initiated an investigation by the organization and the volunteer was removed from further counseling of female clients. A molehill had been enlarged into a mountain because of a lack of sensitivity on the part of the elderly volunteer.

SERVICE This term has two meanings for entrepreneurs: Work done by one person or group that benefits another (businesses of this kind sell expertise and assistance rather than concrete or tangible goods), and the concern a business has for the continued operation and usability of its products after their sale (especially big-ticket items like machinery, appliances, homes, automobiles, TVs, and computers). Our economy, experts have been saying for years, is turning more and more into a service economy and the production of goods is shifting to countries where labor is cheaper and more cost-effective. Quality is as important in service industries as it is in the manufacture of goods. In personalized and professional services—giving accounting and legal advice, rendering medical services, making repairs—quality may be even more important. Entrepreneurs going into service businesses should check their capabilities and performance against the 10 points on the checklist below. For survival and success they should obey them as though they were Commandments.

1. Reliability: Customers can depend on you. This is No. 1.

2. Responsiveness: You are ready, willing, and able.

3. Competence: You are skilled and knowledgeable in your field.

4. Access: It is easy for customers to reach you.

5. Courtesy: You are, always, a public relations person.

6. Communication: You listen, inform, and keep in touch.

7. Credibility: Honesty and believability keep you in business.

8. Security: Financial and physical protection are assured.

9. Empathy: You understand your customer or client.

10. Evidence: You provide tangible evidence of your service.

Image in a business of intangibles is even more important than in a business of tangibles. (See also *Prestige* and *Public Relations.*)

SHOPPERS These tabloid-format papers, which contain either all or mostly advertising, are distributed free in limited neighborhoods. Shoppers can be produced by or for neighborhood shopping centers, large stores, or chain stores. Some shoppers are produced by publishing companies for large areas, or regular newspaper companies may run them as supplements to a daily or weekly newspaper, to compete against an independently published shopper. Because shoppers contain no or very little news, they are cheaper to produce than newspapers and their advertising rates reflect the lower costs. It can be argued that newspapers with news content and features attract more readers and therefore make the ads in them more productive. On the other hand, news organizations themselves have shown through surveys that ads in any medium that has more than 48 pages get diminished reader-attention. Much depends on the shopper's appearance and layout: how neatly and professionally it is designed; how attractive its front page is; how and where it is distributed. The best-looking publication strikes out if its distribution is not professionally handled. When shoppers are professionally designed, with quality ads and an attractive front "cover," are delivered by mail or deposited at customers' doors (preferably in a plastic bag to protect them from the elements), and contain at least some public service material (consumer columns and/or classified ads), they can be as effective as newspapers. They are usually lower in price for comparable ad space and circulation. Some shoppers have been known to have circulation in the hundreds of thousands and have gained support from large and prestigious stores; more often, merchants in a shopping mall band together to produce a cooperative shopper, when the local newspaper does not serve the market adequately. Each outlet should be analyzed individually and objectively.

Shopping Centers

These market centers are collections of retail stores and services that have a common parking area and are under central management and ownership. They may be open malls, closed malls, or a combination of both. Closed malls are usually larger; stores are accessed from the inside of an air-conditioned mall. Open centers, often called strip centers, have store entrances to the outside or the parking lot. Obviously, the closed centers are the more deluxe and expensive ones, but the increased traffic and customer comfort have proven worth the additional investment for those stores that could afford the rent and had a credit rating that was acceptable to the mall's management. An entrepreneur who is considering leasing space in shopping centers has various options. Stores in small, open, strip or neighborhood centers (usually under 300,000 square feet) are more readily available, especially to first-time startups whose credit is limited. Turnover is greater and peripheral costs are lower. The variety of stores is limited; usually customer traffic originates from a confined area. Larger regional malls are expensive; besides basic rental there are additional costs for merchants' association participation, maintenance, security, and overage (percentage payments above the basic lease cost). For these reasons the better capitalized chain stores and high-quality, high-markup stores prefer to go into large, closed-mall centers where high traffic can assure greater dollar volume, joint promotion opportunities, and superior management. Major department stores are usually the "anchor" units in large shopping centers. Small entrepreneurs might be able to obtain kiosks or display/sales carts at moderate rentals and thus take advantage of major mall operations. (See also *Merchants' Associations.*)

SHORT-TERM LOANS

These actually form a line of credit by allowing repeated borrowing, up to an amount previously set by the bank. The borrower repays and reborrows as often as required. An annual review is conducted; depending on repayment performance, a borrower's credit line might be increased. Because of the repetition of the borrowing and repayment process several times during the year, this type of short-term loan is also called a *revolving line of credit.* These loans allow maintenance of an even cash flow with which to efficiently operate a business. They must at all times be secured by adequate collateral—property, equipment, personal investments, and nonseasonal inventory. With a revolving line of credit, an owner can take advantage of favorable seasonal purchasing opportunities or discounts. Short-term loans can tide a company over until business flow increases or customers pay their bills. Businesses that have a pronounced cyclical cash flow need this type of credit. It is particularly pertinent to large farm operations, dealers who stock new models at certain times of the year or who buy for fashion seasons or holidays. Usually the maximum period of a short-term loan is one year. Remember that the lower the amount borrowed and the sooner it is paid back, the more money the business saves on interest charges. (See also *Term Loans.*)

SITE SELECTION

Location, *location,* and LOCATION are the three most important reasons for determining where to open an enterprise, according to most realtors. This is especially true for a retail business that depends on customer traffic and for service businesses. More specialized and exclusive businesses or services can survive well in lower-traffic areas or in locations that are not "100 percent." However, off-beat locations are expensive because more money must be invested in promoting the business. Will space at a prestigious address or in a professional building or an enclosed shopping mall be more expensive because of its location and its peripheral services? Paying a higher rental in a well-located mall or building that has natural traffic, lots of easy parking, and a merchants' association that provides ample, economical advertising opportunities can be less expensive. The better location can produce more business so that the higher rent actually becomes a smaller percentage of operating costs. There are so many considerations in finding the right location that the solution to this problem can sometimes be the make-or-break factor during the first years of business operation. In addition to checking the 25-point checklist on pages 180–181, entrepreneurs can get help in the site selection process from a good realtor who is willing to spend some time giving advice, from the local chamber of commerce, or from a knowledgeable SCORE/SBA counselor. None of these resources costs any money. What is very costly, however, is to make a mistake in finding the right location—to discover after a lease is signed that zoning, traffic, or competition limits a business's plans. The lease itself requires careful perusal. A 5-, 10-, or 15-year lease on a business, or the cost of constructing a facility, will probably be the single largest investment of an owner's entrepreneurial career. It deserves full attention and the help of competent counsel. This 25-point checklist can be a valuable start:

Site Selection Survey Checklist:

1. Location: How is the site located in relation to customers?
2. Materials: Are supplies, especially raw materials, readily available?
3. Employees: Are they available and adequate?
4. Public transportation: Is it available? At what cost?
5. Road pattern: Is it convenient for vehicular or foot traffic?
6. Traffic count: How many vehicles and/or pedestrians pass by?
7. Parking: What is its availability? Cost?
8. Pay scales: What do other businesses pay their employees?
9. Ethnic considerations: What kind of people are in the area? Would they make good employees? Trainees?
10. Schools: What kinds are in the area? Can they be a labor pool?
11. Utilities: Are they easily available? At reasonable rates?
12. Taxes: What are the local rates? Are there any incentives for startups?
13. Business climate: How has the neighborhood supported other merchants? What is its history relative to businesses?
14. Expansion: Is more room available on the premises? Will the neighborhood expand through roads, schools, or utilities?
15. Construction: Have engineers checked the water, soil, and utility conditions? Adjacent properties? Zoning?
16. Municipal services: Does the city or town provide a police department? Fire department? Water and sewerage?
17. Insurance: Is it available at this location? Rates? Restrictions?
18. Employee housing: If this becomes a factor, is it available? What type? At what costs?
19. Environmental factors: Are there restrictions on pollution? On construction?
20. Future value: Will this site retain its value?

21. Competitors: Where they are located? How long have they been there? How strong are they? (Sometimes competitors can be beneficial, as in a shopping mall.)

22. Mortgage money: Is it available and at what rate and duration? (The lender's opinion can be valuable in this instance.)

23. Trade support: Is there a local Chamber of Commerce? Merchants' association? Other pertinent trade group?

24. Media: What advertising/publicity channels exist in the area? What are their rates? Circulation or coverage?

25. Storage: Are there adequate on-premises facilities? Are affordable warehouse facilities available nearby?

SMALL BUSINESS ADMINISTRATION (SBA)

The 4,000 employees of the SBA serve entrepreneurs through more than 100 offices throughout the United States. This independent agency was created by Congress to help the millions of small businesses (generally, those with income of less than $5 million a year) and in particular to stimulate the formation of new small businesses. The assigned tasks of the SBA are: to be the official information agency that will help entrepreneurs through the maze of the federal bureaucracy; to help in obtaining government contracts; to offer management assistance; to dispense low-cost literature; to supervise counseling services by client-agencies; and to process and guarantee loans through SBA-approved lender banks. In some selected cases the SBA offers disaster loans to small commercial, industrial, and agricultural enterprises, or even grants direct financial assistance to disabled persons and disabled veterans. The SBA promulgates special programs for minorities, women, and veterans, and operates an Answer Desk which parries over 250,000 calls annually from the American public. Direct small business counseling on management, marketing, financing, and any one of the myriad problems that beset entrepreneurs is performed by three SBA-sponsored organizations:

- SCORE (Service Corps of Retired Executives)—a 25-year-old volunteer service of considerable help to more than 2,500,000 entrepreneurs; located at 750 offices in all states.
- SBDC (Small Business Development Centers)—cosponsored by and located primarily in large universities in 42 states.
- SBI (Small Business Institute)—in-depth student and faculty counseling to select small business clients.

All three organizations are listed in the blue pages of the telephone book under Small Business Administration. To locate any of the above or the nearest SBA office, contact: (800) 368-5855.

The SBA is the federal government's champion of and ombudsman for small business; it is the entrepreneur's best friend in Washington, in hundreds of locations from coast to coast, and in some off-shore locations. Yet it is a strange organization that displays both the best and the worst of our government. The emphasis on small business support in recent years—following the "discovery" that small business employs far more people, produces far more products and services, and contributes far more to the nation's gross national product (GNP) than had previously been surmised—has been nothing short of phenomenal. As an example, a few years ago, more than 50,000 people called the SBA's Answer Desk to get information on how to get a government loan, how to find a certain department, how to get on a federal government procurement list, and so on. In 1988, after the Answer Desk became overwhelmed and the four to six permanent and volunteer answer-persons could no longer field the avalanche of calls, an electronic system was installed. In 1989, more than 250,000 calls were logged by voice recording methods. But were the callers better served? This writer, for one, finds the new system totally frustrating and resultless. In another example, the SBA's many excellent brochures and "Management Aids" used to be free. Now they cost 50¢ to $1.00 and are often in short supply. This is the price of America's numerical growth. A persistent entrepreneur who contacts one of the SBA branches listed in Appendix D, or a nearby SCORE or SBDC office (see Appendix A), can get some wonderful assistance from this umbrella organization. A complete list of current SBA regional and district offices can be found in Appendix D.

SMALL BUSINESS DEVELOPMENT CENTER (SBDC)

A management assistance program was initiated by the SBA in 1977 that works primarily through universities. There are now 54 SBDCs in 47 states; they are the lead centers for a network of more than 600 service locations. SBDC assistance is specifically tailored to each local area and the needs of individual clients. Each center has a director, some staff members (all of whom are paid), and a cadre of volunteer and part-time personnel from local academia, chambers of commerce, legal and banking circles, professional and trade associations, and SCORE. Funding is accomplished through a $40 million budget voted each year by Congress, plus matching funds from the local university or sponsor. Clients are charged for some services when management assistance is prolonged; fees are decided upon within each office. Counselors are: paid professionals on the staff of the local SBDC office, volunteers, graduate students, and undergraduates. While the SBDC holds elementary startup workshops, its strength is indubitably in its capacity to use research, computer resources, and the facilities of the academic institutions with which its offices are affiliated. SBDC people work with SCORE (whose counselors are retired business and professional people for the most part), as well as with Small Business Innovative Research (SBIR) clients in the innovation and research areas. Further information may be obtained from the nearest SBA office. See also Appendix A.

SMALL BUSINESS INNOVATION RESEARCH (SBIR)

Established in 1982, the SBIR, a technology office within the Small Business Administration (SBA), is a coordinating agency that draws on the expertise of 11 federal agencies. During 1988, SBIR funded 2,724 research and development agreements totaling $389,100,000. This money is directed to small hi-tech enterprises, which have traditionally been responsible for most of the nation's new products, processes, and technologies and are among the most cost-effective performers of research and development. They are regarded as being capable of turning research results into new products that help keep America competitive in the global marketplace. By the end of 1990, it is estimated, more than $2 billion will have been awarded to SBIR companies. The 11 participants in the SBIR program are the Departments of Agriculture, Commerce, Defense, Education, Energy, Health and Human Services, and Transportation; the Environmental Protection Agency, NASA, National Science Foundation, and Nuclear Regulatory Commission. Three phases are available as follows:

Phase I: Awards averaging $50,000 are made for research projects to evaluate the scientific and technical merit and feasibility of an idea.

Phase II: Projects with the most potential are funded to further develop the proposed idea for one or two years. Most awards in this phase are for up to $500,000.

Phase III: An innovation is brought to market by private-sector investment and support, all without SBIR funds. When appropriate, Phase III may involve follow-on production contacts with a federal agency for future use by the federal government.

To get on the SBIR mailing list of presolicitation announcements, send for Form 1386 or request the nearest SBA District Office for one in person or by mail. "Proposal Preparation for Small Business Innovation Research (SBIR) Form SBIR T 1" is an 18-page booklet also available upon request. For more information on contacting the SBA, see Appendixes A and D.

SMALL BUSINESS WEEK   The Small Business Administration (SBA) sponsors this annual event, usually in the first part of May. In 1990 the 27th celebration, held in Washington, DC, had the theme "Small Business: Leading America into the 21st Century." The Week honors the 19 million small business in the United States, which employ half of the nation's workforce. Awards are presented to a Small Business Person of the Year in each state, the District of Columbia, and Puerto Rico/Virgin Islands. The 52 Small Business Persons of the Year are invited to a celebration in Washington where the one national Small Business Person of the Year is then chosen. Six national Small Business Advocates of the Year are also selected—an exporter, a young entrepreneur, a prime contractor, a subsubcontractor, and two corporations that started small and with SBA assistance grew into large businesses. Nominations of persons eligible for the above awards (and its attendant publicity) should be submitted to the SBA prior to November 15 of the previous year. A 23-page booklet describing the entire selection process is available from SBA district offices in 65 locations across the country.

SPEECHMAKING   Being invited by a local school, ladies' organization, service club, or chamber of commerce to give a brief talk about one's own business, profession, or experience has caused many entrepreneurs, even brilliant business tacticians and innovators, to freeze up when the occasion begins. In a one-on-one discussion with a friend, neighbor, or peer, the same entrepreneur would be able to deliver an outstanding, erudite, and cogent account. Making an "impromptu" speech does not have to hold any terrors. The audience *wants* to hear what the speaker has to say and the speaker *knows* what to say; whether there are two or 200 people listening, the speech is still the same. Why panic? Any entrepreneur called upon to give a talk should pick a topic that is known inside out. Notes should be prepared on 3" x 5" cards even for an extemporaneous talk. The introduction is most important because it sets the mood for the rest of the talk. A long joke, especially a shaggy dog story, is a poor start but a brief, *pertinent* one-liner or anecdote can be appropriate. Illustrated material that can easily be seen by the audience provides a break in the presentation format and a "tool" for developing ideas. The main body of the talk needs to inform, instruct, persuade, and inspire. The summation reviews briefly the information presented and repeats the most important and salient points; if it is a sales-oriented talk the summation asks for some kind of action, or an order. Mark Twain said, "It takes three weeks to prepare a good ad-lib speech." A good speaking pace is about 100 words a minute and the finest conclusion is the audience's applause.

Standard Rates and Data Service (SRDS)

This is the bible of the advertising media trade. Its monthly catalogs are the size of telephone books and contain information about newspapers, consumer magazines, business magazines, radio, television, direct response, agricultural and international media, and other information that should be studied before any money is invested in advertising. Advertising agencies subscribe to these media information directories; most libraries have them in their reference sections. Because the SRDS books cover media categories and each volume is divided inside into smaller categories, information is relatively easy to obtain. If an owner works through an advertising agency in creating ads, the agency will furnish a media study and schedule, complete with circulation of each medium, costs, and comparative costs (how much it costs to reach 1,000 readers or viewers, or similar objective comparisons, with other media). For an owner planning to research advertising, SRDS can show what publications or other media are available in a particular field or geographical area, where they are located, who runs them, how much they cost, what various sizes or time segments are available and at what price, what the deadlines are, and what audience composition and circulation exist in various parts of the country. Many of the media have regional or sectional editions. As an example, *The Wall Street Journal* has no less than a dozen editions nationwide. Its total circulation is more than 2 million and a page costs over $100,000, but an ad can be run only in the Baltimore/ Washington area (circulation of below 100,000) at a cost of less than $6,000 per page.

Startup Advice

The information noted here was suggested by major accounting professionals and pertains, to a large degree, to the formulation of a business plan, which is considered the first step in organizing and funding a new business. (See also *Business Plan.*)

- Potential investors and major bank loan officers receive hundreds of loan applications and business plans. The door to the business plan, the Executive Summary, is like an introduction to a book. It should be concise (no more than three pages), contain the heart of the business proposal, answer the investor's question, "What's in it for me?", and be followed by a brief table of contents.

- Since the new business does not have a track record, the analysis of the market and the estimates must be thorough, critical, logical, and probable—not just possible.

- The definition of the business and its goals should be crystal-clear, to avoid confusing the reader.

- Descriptions of how the owner plans to beat a path to the market, who will do each job, and how the owner plans to pay for it all should be exact.

- Prognostications are as yet theoretical; they must coincide with financial projections. Any inconsistencies will be quickly spotted and will leave a bad impression on lenders.

- Avoid criticism of the competition; stick to the facts. It is more important to give cogent rationales for entry into the marketplace and plans to achieve success and profits.

- Creativity in financing proposals is appreciated as long as it remains objective. Always bear in mind that the readers, who are potential financial backers, are concerned with *their* interests.

- Retention of good legal and accounting advisors will help to assure financiers that a proposed business is soundly structured and will not lead to unforeseen liabilities in the future.

- Excessive documentation, exhibits, and appendixes should not be part of the body of the business plan. As a separate addendum they make the presentation look less formidable.

STARTUP CHECKLIST A comprehensive and practical checklist titled "What Is Needed to Operate a Good Small Business" is distributed by the SBA and is given here verbatim. Keep a special bookmark in this page.

If you are thinking of going into business, the following requirements must be considered for a successful operation:

1. *TYPE OF BUSINESS OR SERVICE:* You must have training or experience in the type of business under consideration. You cannot hire a person that has the experience you lack, in hopes that his knowledge will make the business go.

2. *CAPITAL:* It takes money to start a business. To borrow money is possible, but only if you have sufficient funds of your own in cash, inventory or equipment to provide a reasonable equity for loan consideration. Sufficient funds should be available to meet overhead, take advantage of discounts and ability to arrange credit to eliminate immediate financial problems and worry.

3. *LOCATION:* Space leased or owned must be sufficient to meet the needs of the business considered. Location should be convenient for the customers serviced, with adequate parking facilities.

4. *PRODUCT OR SERVICE:* Reasonable assurance should be evident that there is a need for the product or service offered, or that a demand can be developed through advertising to provide a profitable return on your time and money involved.

5. *BOOKKEEPING:* A system must be in use to reflect all transactions of the business, to provide records of the operation and data for the preparation of reports to meet city, state and federal requirements.

6. *RECORDS:* Reports should also be prepared for internal use covering receivables, payables, inventory, payrolls, insurance, . . . financial statements as needed, and, if possible, monthly operating statements.

7. *MANAGEMENT:* Experience in management will contribute much to a successful operation. If lacking, it may be developed by understanding and using the reports listed under Item (6). Most business failures are due to *POOR MANAGEMENT.*

8. *PERSONNEL:* Sufficient [staff], experienced in the business, should be available to service customers and carry on during the absence of the owner.

9. *INVENTORY:* Inventory should be ample in quality and quantity to meet customer demand.

10. *ADVERTISING:* Advertising is necessary to make a business grow. Do not contract for paper space, radio or television time without experienced help. It's not the media that counts—it's the grey matter that goes into it.

11. *TAX PAYMENTS:* Be sure all payments are made on time. The Internal Revenue Service (IRS) has tightened its regulations on the prompt payment of withholding monies.

12. *ATTORNEY:* Every business should have an attorney to call upon as needed. This especially applies to leases, partnership agreements—particularly on a 50–50 basis to assure a satisfactory prearranged buy and sell signed agreement. Also, if a corporation is being considered.

13. *LICENSE AND REGISTRATION REQUIREMENTS:* You must be sure the business you are considering is properly licensed and registered to meet legal requirements. A checklist is available for guidance in this area.

14. *SCORE (SERVICE CORPS OF RETIRED EXECUTIVES):* Score is an organization of retired persons who have volunteered to assist, at no charge, individuals in business or considering a business venture.

STARTUP COSTS   These are the total amount of available cash needed to pay for all initial expenses until the money earned by the new business from sales of products or services exceeds the immediate requirements of the business's operation. Startup costs can fluctuate wildly, depending on the size of the planned business, the length of time it will take to produce marketable products or services, competition, and a great many other variable factors. Even after all estimates are accounted for, it is wise to add 25 percent for unforeseen expenses, delays, inflation, strikes, competitive pressures, and so on. Startup costs should include: rent and utility deposits, office equipment and supplies, machinery and parts, rolling stock (cars, trucks), leasehold improvements that might not have been apparent earlier, working capital until new money is generated through business activities, inventory requirements due to public demand or style changes, and personal needs. The latter are often overlooked; or projections of income, prepared prior to the startup, are too optimistic; or personal emergencies require additional money. The following are minimum estimates for a small startup enterprise with an estimated asset value of $100,000:

Manufacturing Enterprise		Retail Operation
$ 5,000	Deposits	$ 4,000
* 20,000	Furniture, equipment	25,000*
10,000	Machinery, equipment	5,000
* 30,000	Transportation equipment	20,000*
12,000	Leasehold improvements	10,000
2,000	Professional fees	2,000
5,000	Advertising	5,000
20,000	Inventory	35,000
10,000	Working capital	5,000
$114,000	Totals	$111,000

* Could be considerably less if leased rather than purchased.

Wholesale Business		Service Business
$ 10,000	Deposits	$ 4,000
* 10,000	Furniture, equipment	15,000
* 25,000	Machinery, equipment	—
* 30,000	Transportation equipment	**
10,000	Leasehold improvements	10,000
2,000	Professional fees	2,000
3,000	Advertising	3,000
50,000	Inventory	**
25,000	Working capital	25,000***
$165,000	Totals	$59,000

* Some machinery and rolling stock can be leased rather than purchased.
** If the service business utilizes delivery and some parts supplies, $20,000 to $50,000 might be needed additionally.
*** This is primarily for the owner's personal living costs.

STARTUP LOANS

Nearly 75 percent of all new entrepreneurs start with some of their own saved-up money. Twenty-three percent use only their personal funds. The average investment in a new enterprise is just a little over $1,500. (See *Seed Money.*) Many new enterprises require more capital, however, and when a startup owner approaches a bank for a commercial loan or a guaranteed loan, the borrower's application will normally be rejected unless some of his or her own capital is in the "loan package." One other vital ingredient must be part of a startup loan application: management expertise. Loan officers are emphatic on this point for two valid reasons:

1. It has been shown that lack of management expertise is the single biggest cause of business failures; an inexpert owner-manager jeopardizes the loan that might have been made by the bank;

2. During a number of years, a decade or more ago, when banks and the Small Business Administration (SBA) were rather loose with loans and often lent money based on minority needs rather than business expertise, the bankruptcy rate was unconscionably high.

Small banks are still easier to approach when a startup loan is needed; larger or multibranch banks are more impersonal, require OKs from higher officials at the main office, and often rely on the backup of an SBA guarantee. In all cases, a complete, credible, verifiable business plan is required as proof to the loan officer that the applicant knows where he or she is going. If a startup business can qualify for an economic development debenture (with SBA backing), the owner needs to put up only 10 percent of the total investment.

However, the owner must prove that one new job is created in the company for every $15,000 in bonds sold by this means (504 Loan Program). High-profit, fast-growth startups may want to look into venture capital financing.

According to the National Federation of Independent Business, the major sources of small-business startup loans are:

Personal savings	23%
Institutional lenders	7
Individual investors	3
Friends and relatives	2
Government sources	1
Venture capital	less than .5

Other sources were combinations of the above; the majority combined personal savings with loans from institutional lenders (banks).

The SBA Office of Public Information, in a publication entitled "SBA Business Loans," gives these step-by-step procedures for preparing for and filing a startup loan application:

1. Write a detailed description of the business to be established.

2. Describe your experience and management capabilities.

3. Prepare an estimate of how much money you and/or others have to invest in the business, and how much you will need to borrow.

4. Prepare a financial statement listing all your current personal assets and liabilities.

5. Prepare a detailed projection of earnings anticipated for your first year in business.

6. List collateral you can offer as security for the loan, including an estimate of the present market value of each item.

7. Take all the above with you to your banker. Ask for a direct loan. If the direct loan is declined, ask the bank to (a) give you a loan under SBA's Loan Guaranty Plan, or (b) participate with SBA in a loan. If the bank is interested, ask the banker to discuss your application with the SBA. In most cases, SBA deals directly with the bank on these two types of loans.

8. If neither the guaranty or participation loan is available to you, visit or write the nearest SBA office in your area. Take your financial information with you on your first office visit or include it in your first letter.

STATE SMALL BUSINESS CONFERENCES
Many states hold from one to 15 statewide or regional conferences to discuss problems of their resident small business owners and farmers. Some are "listening" conferences at which government representatives obtain feedback from citizens; others offer information about state programs in the areas of state and federal counseling services and financial assistance. Entrepreneurs planning to establish a business, seeking help or information, or interested in expanding an existing business, should inquire about dates and locations of conferences in their state during the current year. See Appendix E for details.

STATIONERY
This representative and messenger of an owner or a company may be merely a piece of paper, but it speaks as loudly and succinctly as an emissary making a presentation in person. No matter what message is being delivered, if it is important enough to be created, reproduced, and sent, then it is vital enough to be as excellent as affordably possible. The cost of a letter can be 50 cents or up to $10, when costs of good letterhead paper, envelope, enclosure, stamp, addressing and franking, dictation or writing time, transcription, copying, and filing by a secretary or other assistant are all included. Even for a computer or FAX message, the cost is considerably higher than its physical form might suggest. (What about the amortization of the machinery that produces the message and the supplies that are needed?) The design, typeface, and paper stock of company stationery need considerable thought; much, of course, depends on the nature of the mailing piece. A personal, individualized letter will obviously be expensive and subject to great care. The paper stock will be of better quality than ordinary bond paper (at a cost of 2 to 6 cents more); it might be an elegant pastel color; the typeface of the letterhead may be selectively designed; an artist or typographer may be hired to create a presentation that is distinctly the company's. Mass mailings can be produced on lesser quality stock, but the message and the content of the mailing packet need to be carefully created and the mailing list carefully selected and screened. Addressees change on an average of once every five years; personnel moves within companies occur even more frequently.

STELA (SYSTEM FOR TRACKING EXPORT LICENSE APPLICATIONS)
This computer-generated voice unit interfaces with the Department of Commerce's Export Control Automated Support System (ECASS) data base. It provides current information on the status of an export license application, showing exactly where an application is in the system,

and for how long it has been in the works. It can also give an exporter authority to ship goods for applications that are approved without conditions. Exporters receive a hard copy of the license later by mail but they can ship goods with STELA's approval before receiving the hard copy. Exporters can call STELA on a touch-tone telephone at (202) 377-2752. STELA will answer, "Hello, I'm STELA, the Department of Commerce export license system. Please enter your license application number or hang up." Using the push buttons on the phone, the exporter can enter the license application number. A synthesized voice will then come on and will give the status of the application. STELA can also handle questions about changes in the applications. For each inquiry, the application number of that particular must be punched. STELA is open daily for 16 hours (Mondays through Fridays, 7:15 A.M. to 11:15 P.M. ET) and for eight hours on Saturdays (8:00 A.M. to 4 P.M.). Since the STELA data base is updated each night, inquiries should only be made once a day. The location of STELA is the Bureau of Export Administration, Office of Export Licensing, Department of Commerce, HCHB Room 1099D, Washington, DC 20230. To reach an export consultant, phone: (202) 377-2753. (See also *ELAIN.*)

STORE DESIGN There are two key areas for store design—the front or facade and the interior. Both require a specialist from the installation company, an architect/designer who specializes in store design work, or a professional from the store fixture company. Sometimes a lease contains restrictions or demands that must be considered in the exterior design. This is particularly true for a store leased in a shopping center where either frontal facades or overhead signage must have a measure of uniformity. Store locations in closed malls are especially subject to lease parameters. Security also dictates both external and internal design. In a crime-prone area the exterior design might demand smaller display windows, shatterproof glass, metal grillwork, or no display windows at all. Interior layout must accommodate several factors: adequate space and lighting to display merchandise for optimum exposure and selling, convenience of access, space for backup inventory (storage), safety of merchandise (secured cases for jewelry; refrigerated cases for foods, flowers, pharmaceuticals, and confections; closed-circuit TV monitoring security systems), and traffic pattern. Some store owners prefer the classic grid layout found in most supermarkets— row after row of merchandise, allowing maximum quantitative displays. Others prefer a free-form layout that lets customers wander around serendipitously. The latter mixes a number of different display fixtures to give the store interior a less monotonous appearance, adapting different styles and shapes of fixtures to various lines of merchandise. Many store owners keep security in mind by limiting the height of displays to chin-level; security personnel can then observe customers over the top of the displays. Store design is dictated largely by function: *sales.*

STRATEGIC ALLIANCES   This form of networking or brainstorming involves the formation of an informal network of like-minded individuals who can act as a sounding board for each other's ideas and business problems. In principle they form an informal board of directors. Especially through cooperative marketing, they cross-promote the interests of each member of the alliance. Many promotions in the vacation and recreation industry use strategic alliance techniques. An airline may offer a package that includes round-trip tickets to London, a hotel for one night in London, and a rental car for three days—all at one package price. Three different companies share in the promotion and benefit by less expensive per-share advertising costs. Chances are, the customer will stay more than one night at the hotel or keep the car for more than the package period. The key to strategic alliances is to find similar or compatible businesses. The opportunities are endless, especially among small businesses, the professions, and interrelated services. The concept can be carried even further. In Virginia a group of 20 or more businesspeople meets for breakfast every two weeks. Each tells about new clients, especially those who have just opened up business, proposes to other breakfast club members what other products or services the new client might need, and suggests that relevant sales calls on the new enterprise be arranged. Specialty stores that do not carry jewelry or shoes, for instance, might borrow those items for use in their window or interior displays—giving credit to the allied, but different, businesses that have supplied them. A retailer might create an alliance with a distributor or manufacturer by stocking the supplier's merchandise on favorable terms, for an extended payment period, or on consignment. Another way to maximize the advantages of alliances is for a group—commercial or professional—to buy all its services from one source and thus obtain better prices or terms for all participants. This agreement could apply to banking, equipment and vehicle leasing, newspaper promotion, and any number of commercial, personal, and medical services.

STRESS MANAGEMENT   Every occupation and human relationship has its stresses. Entrepreneurs especially are prone to them. If it is uncontrolled, continual stress can result in ulcers, alcoholism, elevated cholesterol, heart attack, or "burn-out"—the total decline and death of motivation to continue working. How does one control one's behavior and continue to function at optimum effectiveness? Hard work never killed anybody, says a Victorian adage; but being too tough on oneself, tackling more than one's capacity to perform, trying to do everything by oneself, wasting too much time on details—all these pitfalls can lead to being "stressed out" and eventually can burn up the motivation to continue. The entrepreneur who runs a business is the most expensive person on the payroll and the most important one. Stress management experts have isolated 12 areas that every entrepreneur should read and remember—and practice:

1. Organize. Set realistic goals and manage time so that the most important tasks are done first.
2. Focus. Do what's meaningful.
3. Delegate. Don't sweat the small details; let others handle them.
4. Communicate. Don't bottle up problems; share them.
5. Socialize. Network personally and for the enterprise.
6. Reorganize. If things don't work out one way, try another.
7. Explore. Search and research for new ideas and methods.
8. Escape. Everyone needs a period of rest; a good goal is to look forward to each vacation.
9. Relax. Take mental breaks with music, books, and friends.
10. Moderate. Take care of the business's most important person by avoiding abuses of alcohol, stimulants and food.
11. Monitor. The owner's physical condition and mental state are important. Keep track of them.
12. Detach. When away from business, be *away.* Stop worrying during nonwork time.

Success

This is such an elusive term that it is difficult to have a general definition. To one it is money, to another personal achievement; to one it is glory and kudos, to another the establishment of an estate for his or her children. From an entrepreneurial viewpoint, however, we shall attempt to define the steps that appear to make for success in small, independent businesses:

- Be a jack-of-all-trades: entrepreneur, manager, technician.
- Know the business and know the competition.
- Know the product and market thoroughly and trust well-thought-out judgments—but leave a little room for new ideas.
- Know the business's strengths and weaknesses and deal with customers from a position of strength.
- Be sensitive to the needs of customers and do not be afraid to reach and teach them about a product or service.

- Create and continually update a personal business plan, especially on cash flow; it is the road map to success, for without it the business can get lost.

- "Know thyself" and do not wait till it's too late to ask for help and moral support.

- Select staff members carefully, for they are personal extensions of an owner; reward them bountifully for a job well done.

- Each employee is an individual and should be treated accordingly.

- Read, read, and read. Newspapers (especially the business pages), trade publications, and business magazines will help with understanding the Big Picture.

SUGGESTION BOX   A device to solicit opinions from employees covertly could be a simple shoe box with a slot in it and a sign stuck on it, or an elaborate treasure chest. The use of such a device should be promoted through posters, newsletters, pay-envelope enclosures, word-of-mouth, conspicuous placement (near the time clock, payroll office, locker room, lunch room, and so on), and perhaps an award incentive system. Even entrepreneurs who make it known that they are always available do not get enough feedback. Suggestion boxes offer the privacy and confidentiality that will help to loosen up ideas from employees. One owner keeps a lock on his suggestion box and lets it be known that he is the only one who has the key. He has stated that this device "is a safety valve for people who feel threatened or ignored." A suggestion box shows employees that they have a voice around the workplace and a direct link to the top. A well-used suggestion box is thought to be a great morale-builder within an organization, as well as a potential fount of new ideas.

TARGET MARKETING Manufacturing, promoting, and selling to a specific, narrow segment of the public is a definite trend of the 1990s. Major changes in this nation's demographics and behavior patterns are creating more and more "specialists" in marketing. These are some of the trends that entrepreneurs must watch:

- Women will have greater influence in buying decisions.
- Minority and immigrant populations will grow in percentage.
- Dual-income families will increase to include 68 percent of all married women, 20 million of whom will be mothers of school-age children.
- Home-based businesses will increase vastly.
- Concern for the environment will spur "social conscience" marketing.
- Fast-food operations will continue to diversify and cafeteria-style restaurants will make a comeback.
- Older people will get back into the marketplace, either as part-time employees or as entrepreneurs of small businesses that are usually different from their previous occupations.
- Youthful purchasers will become more mature, have more discretionary income, and make more of their own purchasing decisions.

Target marketing is not all intuition, even though the latter has a firm niche in entrepreneurship. It must be backed by thorough and pragmatic research. Even large corporations fail to follow this advice occasionally, as proven by Ford Motor Company's Edsel and the Coca-Cola Company's "Coke." The sound entrepreneur will distinguish between a fad and a trend. Most trends can be spotted by analytically watching consumer magazines and television programming and by consulting with typical industry representatives. Add to these good merchandising sense, patience, experience, and a good gut feeling, and most entrepreneurs can become reasonably successful marketers who shoot at the right target. Specialization or target marketing appears to be the trend of the future.

T_{AX} In entrepreneurial planning, the levy imposed by each governmental entity is the single most important impediment impacting upon the businessperson's financial goals. Tax payments deserve greater attention in planning than ever before. A decade ago, when the country suffered through a 12 percent inflation, taxes were eroding business income as much as 70 percent. In 1989 inflation had been pared down to 5 percent and the average business tax rate was 28 percent. It might have seemed like a victory but it has actually been only a Pyrrhic one. During the years since the Tax Reform Act of 1986 and its amendments, more tax deductions have been withdrawn but more opportunities exist for deferring taxes on some income. Planning and a good accountant are essential. The first fact to recognize in entrepreneurial planning is that the more taxation a business postpones, the more money it can retain. For example, if a business accumulates $50,000 in assets and invests it as a lump sum in a 10 percent interest-bearing instrument, in a 28 percent tax bracket, the tax is $1,400 on the $5,000 interest earned. If the interest is left in the account, the investment will grow in 10 years to $100,000, and in 20 years it will double again to $200,000. If that same $50,000 were invested in a nontaxable bond or plan, the holder would wind up with $400,000 in about 21 1/2 years. Tax at 28 percent would be paid on the total gain all at one time—or less than $100,000. The holder will have more than $300,000 left rather than the $200,000 under the pay-tax-as-you-go plan. One of the long-term investments favored by financial planners is the fixed annuity, which offers safety, interest reinvestment, and tax deferment.

TAX PLANNING Perfectly legal and systematic analyses of different tax options can often minimize the amount of taxes a business will pay to the Internal Revenue Service. In addition to having a good accountant who advises on a continual basis but is especially involved toward the end of the business's fiscal year, an entrepreneur can take a number of steps to minimize the tax bite and maximize profits:

- If married, figure out whether it is advantageous to file separately or jointly with a spouse.
- Determine the best time to effect the sale of an asset, depending on current and projected tax regulations.
- If retirement funds are being withdrawn determine the number of years over which the withdrawal will be more advantageous.
- For outside income, or payments coming from clients toward the end of the year, determine whether to make deposits as received or hold them till after January 1. Do the same with paying bills at the end of the year.

- Determine the timing and amounts of gifts to be made.
- If income is on the high side of the 28 percent tax bracket, current income could force filing in the 33 percent bracket (or a change from 15 percent bracket to the 28 percent).
- If the 65-year age bracket is approaching, will income deferred until after the 65th birthday be advantageous or not?
- Will it be advantageous to hold some deductions from this year until the next one? Take standard deductions instead?
- Business debts, unlike personal debts, can be written off against revenues even if only partially uncollectible.
- Check inventory before the year is over and determine how to liquidate surplus goods—by giving them to charity and taking a deduction, or to a liquidator for distress sale.
- Deposit to a Keogh account by December 31; for an IRA account, deposits made until tax filing time get the tax deferment.
- Is any business-related equipment needed? Should the acquisition be made now? The accountant and owner can tell.

TAX REFORM ACT   Under this federal law, enacted in 1986, a clause referred to widely as "Section 89" required businesses that offer employee benefits such as health insurance to prove that their plans did not discriminate against lower-paid workers. Section 89 was especially onerous to small entrepreneurs. Large businesses found the law to be burdensome and corporations felt it was unnecessary when they were equal opportunity employers. Late in 1989 all businesses represented in Washington by lobbies ganged up on Congress and forced the revocation of Section 89. Small businesses were led in this "revolt" by the National Federation of Independent Business (NFIB). The House subsequently voted to repeal this section by a vote of 390–36. The vote got support from two prominent members of Congress, Small Business Committee Chairman John J. LaFalce (D-NY) and Senate Finance Committee Chairman Lloyd Bentsen (D-TX). In wiping the three-year-old antidiscrimination law off the federal books, Congress also eliminated a pending amendment that would have put worker representatives on pension boards. Providing even and humane benefits to employees now becomes a matter of the entrepreneur's conscience and will be guided by economic necessity and competition for good employees, rather than by Congressional mandate.

TELECOMMUNICATIONS   As a means of transmitting information from a terminal—a telephone, computer, facsimile, video—to a customer, supplier, colleague, branch office, sales staff, or prospect who has a receiver unit anywhere in the world, telecommunications are instantaneous and interactive. They can deliver data or hard copy strategically and efficiently in order to achieve specific business objectives, seize new opportunities, overcome barriers to business growth, and control costs—especially personnel costs—for improved profitability. Telecommunications can multiply the effectiveness of face-to-face sales calls; expand executive time through teleconferences; enable businesses to exchange hard-copy documents and electronic data through facsimile transmissions and computer-to-computer dial-up connections. 800 and 900 lines are finding more and more utilization in small business communication, in effect extending business hours beyond the traditional 40-hour workweek. A useful reference is the brochure "A Planning Tool for Small Business Growth" (#FB1657-01) obtainable from the nearest AT&T office or phone: (800) 222-0400, ext. 339.

TELEVISION

For the small entrepreneur with a limited advertising budget, TV is a Cadillac making deliveries. It is a powerful and effective medium, but both the air time and the production of commercials are very expensive. Cable TV is more reasonable because it is still quite new, remains competitive, and has a limited audience. TV was a bit of magic when the first public telecast opened the New York World's Fair in 1939. President Franklin D. Roosevelt spoke on the giant screen from 250 miles away, delivering his message to an incredulous audience that responded with a standing ovation—whether for FDR or the medium, we do not know. TV is still magical, a dramatic advertising medium that conquers both sight and sound. Its mercantile impact is immediate, though six repetitions of commercials are said to cause audience saturation. As TV has become more popular and more sophisticated, its real cost has skyrocketed but so have its ranks of advertisers. Up to six separate commercials are bunched up between shows, even though viewers often head for the refrigerator or study their *TV Guide* for other programs during that break. Those advertisers who can afford prize-winning commercials—really staged performances, or elaborate cartoon shows—outdistance any local advertiser for attention and results. Small advertisers with limited budgets are then left to explore cable TV, late-night programs, or the shoppers' network programs that demonstrate only merchandise and sell directly, or to turn to radio and local print media. For someone who has the money and can afford to prospect for customers everywhere, TV's 97 percent saturation of sets gives the potential of the only total advertising impact in America.

TEMPORARIES (TEMPS)

Employees can be hired through an agency for a day, a week, or other specific but limited period. Usually all fees and benefits, as well as taxes, are paid by the agency placing the temp. Traditionally temps filled secretarial and clerical positions, but in recent years temp agencies that specialize in professional and executive personnel have sprung up all over the country. For short-term projects or highly specialized contracts, large corporations have resorted to this route in finding the exact persons needed, devoid of the high cost of recruiting, fringe benefits, moving expenses, and long-term obligations. The professionals available for these specialized, short-term assignments are often retirees who are not looking for long-term employment or pension and health care benefits. The temporary agency works effectively as a business matchmaker, and may have a roster of as many as several thousand senior executives and high-technology experts. While the fees are high, even small entrepreneurs might be able to afford the services of a top-notch former corporate executive for a short period of time. Three major agencies in this field are Parsons Associates in Altamonte Springs, Florida; Interim Management Corporation, New York City; and The Corporate Staff in San Francisco.

TERM LOANS These are either intermediate (up to three years) or long-term (over three years but usually not more than 10 years) loans. Intermediate loans are requested for startups, purchase of new equipment, expansion of a property or plant, or an increase of working capital to add a new line or department. Long-term loans are invariably for the same purposes as the intermediate ones but with larger dimensions—major acquisitions, assembly-line equipment, relocation property purchases, and expansions that take a longer time to amortize. Either loan arrangement requires collateral and provisions for monthly or quarterly payback. Agreements with lenders may contain restrictive clauses that help assure the borrower's ability to meet repayment terms: limitations on incurring other debts, amount of dividends paid out, principals' salary increases, and acquisition of other than needed production equipment or inventory. Collateral needs to have a value greater than the amount borrowed and must be of such a nature as to be completely liquid and protected from serious economic variations. Usually such collateral is supplemented by a personal guarantee, which can include personally held stocks, bonds, CDs, and other assets, both personal and business. (See also *Short-Term Loans.*)

TIME MANAGEMENT Managing each day's workhours to achieve optimum productivity is working hard not to waste time. It is an insidious problem for nearly all entrepreneurs, especially those working alone or at home. Distractions and personal needs are everywhere during business hours. The concept that their own time is valuable—that it is, in fact, often the only salable commodity that can be offered—can be hard to get used to. Keeping track of *chargeable* time is similar to inventory control. Knowing what to do *when* and *for whom,* and charging accordingly, can be the difference between survival and bankruptcy. A number of time-management pros propose the following ways to save on personal time and increase profit:

- Make idle time count—while waiting, standing in line, riding to work.
- Combine activities by better planning, such as ganging up prospect and customer mailings, socializing while walking, and so on.
- Plan ahead to avoid delays, disappointments, and duplication of efforts—as in shopping, traveling, and doing chores.
- Group appointments such as for several services or repair people.
- Stock up on standard and nonperishable items when sales on them are in progress.
- Network knowledge. Friends and co-workers might already have needed information or tools.
- Keep an up-to-date calendar and appointment schedule.
- File away things as they accumulate.
- File obvious junk mail immediately—in "file 13."
- Have suppliers ship items directly to customers when possible.
- Learn to delegate. Don't try to do everything: it inhibits growth and leisure time.
- Say No to requests. It's wonderful to be wanted, but often the doers are put upon by the mañanamen. Maybe it's time for others to assume some responsibility. Concentrate on the important tasks—and on numero uno.

Dr. Geri McArdle of the Training Systems Institute, Reston, VA, has identified these helpful steps to conserve entrepreneurial time, organize work better, and make more money in the process:

1. Learn to delegate to qualified workers.
2. Minimize interruptions during the workday.
3. Know the difference between excellence (an achievable goal) and perfection (an unattainable frustration).
4. Develop the ability to say No. Do it tactfully and people will not react negatively.
5. Determine which tasks are absolutely necessary—and which are not.

6. Do the most creative, most important, and most difficult work during the most productive period.

7. Organize available work space so that no time is wasted trying to find things.

8. In working with other people, in or out of an office or home, motivate them to serve the business better, more efficiently, and more economically.

TRADE CREDIT   In an open-account arrangement with suppliers of goods and services, payment for the latter may be made at some agreeable time in the future. For example: You buy $1,000 worth of goods. The supplier sends you a bill that states "Payment due in 30 days." It means that you have 30 days to use the $1,000. If you had to borrow $1,000 from a bank in order to pay in advance or C.O.D. and received an 18 percent, short-term, unsecured loan, you would have to pay $15 for the use of the $1,000 for a 30-day period. Your trade credit with your supplier has "earned" you an extra $15. Multiply this by a hundred times over the course of a year during which you might make $100,000 in purchases, and you have earned a net of $1,500. Trade credit is referred to as a "spontaneous" source of financing because it becomes available as a result of ordinary business transactions. Entrepreneurs should take advantage of it and negotiate the best possible trade terms with all suppliers in the normal course of doing business with them. Not only is trade credit interest-free, but it involves no control on the part of its extender. From the standpoint of the seller, however, trade credit may be a costly, but necessary, sales promotion device. Trade credits are not standardized among various industries. Sometimes they depend on individual negotiations, on quantity purchasing, or on customs. Some industries customarily offer 2 percent after 10 days ($2/_{10}$, net 30) or after 30 days; some give higher percentages. There is another, not easily perceived, advantage to using $2/_{10}$, net 30 trade credit: suppliers will note payment was prompt and according to their terms; that can result in supplies arriving promptly, sometimes ahead of competitors' deliveries.

TRADE SHOWS   Exhibits of merchandise and/or services for the benefit of companies or individuals in a particular trade are usually held in exhibition halls, rooms in hotels, or civic centers. For products such as construction equipment and boats, exhibits may be held outdoors. Attendees can place orders for merchandise or services, usually for resale. The space rented by a manufacturer or sponsor can vary from a simple tabletop display costing $100 to several elaborate, illuminated booths costing several thousand dollars. Most trade shows offer basic 8' × 10' spaces and provide a cloth backdrop and stanchions to separate the space from its neighbors. Tables and chairs may be brought in by the exhibitor or rented from a local leasing company that works with the trade show. Since most of the workers at major trade shows are unionized, getting moving chores and electrical hookups done becomes a costly add-on to the exhibit space. Expenses include hotel space for company representatives, floor space for the trade show's booth, living expenses for the two to three days of the show, and possible shared promotion costs. A trade show bill can run up to a couple of thousand dollars, even for a basic space. Trade shows are, however, a good way to meet new prospects and old customers, try out new merchandise and promotions, and give widespread staff exposure to the market. Companies that attend several trade shows a year often invest in a collapsible display stand that can be custom-made for a specific product or service for a few hundred dollars. A source that lists all national trade shows each year is the *Trade Show Directory* available from Forum Publishing, 383 East Main St., Centerport, NY 11721.

TRADEMARKS

These are insignia or logos that distinguish one manufacturer's goods from any others. A trademark can be a word, phrase, letter, number, picture, or design, or a combination of any of them. It might be used by a person or company in a variety of ways—affixed to the product, displayed in an ad for the product, or on a package or container. Products cannot have a commonly used or generic term for trademarks. Over a period of time, trademarks on products become closely identified with the product, impart prestige and value to it, and become of considerable marketing value. In 1988 the United States Trademark Law was amended and the new provisions went into effect in November 1989. There is no longer a requirement that a trademark must actually have had commercial use before it can be registered—a requirement that had led to some companies setting up phony sales of new products in miniscule numbers just so they could attest that the trademark had been used. To register a new trademark, contact: Trademark Information, Patent and Trademark Office, Department of Commerce, Washington, DC 20231; phone: (703) 557-4636. Ask for the information booklet "Basic Facts About Trademarks." The application for trademark registration must be filed in the name of the owner of the trademark. Owners can file their own application for registration or may be represented by attorneys.

Many companies run continuous ads in trade publications reminding readers that their trademarks are the property of their company. However, popular usage is stronger than ever the Trademark Law. Among the many registered, private trademarks that have become adopted in English parlance (often with no awareness of their owners) are the following:

Most Popular Trademarks:

Band-Aid	(Johnson & Johnson)
Coke and Coca-Cola	(Coca-Cola Co.)
Formica	(American Cyanamid Co.)
Jeep	(Chrysler Corp.)
Kleenex	(Kimberly-Clark Corp.)
Ping-Pong	(Parker Brothers)
Q-Tips; Vaseline	(Chesebrough-Ponds Co.)
Scotch Tape	(3M Corp.)
Styrofoam	(Dow Chemical Co.)
Technicolor	(Technicolor Corp.)
Teflon and Orlon	(E.I. DuPont de Nemours Co.)
Windbreaker	(Men's Wear International)
Xerox	(Xerox Corporation)

A number of older trademarks have wound up in English-language dictionaries. Among these can be found: aspirin, cellophane, celluloid, escalator, kerosene, lanolin, milk of magnesia, shredded wheat, thermos, yo-yo, and, in closing, zipper.

TURNAROUND COMPANY   A company that is headed for financial trouble, already in deep trouble, or just working itself out of trouble is called a turnaround company. The theory is that most companies have multiple lives and that a change in operation or management, or a refinancing, can resuscitate an otherwise viable company. Some investors look for companies in trouble because their stock can be bought advantageously, brought back to profitability, and then sold at a substantial profit. There is even a newsletter called "The Turnaround Letter" published by George Putnam III in Boston, MA. According to this turnaround expect, probably more than half the companies entering such revival efforts become successful again. Investors who are advised to spread their risks around, or diversify, and have the patience to wait three or four years for turnaround efforts to pay off can reap substantial appreciation. One segment of business that is proving difficult to turn around, sometimes even when expert aid is available, is banking and savings and loan companies. In effecting a turnaround for a company, it is best to stick to what that company knows best but to slim it down, concentrate its focus, and bring in new management who have a fresh and unfettered viewpoint. Turnarounds are not limited to stock companies and manufacturers. There are turnaround specialists who will take over a retail business, either under contract or by buying it cheaply, and promote it back to health with innovative merchandising and advertising, and enthusiastic management. Turnaround strategy is almost like buying an old house, renovating it, and reselling it at a sizable profit. Moderate fortunes have been made like this.

TURNOVER RATIOS

Bankers look at these three ratios, but entrepreneurs should also know these figures in order to have a more realistic picture of their business operation. As a general rule, the greater the accounts receivable (what customers owe), the more capitalization is needed to tide the business over until those accounts are paid. Consequently, many businesses try to charge interest on accounts that go beyond a certain deadline, say, longer than 30 days. The three pertinent ratios are:

1. Sales-to-receivables: This ratio determines the average collection period. It tells the owner and the banker how much money is needed to continue in business. Figure this ratio this way: Annual sales (say, $400,000) divided by Number of business days (say, 300) equals Daily sales ($1,333). Accounts receivable in this example are 25 percent, or $100,000. Divide Accounts receivable by Daily sales to find the number of days money is tied up in receivables (Average collection period):

   $$400,000 \div 300 \quad = 1,333 \text{ (Average daily sales)}$$
   $$100,000 \div 1,333 = \quad 75 \text{ (Average collection period)}$$

   How much does it cost to run the business for 75 days? *That's* how much an owner needs to have on hand—or to borrow.

2. Sales-to-inventory: Divide annual sales ($400,000) by current inventory (say, $100,000) to get the number of times that inventory "turns over" each year. In this example it's four times.

3. Sales-to-fixed-assets: This ratio reveals how many dollars in sales are generated by each dollar invested in plant and equipment. If assets are $150,000, divide sales ($400,000) by total assets ($150,000). The answer is 2.67 (400,000 ÷ 150,000).

UNDERCAPITALIZATION Available money may be insufficient to operate a business effectively, especially during seasonal surges, emergency conditions, slow collection periods, management miscalculations, competitive pressures, inflation, and other uncontrollable external pressures. While undercapitalization is one of the major causes of business closings, this might be due in part to disappointment of entrepreneurs' expectations. Owners may find that business independence is not as lucrative as anticipated or that salaried employment could be more profitable and less risky. Lack of "sufficient" money is often a subjective criterion. What is an adequate return to one entrepreneur is inadequate to another. Frequently capital that should have been conserved for unforeseen but unplanned expenses is squandered on frills, heavy purchases, premature expansion, superfluous hiring, or increases in the cost of working capital. Then, of course, undercapitalization is blamed, rather than poor management judgment or inexperience. There is a certain pace of growth in every business and each entrepreneur must determine and learn what that pace is—and err on the side of conservatism, if capital supply is limited or uncertain. Generally, there are several steps to transform undercapitalization into tangible assets:

1. Avoid grand-opening posturing, overblown staffs, and grandiose advertising and decor.
2. Borrow money only to the extent needed.
3. Expand only as it can be afforded and be sure of each step.
4. If earlier personal experience was in a big organization, go easy. A small business won't have the people or the money to tide it over problem periods.
5. Minimize the entrepreneurial risk by gaining more experience.
6. Keep a tight rein on inventory. Make sure to achieve optimum turnover and get rid of slow-moving merchandise that drains cash availability.

UNITED STATES CUSTOMS SERVICE

For entrepreneurs eyeing the export–import business, knowing the rules, regulations, idiosyncrasies, and even helpmates of this branch of the Treasury Department will be vital and remunerative. (See *Foreign Trade Zones [FTZ]*.) The Customs Service employs nearly 15,000 people whose job it is to administer and collect duties, taxes, fees, and penalties on imported merchandise and to monitor and penalize those who try to bring contraband goods into the United States. It maintains an extensive network of ports and points-of-entry and issues licenses to brokers who handle the importing of foreign goods. The rules that American importers and their foreign contacts must know and observe include:

- All information required on customs invoices must be in clear, legible English.
- Each item in a shipment must have an identification number corresponding to the number shown on the customs invoice.
- Each package must indicate the country of origin.
- Rules issued by the Customs Service regarding invoicing, packaging, marking, labeling, and so on, are to be forwarded to the shipper by the U.S. importer and must be followed accurately.

The Customs Service can be contacted at the Department of the Treasury, 1301 Constitution Avenue, NW, Washington, DC 20229; phone: (202) 566-8195. Specialists who can provide specific information on each product category are called customs commodity experts. They are located at 6 World Trade Center, Room 425, New York, NY 10048; phone: (212) 466-5821. There are no fewer than 60 specialists, covering every industrial classification; callers should be sure to ask for the specific one assigned to a special trade.

UNITED STATES HISPANIC CHAMBER OF COMMERCE (USHCC)

Formed in 1979, the USHCC is the sole nationwide network of businesses within the Hispanic community of the United States, as well as companies wanting to be identified as catering to the Hispanic community. With nearly 20 million Hispanic citizens, this group has become the fastest growing minority in the country. Nearly 400,000 enterprises are now identified as Hispanic; there exist over 200 Hispanic chambers of commerce and business associations. The USHCC publishes an annual business directory listing up to 10,000 Hispanic business enterprises (HBEs) in all sectors of the manufacturing and service industries. The directory is organized by states, according to Standard Industrial Classification (SIC) codes, and cross-referenced against an Automated Vendor Profile Matching System, an electronic data bank through which corporations can access data on HBEs and research potential business opportunities. The directory is about $28, delivered; mailing labels of its complete listings are available for $500. One of the other objectives of the USHCC is to assist HBEs in business ventures in Latin America. For $5 to $25 publications and studies are available on Hispanic business communities in Texas, Los Angeles, Miami, Atlantic seaboard cities, Washington, DC, San Francisco, San Diego, Arizona, Colorado, and Indiana. Membership starts at $100 annually. National headquarters of the USHCC is at 4900 Main Street, Suite 700, Kansas City, MO 64112; phone: (816) 531-6363. A Western office is located at 5400 E. Olympic Boulevard, Suite 308, Los Angeles, CA 90022, and the Eastern office is at 111 Massachusetts Avenue, NW, Suite 200, Washington, DC 20001.

UNITED STATES SMALL BUSINESS ADMINISTRATION
See *Small Business Administration (SBA)*.

VENTURE CAPITAL Money is often invested in enterprises that have some element of risk but have the potential of reaping considerable profit. Venture capitalists invest about $1 billion a year in various enterprises—mostly existing, expanding businesses that are novel and interesting enough to promise high profit returns and a fairly short-term buyout or opportunity to go public. Emerging growth and high-technology companies are prime prospects for venture capital infusion. Invariably, the investors will take a major portion of the company's equity. Venture capitalists are not money lenders in the traditional sense but seek to buy into a company that promises quick and high returns. When private money or normal bank loans are unavailable, venture capital is often the only way to get a fast-track product or service off the ground. The entrepreneur's thinking then is that half a loaf is better than none. To reach a venture capitalist, whether an individual, a small investment group, or a large insurance company, the entrepreneur must go through much the same procedures as for a bank loan—prepare a meticulous business plan and show proof positive that projections are or at least appear to be valid. While making more money is the name of the game for venture capitalists, they add the elements of adventure and thrill. They have already been there: most of them have been or are successful businesspeople. The $1 billion a year that this group invests into ventures is money they can afford to lose—but the best bet is that few will lose. For more information see *Venture* and *INC.* magazines, which usually feature many ads from venture firms.

For small financing (under $1 million), the following venture capital organizations might be of assistance:

Association of Venture Capital Clubs, 524 Camino Del Monte Sol, Santa Fe, NM 87501; phone: (505) 983-3869 (no fee, brochure available)

Basic Search, Inc., Park Place, 10 West Streetsboro Street, Hudson, OH 44236; phone: (216) 656-2442

International Venture Capital Institute, Inc., P.O. Box 1333, Stamford, CT 06904; phone: (203) 323-3143 (Directory of Venture Capital Clubs, lists 100 U.S. clubs and 15 foreign ones)

National Association for Female Executives, 127 West 24 St., New York, NY 10011; phone: (212) 645-0770 (Venture capital funding for women entrepreneurs)

National Association of Small Business Investment Corporations, 618 Washington Building, Washington, DC 20005 (Free directory of members available)

National Venture Capital Association, 1225 19th Street, NW, Suite 750, Washington, DC 20036 (Free directory of members available)

Nebraska Business Development Center, 1313 Farnam Street, Suite 132, Omaha, NE 68182 (List of over 60 VC clubs free; send self-addressed #10 envelope with 45 cents postage)

"Raising Venture Capital," Deloitte Haskins Sells, 1114 Avenue of the Americas, New York, NY 10036

Seed Capital Network, Inc., 8905 Kingston Pike, Suite 12, Knoxville, TN 37923

Venture Capital Network, P.O. Box 882, Durham, NH 03824; phone: (603) 862-3556

VIDEO DISPLAY TERMINAL (VDT) This computer input/output device is made up of a keyboard and a cathode-ray-tube display and either includes a microcomputer or has a computer link to a separate computer. The VDT has occasionally been accused of causing eyestrain and other ill effects. One study published in the *American Journal of Industrial Medicine* in 1988 found that pregnant women who used a VDT more than 20 hours a week suffered twice as many miscarriages as non-VDT workers during the first 12 weeks of pregnancy. While no adverse effects were confirmed by the Office of Safety and Health Administration, OSHA proposed that VDT operators should avoid excessive discomfort and fatigue from the prolonged use of VDTs. Vision problems are a reality, however. It has been suggested by sight specialists that either blue or green screens should be used on VDTs or special filtering glasses should be worn. One legislative intervention is already on the books in Suffolk County, New York: VDT operators must limit their weekly use to 26 hours. To protect VDT operators, owners are urged to provide appropriate eyewear that will screen out adverse reaction to screen glare, adjustable chairs so that the VDT can be viewed most advantageously, adequate exterior lighting, an adjustable keyboard shelf, and, if feasible, instruction on doing eye exercises recommended by an ocular specialist.

VISUAL AIDS Images are presented to accompany some written or oral presentations. They may be easel displays, projected pictures or graphs, items written on a blackboard, blown-up clips from a newspaper or magazine, a slide showing, or a TV screen projection. People generally remember best what they can hear *and* see—hence, visual aids tend to make for greater impact of oral presentations. But there are a number of caveats. Visual aids used improperly can be counterproductive. Here are some simple rules to bear in mind when using visual aids during sales and entertainment presentations:

1. Don't use a visual display to distract the audience's attention. Use it only to enhance and to elaborate on the points being made.

2. In the first few minutes of a presentation, get the audience's attention with humor, small talk, or a question to involve them.

3. Make sure the visual is readable from anywhere in the room.

4. Make up transparencies horizontally—they're easier to read.

5. Use a frame to keep the projection centered.

6. Move from the projector to the screen occasionally, but be sure not to block the projection.

7. Watch the audience closely for signs of unrest, raised hands, puzzled looks. Ask questions in between.

8. When the visuals are not in use, turn off the projector or turn the flip chart to a blank page and walk away from it so that the audience will not be distracted.

WASTE DISPOSAL Businesspeople need to be concerned with getting rid of paper, cardboard, plastic packaging, metal containers, and all the various throwaway materials with which America achieves its great distribution system. Hiring the lowest bidder to collect daily waste or to empty a dumpster (in a shopping center, this cost is part of the management fees) is really the least of the problems, although it does cost money. Recycling can eliminate some of the refuse—and perhaps even make it profitable. (See *Recycling* for some ideas.) Alternatives are to analyze whether biodegradable materials can be purchased in the first place, or whether the disposable material can be reused somehow, or compacted or broken up into smaller disposal units. It makes little sense to achieve instant foods and quick-use convenience products, but then wrap them in containers that last for centuries or for which no more landfills exist. Ecologically sensitive entrepreneurs will be aghast to learn that on an average business day the American consumer is on the receiving end of 5,000 tons of generally unsolicited promotional mail, 20 million catalogs from stores and mail order companies, 65 million newspapers weighing 25,000 tons, 187,000 tons of paper, 150,000 tons of bags and cardboard boxes, and 1.3 million convenience food cartons. And all this unmitigated garbage does not include a half-million old tires and 300,000 appliances of various kinds. If landfills could be manufactured, they would make one of the great entrepreneurial opportunities.

WOMEN IN BUSINESS   The emphasis on helping women to enter the world of entrepreneurship began in earnest on June 22, 1983, when President Ronald Reagan signed Executive Order 12426. It called upon federal agencies to increase procurement from women-owned businesses and generally to provide financial and management assistance to women. The Department of Commerce and the Small Business Administration have special departments set up to implement this Executive Order. "Ask Us, U.S. Department of Commerce Programs to Aid Women Business Owners" is a valuable 42-page booklet that is a good start in taking advantage of this Order. The booklet may be obtained from a local Department of Commerce office or by writing to: Office of Small and Disadvantaged Business Utilization, Room H6411, U.S. Department of Commerce, Washington, DC 20230; phone: (202) 377-5614. (See Appendix B for a complete list of federal contacts.) The Small Business Administration, through its Women's Business Opportunities (WBO) section, offers helpful management advice for startup and operating enterprises owned and/or managed by women. A complete list of regional SBA offices can be found in Appendix D. The SBA/WBO also conducts several seminars yearly on such topics as credit, procurement, and networking. To obtain the latest information on WBO programs, contact the nearest SBA office or write SBA/WBO, 1441 L Street, NW, Washington, DC 20416; phone: (202) 653-8000. (See also *Government Procurement*.)

YOUNG ENTREPRENEURS' ORGANIZATION (YEO)   This organization was formed as a natural outgrowth of the collegiate entrepreneurial group. The YEO's mission is to "build bridges" between the collegiates and the over-35 "alumni"—the older, established entrepreneurs. Occasional meetings are held with the latter as well as with entrepreneurs overseas. Chapters are being established in Latin America and Japan. Participation criteria in YEO include annual revenues in excess of $1 million, being under 35 of age, and having a willingness to share experience and know-how with others. Two annual meetings are held by the approximately 300 members. In addition, the national director, Verne C. Harnish, publishes a newsletter, arranges overseas entrepreneurial tours, conducts a four-day Leadership Summit, and publishes a descriptive, illustrated directory. Annual dues are $450. Offices are at 1221 Pennsylvania Avenue, NW, Washington, DC 20003; phone: (202) 544-7100.

ZENZ CASE   If a seller is planning to buy a going business with income realized from a sale then the landmark case of *Fern R. Zenz v. John J. Quinlivan,* 213 F.2d 914 (1955) will be pertinent in negotiations and as a reference for the attorney handling the acquisition. In the *Zenz* case, the taxpayer was the widow of a man who had been engaged in sewer construction and excavating work. Eventually, the widow sought to dispose of her inherited company to a competitor. The prospective buyer did not want to assume the tax liabilities which, it was believed, were inherent in the accumulated profits and earnings of the corporation. To avoid acquiring the accumulated profits and earnings as future taxable dividends, the buyer purchased only part of the widow's stock for cash. Three weeks later, after corporate reorganization, the corporation purchased the balance of the widow's stock as treasury stock, which offset substantially all of the accumulated earnings and surplus of the corporation. The widow identified the amount received from the purchaser and from the corporation as proceeds from the sale of a capital asset and reported the resulting gain as a capital gain. The Internal Revenue Service (IRS), however, held that the corporation had made a distribution that was "essentially equivalent to a dividend." The District Court upheld the IRS, finding that the widow had employed a circuitous approach to avoid tax consequences. The Circuit Court, in reversing the District Court, stated that "the use of corporate earnings and profits to purchase and make payment for all of the shares of a taxpayer's holdings in a corporation is not controlling . . ."—and henceforth, the IRS accepts the *Zenz*-type liquidation (Rev. Rul. 55-745).

ENTREPRENEURIAL RESOURCES

This resource list gives the locations, as of 1989, of state agencies and state-located offices that can be of assistance to entrepreneurs, whether they are starting an enterprise or are already in business. The most important offices in each of the 50 states, the District of Columbia, and Puerto Rico are listed. Information on offices that may be nearer to the location of an entrepreneur's home or business is available from those given here. There are more than 100 SBA offices, about 600 SBDCs, and over 750 SCORE locations. Several thousand chambers of commerce or similar organizations are available, of which about 4,500 are members of the U.S. Chamber of Commerce. One chamber office is listed for each state. The abbreviations used are:

CoC	Chamber of Commerce
DO	Development Office
FIC	Federal Information Center
ITA	International Trade Administration (Commerce Department)
OFed	Other federal offices
OSHA	Occupational Safety and Health Administration
SBA	Small Business Administration Field Office
SBDC	Small Business Development Center
SCORE	Service Corps of Retired Executives

If any desired information cannot be located among the several hundred resources listed here, call the SBA's national Answer Desk on its free hotline: 1 (800) 368-5855.

ALABAMA

DO: State Capitol, Montgomery 36130; (205) 263-0048

Services: Business development, financial assistance, procurement assistance, minority/women opportunities

Publications: *Alabama Developing News; Alabama International Directory; Alabama Exporting Guide; Alabama: Products for the World*

SBA: 2121 8th Ave. N., Suite 200, Birmingham 35203; (205) 731-1344

OFed:	(Birmingham) FIC, (205) 322-8591 ITA, (205) 731-1331 OSHA, (205) 731-1534
SBDC:	University of Alabama, School of Business, 901 15th St. S., Suite 143, Birmingham 35294; (205) 934-7260
CoC:	Business Council of Alabama, 468 S. Perry St., P.O. Box 76, Montgomery 36195; (205) 834-6000
SCORE:	Birmingham—901 S. 15th St.; 934-6868 Florence—c/o Chamber of Commerce; 764-5372 Mobile—c/o Chamber of Commerce; 433-8614 Tuscaloosa—c/o Chamber of Commerce; 758-7588

ALASKA

DO:	Division of Business Development, P.O. Box D, Juneau 99811; (907) 465-2027 Services: Business development, financial assistance, procurement assistance; international trade (907) 561-5585 Publications: *Focusing on International Trade*
SBA:	8th and C Sts., Module G, Room 1068, (mailing address: 701 C St., Box 67) Anchorage 99513; (907) 271-4022
OFed:	FIC, (907) 271-3650 ITA, (907) 271-5041 OSHA, (907) 271-5152
SBDC:	Anchorage Community College, 430 W. 7th Ave., Suite 115, Anchorage 99501; (907) 274-7232
CoC:	Alaska State Chamber of Commerce, 310 Second St., Juneau 99801; (907) 586-2323
SCORE:	P.O. Box 848, Soldotna 99669 (or contact **SBA**)

ARIZONA

DO:	Office of Community Finance, Dept. of Commerce, 1700 W. Washington St., 4th Fl., Phoenix 85007; (602) 255-5705 Services: Business development, financial assistance, procurement assistance; international trade (602) 255-5374 Publications: *Directory of Exporters, Arizona Directory of International Services*
SBA:	2005 N. Central Ave., Phoenix 85004; (602) 261-3732; 300 W. Congress St., Tucson 85701; (602) 629-6715
OFed:	(Phoenix) FIC, (602) 261-3313 IRS, (602) 261-3861 ITA, (602) 261-3285 OSHA, (602) 261-4858

SBDC:	Gateway Community College, 108 N. 40th St., Phoenix 85034; (602) 392-5224
CoC:	1366 E. Thomas Rd., Suite 202, Phoenix 85012; (602) 261-3843
SCORE:	Phoenix—2005 N. Central, 5th Fl., 85004; (602) 261-3843
	Prescott—P.O. Bldg., Suite 8, 86302; (602) 778-7438
	Tucson—301 W. Congress, Fed. Bldg., 85715; (602) 629-6616

ARKANSAS

DO:	1 State Capitol Mall, Room 4C-300, Little Rock 77201; (501) 682-3358
	Services: Business development, financial assistance, procurement assistance; international trade (501) 371-7678
	Publications: *Arkansas Guide to Export Services; Arkansas International Marketers Newsletter* (quarterly); *Starting a Small Business in Arkansas*
SBA:	320 W. Capitol Ave., #601, Little Rock 72201; (501) 378-5871
OFed:	(Little Rock)
	FIC, (501) 378-6177
	IRS, (501) 378-5685
	ITA, (501) 378-5794
	OSHA, (501) 378-6291
SBDC:	University of Arkansas, 100 S. Main St., Suite 401, Little Rock 72204; (501) 371-5381
CoC:	100 Main St., Suite 510, Little Rock 72203-3645; (501) 374-9225
SCORE:	Little Rock—c/o SBA, Suite 602, 320 W. Capitol Ave.; (503) 378-5813

CALIFORNIA

DO:	1121 L St., Suite 600, Sacramento 95814; (916) 445-6545
	Services: Business development, financial assistance, procurement assistance, minority /women opportunities; international trade (916) 324-5511
	Publications: *California Service Exports: Emerging Global Opportunities, California Manufactured Exports*
SBA:	350 S. Figueroa St., Los Angeles, 90071; (213) 894-2956; 211 Main St., 4th Fl., San Francisco, 94105; (415) 974-0649

OFed:	FIC, Los Angeles (213) 894-3800
	IRAS, San Francisco (415) 556-0880; Los Angeles (213) 894-4574
	ITA, San Francisco (415) 556-5860; San Diego (619) 557-5395
	OSHA, Long Beach (213) 514-6387; San Francisco (415) 556-7260
SBDC:	n.a.
CoC:	1027 10th St., Sacramento 95808; (916) 444-6670
SCORE:	Fresno—2202 Monterey St., Suite 108; (209) 487-5605
	Los Angeles—Suite 190, 339 N. Brand Blvd.; (213) 894-3016
	San Diego—c/o SBA (Suite 4-S-29), 880 Front St.; (619) 557-7269
	San Francisco—c/o SBA 211 Main St., 4th Fl.; (415) 974-0599
	Santa Ana—901 Civic Center Dr., #160; (714) 836-2709
	Santa Barbara—3227 State St.; (805) 563-0084
	Santa Rosa—3033 Cleveland Ave., Suite 11; (707) 525-9967

COLORADO

DO:	1525 Sherman St., Room 110, Denver 80203; (303) 866-3933
	Services: Business development, financial assistance, procurement assistance; international trade (303) 866-2205
	Publications: *Doing Business in Colorado, Colorado Foreign Trade Directory,* "Business Startup Kits"
SBA:	One Denver Pl. N Tower, 999 18th St., #701, Denver 80202; (303) 294-7149
OFed:	(Denver)
	FIC, (303) 844-6575
	IRS, (303) 825-7041
	ITA, (303) 844-3246
	OSHA, (303) 844-5285
SBDC:	Colorado Community College, 600 Grant St., #505, Denver 80203; (303) 894-2422
CoC:	1860 Lincoln St., #550, Denver 80295-0501; (303) 831-7411
SCORE:	Denver—721 19th St.; (303) 844-3985
	Pueblo—c/o Chamber of Commerce; (303) 547-2762

CONNECTICUT

DO: 210 Washington St., Hartford 06106; (203) 566-4051

Services: Business development, financial assistance, procurement assistance, minority/women opportunities; international trade (203) 566-3842

Publications: *Establishing a Business in Connecticut, Connecticut Women & Minorities in Business*

SBA: 330 Main St., 2nd Fl., Hartford, 06106; (203) 240-4700

OFed: (Hartford)
FIC, (203) 527-2617
ITA, (203) 240-3530
OSHA, (203) 240-3152

SBDC: c/o University of Connecticut, Room 422, 368 Fairfield Rd., Storrs 06268; (203) 486-4135

CoC: 370 Asylum St., Hartford 06103; (203) 547-1661

SCORE: Bridgeport—180 Fairfield Ave.; (203) 335-3800
Hartford—c/o SBA, 330 Main St.; (203) 240-4640
New Haven—25 Science Park; (203) 865-7645

DELAWARE

DO: 99 King's Highway, P.O. Box 1401, Dover 19903; (302) 736-4271

Services: Business development, financial assistance, procurement assistance, minority/women opportunities; international trade (302) 571-6262

Publications: "Small Business Start-Up Guides," *Export Directory*

SBA: J. Caleb Boggs Fed. Bldg., 844 King St., #5207, Wilmington 19801; (302) 573-6295

OFed: (see **Pennsylvania**, Philadelphia area)

SBDC: University of Delaware, Suite 005, Purnell Hall, Newark 19716; (302) 451-2747

CoC: One Commerce Center, Suite 200, Wilmington 19801; (302) 655-7221

SCORE: Wilmington—1 Rodney Sq., Suite 410; (302) 573-6552

DISTRICT OF COLUMBIA

DO: 1111 E St., NW, 7th Fl., Washington 20004; (202) 727-6600

Services: Business development, financial assistance, procurement assistance, minority/women opportunities; international trade (202) 727-1576

Publications: *Small Business Annual Report, Export Guide, International Resource Guide*

SBA:	1111 18th St., NW, 6th Fl., Washington 20036; (202) 634-6197
OFed:	FIC, (202) 655-4000
	IRS, (202) 488-3100
	ITA, (202) 377-3181
	OSHA, (202) 523-8148
SBDC:	(202) 636-5151
CoC:	(202) 463-5580
SCORE:	(202) 653-6279 (National Office)

FLORIDA

DO:	107 W. Gaines St., Tallahassee 32339-2000; (904) 488-9357; in state: (800) 342-0771
	Services: Business development, financial assistance, procurement assistance, minority/women opportunities; international trade (904) 488-5280
	Publications: *New Business Guide and Checklist*
SBA:	700 Twiggs St., Room 607, Tampa 33602; (813) 228-2594
OFed:	FIC, Miami (305) 356-4005; Jacksonville (904) 354-4756; Tampa (813) 229-7911
	ITA, Miami (305) 536-5267; Jacksonville (904) 791-2796
	OSHA, Ft. Lauderdale (305) 527-7292; Jacksonville (904) 791-2895
SBDC:	University of West Florida, 1000 University Blvd., Bldg. 38, Pensacola 32514; (904) 474-3016
CoC:	136 S. Bronought St., Tallahassee 32302; (904) 222-2831
SCORE:	Coral Gables—1320 S. Dixie Highway; (305) 536-5833
	Ft. Lauderdale—105F Fed. Bldg., 299 E. Broward Blvd.; (305) 527-7263
	Jacksonville—c/o SBA, Fed. Bldg., 400 W. Bay St.
	Orlando—455 Fed. Bldg., 80 N. Hughey Ave.; (407) 648-6476
	Tampa—c/o SBA, Room 607, 7000 Twiggs St.; (813) 225-7047

GEORGIA

DO:	230 Peachtree Rd. NW, Atlanta 30303; (404) 656-3584
	Services: Business development, procurement assistance, minority/women opportunities; international trade (404) 542-6789
	Publications: *How to Start A Business in Georgia, Targeting a Small Business for Export Assistance, Training Modules on Export Assistance*
SBA:	1375 Peachtree St. NE, Atlanta 30367; (404) 347-2797

OFed:	FIC, Atlanta (404) 331-6891
	ITA, Atlanta (404) 347-7000
	OSHA, Tucker (404) 331-0353
SBDC:	University of Georgia, 1180 E. Broad St., Chicopee, Athens 30602; (404) 542-5760
CoC:	1280 South CNN Center, Atlanta 30303; (404) 223-2264
SCORE:	Atlanta—c/o SBA, 6th Fl., 1720 Peachtree Rd. NW; (404) 347-2396
	Savannah—125 Bull St., Suite 8B; (912) 248-4335

HAWAII

DO:	250 South King St., Room 724, Honolulu 96813; (808) 548-7645
	Services: Business development, financial assistance, procurement assistance, minority/women opportunities; international trade (808) 548-3048
	Publications: *Starting a Business in Hawaii, Hawaii Business Regulation, Hawaii Business Abroad*
SBA:	300 Ala Moana, Room 2213, (P.O. Box 50207) Honolulu 96850; (808) 541-2977
OFed:	(Honolulu)
	FIC, (808) 541-1365
	IRS, (808) 541-1040
	ITA, (808) 541-1782
	OSHA, (808) 541-2685
SBDC:	n.a.
CoC:	Dillingham Bldg., 735 Bishop St., Honolulu 96813; (808) 531-4111
SCORE:	Honolulu—300 Ala Moana Blvd., Room 2213; (808) 546-5154

IDAHO

DO:	State Capitol, Room 108, Boise 83720; (208) 334-3416
	Services: Business development, financial assistance, procurement assistance; international trade (208) 334-2470
	Publications: *How to Start a Small Business in Idaho, International Trade Directory*
SBA:	1020 Main St., #290, Boise 83702; (208) 334-1696
OFed:	(Boise)
	ITA, (208) 334-9254
SBDC:	Boise State University, College of Business, 1910 University Dr., Boise 83725; (208) 385-1640

CoC: 805 Idaho St., Suite 200, Boise 83701; (208) 343-1849

SCORE: Boise—c/o SBA, 1020 Main St., #290; (208) 334-1780

ILLINOIS

DO: 620 E. Adams St., Springfield 62701; (217) 785-6282; in state: (800) 252-2923

Services: Business development, financial assistance, procurement assistance, minority/women opportunities; international trade (312) 917-7166

Publications: *There's No Business Like Small Business in Illinois, Starting a Small Business in Illinois*

SBA: Four North, Washington Bldg., Old State Capital Plaza, Springfield 62701; (217) 492-4416

OFed: FIC, Chicago (312) 353-4242

IRS, Chicago (312) 435-1040

ITA, Chicago (312) 353-4450

OSHA, Calumet City (312) 891-3800; Peoria (309) 671-7033

SBDC: 620 E. Adams St., 5th Fl., Springfield 62701; (217) 785-6174

CoC: 20 N. Wacker Dr., Chicago 60606; (312) 372-7373

SCORE: Carbondale—615 S. Washington; (618) 536-2424

Chicago—437 Dirksen Bldg., 219 S. Dearborn; (309) 353-7723

Peoria—Chamber of Commerce, 124 S.W. Adams St., Suite 300; (309) 676-0755

Springfield—509 West Capitol; (217) 492-4416

INDIANA

DO: One North Capital, Suite 700, Indianapolis 46204-2288; (317) 232-3527; in state: (800) 824-2476

Services: Business development, financial assistance, procurement assistance, minority/women opportunities; international trade (317) 232-8846

Publications: *Guide to Starting a Business in Indiana,* "ORR/MUTZ: Economic Development Package," *International Trade Services Directory*

SBA: 575 N. Pennsylvania St., Room 78, Indianapolis 46204; (317) 269-7272

OFed: FIC, Indianapolis (317) 269-7373; Gary/Hammond (219) 883-4110

IRS, Indianapolis (317) 269-5477

ITA, Indianapolis (317) 269-6214

OSHA, Indianapolis (317) 269-7290

SBDC: One North Capitol, Suite 200, Indianapolis 46204; (317) 634-1690

CoC:	Same as **SBDC**; (317) 634-6407
SCORE:	Fort Wayne—130 Fed. Bldg.; (219) 422-2601
	Indianapolis—589 New Fed. Bldg., 575 N. Pennsylvania St.; (317) 226-7264
	South Bend—300 N. Michigan St.; (219) 282-4350
	Terre Haute—c/o Chamber of Commerce, 2225 Wabash Ave.; (812) 232-2391

IOWA

DO:	200 E. Grand Ave., Des Moines 50309; (515) 281-8310; in state: (800) 532-1216
	Services: Business development, financial assistance, procurement assistance, minority/women opportunities; international trade (515) 281-7258
	Publications: *World Trade Guide, Exporter's Directory*
SBA:	The Federal Bldg., 210 Walnut St., Room 749, Des Moines 50309; (515) 284-4422
OFed:	(Des Moines)
	FIC, in state only: (800) 523-1556
	IRS, (515) 283-0523
	ITA, (515) 284-4222
	OSHA, (515) 281-3606
SBDC:	Iowa State University, Chamberlynn Bldg., 137 Lynn Ave., Ames 50010; (515) 292-6351
CoC:	706 Employers Mutual Bldg., 717 Mulberry St., Des Moines 50309; (515) 244-6149; in state: (800) 532-1406
SCORE:	Cedar Rapids—373 Collins Rd., NE, 52402; (319) 399-2571
	Des Moines—c/o SBA, 579 Federal Bldg., 210 Walnut St. 50309; (515) 284-4760
	Dubuque—770 Town Clock Plaza, 52001; (319) 557-9200
	Sioux City—320 6th St., Room 223, 51101; (712) 233-3397

KANSAS

DO:	400 SW Eighth Street, 5th Fl. Topeka 66603; (913) 296-5298
	Services: Business development, financial assistance, procurement assistance, minority/women opportunities; international trade (913) 296-4027
	Publications: *Guide to Starting a Business in Kansas*
SBA:	110 E. Waterman St., Wichita 67202; (316) 269-6273
OFed:	FIC, in state only: (800) 432-2934
	IRS, Wichita (316) 269-6401
	ITA, Wichita (316) 269-6160; Kansas City, MO (816) 374-3142
	OSHA, Wichita (316) 269-6644

SBDC: Wichita State University, 1845 Fairmont, 201 Clinton Hall,
                        Wichita 67208; (316) 689-3193

CoC: 500 Bank IV Tower, One Townsite Plaza, Topeka 66603;
                        (913) 357-6321

SCORE: Wichita—c/o SBA, 110 E. Waterman, 67202; (316) 269-
                        6273

KENTUCKY

DO: Capitol Plaza Tower, 22nd Fl., Frankfort 40601; (502) 564-
                        4252; in state: (800) 626-2250

                        Services: Business development, financial assistance,
                        procurement assistance, minority/women opportunities;
                        international trade (502) 564-2170

                        Publications: *The Entrepreneur's Guide, Kentucky Export
                        Guide, Kentucky International Trade Directory*

SBA: 600 Federal Pl., Room 188, Louisville 40202 (mailing
                        address: P.O. Box 3527, 40201); (502) 582-5971

OFed: (Louisville)
                        FIC, (502) 582-6261
                        ITA, (502) 582-5066
                        OSHA, (502) 564-6895

SBDC: University of Kentucky, 18 Porter Bldg., Lexington 40506;
                        (606) 257-1751

CoC: Versailles Rd., P.O. Box 817, Frankfort 40602;
                        (502) 695-4700

SCORE: Lexington—1460 Newtown Pike, 40511; (606) 231-9902
                        Louisville—600 Fed. Bldg., Room 188, P.O. Box 3527,
                        40201; (502) 582-5976

LOUISIANA

DO: P.O. Box 94185, Baton Rouge, 70804-9185; (504) 342-5365

                        Services: Business development, financial assistance,
                        procurement assistance, minority/women opportunities;
                        international trade (504) 342-9232

                        Publications: *Small Business Financing in Louisiana,
                        Economic Advantages of Doing Business in Louisiana, Guide
                        to International Business for Louisiana Companies*

SBA: 1661 Canal St., #2000, New Orleans 70112;
                        (504) 589-2354

OFed: FIC, New Orleans (504) 589-6696
                        ITA, New Orleans (504) 589-6546
                        OSHA, Baton Rouge (504) 389-0474

SBDC: Northeast Louisiana University, College of Business,
                        Administration Bldg. 2-57, University Dr., Monroe 71209;
                        (318) 342-2464

CoC:	P.O. Box 80258, Baton Rouge 70898-0258; (504) 928-5388
SCORE:	Baton Rouge—P.O. Box 3217, 70821; (504) 381-7125
	New Orleans—c/o SBA, 1661 Canal St., Suite 2000, 70112; (504) 589-2354
	Shreveport—c/o Chamber of Commerce, 400 Edwards St., 71120; (318) 677-2500

MAINE

DO:	State House, Augusta, ME 04333; (207) 289-2659; in state: (800) 872-3838
	Services: Business development, financial assistance, procurement assistance; international trade (207) 622-0234
	Publications: *Doing Business in Maine,* "Business Expansion Resource," *International Commerce Training Guide*
SBA:	40 Western Ave., Fed. Bldg., #512, Augusta 04330; (207) 622-8378
OFed:	(Augusta)
	ITA, (207) 622-8249
	OSHA, (207) 622-8417
SBDC:	University of Southern Maine, 246 Deering Ave., Portland 04102; (207) 780-4423
CoC:	126 Sewall St., Augusta 04330; (207) 623-4568
SCORE:	Augusta—c/o SBA, 40 Western Ave., 04330; (207) 622-8508
	Lewiston/Auburn—c/o Chamber of Commerce, 179 Libson St., Lewiston 04240; (207) 782-3708
	Portland—66 Pearl St., Room 210, 04101; (207) 772-1147

MARYLAND

DO:	45 Calvert St., Annapolis 21401; (301) 974-2946; in state: (800) 654-7336
	Services: Business development, financial assistance, procurement assistance, minority/women opportunities; international trade (301) 333-4295
	Publications: *Guide to Business Regulation, Suggestions for Developing a Business Plan, Export Guide, Maryland Resource Directory*
SBA:	10 N. Calvert St., 3rd Fl., Baltimore 21202; (301) 962-4392
OFed:	(Baltimore)
	FIC, (301) 962-4980
	ITA, (301) 962-3560
	OSHA, (301) 962-2840
SBDC:	217 E. Redwood St., 10th Fl., Baltimore 21202; (301) 333-6608
CoC:	60 West St., Suite 405, Annapolis 21401; (301) 269-0642

SCORE: Annapolis—6 Dock St., 21401; (301) 268-7676

Baltimore—c/o SBA, Room 453, 10 N. Calvert St., 21202; (301) 962-2233

Hagerstown—14 Public Square, 21740; (301) 739-2015

MASSACHUSETTS

DO: 100 Cambridge St., 13th Floor, Boston 02202; (617) 727-4005

Services: Business development, financial assistance, procurement assistance, minority/women opportunities; international trade (617) 367-1830

Publications: *All the Basic Facts You Need to Know to Start a Small Business, Export Services Directory, Foreign Firm Directory*

SBA: 60 Batterymarch St., 10th Fl., Boston 02110; (617) 223-2023

OFed: FIC, Boston (617) 565-8121

IRS, Boston (617) 523-1040

ITA, Boston (617) 565-8563

OSHA, Waltham (617) 647-8681

SBDC: University of Massachusetts, 205 School of Management, Amherst 01003; (413) 549-4930

CoC: 287 Linden St., P.O. Box 715, Wellesley 02181; (617) 235-2446

SCORE: Boston—10 Causeway St., Room 265, 02222; (617) 565-5591

Fall River—200 Pocahasset St., P.O. Box 1871, 02722; (617) 676-8226

Springfield—1550 Main St., Suite 212, 01103; (413) 785-0314

Worcester—c/o Chamber of Commerce, 33 Waldo St., 01608; (617) 753-2924

MICHIGAN

DO: P.O. Box 30107, Lansing 48909; (517) 373-6241; in state: (800) 232-2727

Services: Business development, financial assistance, procurement assistance, minority/women opportunities; international trade (517) 373-6390

Publications: *A Guide to Starting a Business in Michigan, Michigan International Business Services Directory*

SBA: Patrick V. McNamara Bldg., 477 Michigan Ave. Room 515, Detroit 48226; (313) 226-6075

OFed: (Detroit)

FIC, (313) 226-7016

IRS, (313) 237-0800

ITA, (313) 226-3650

SBDC:	Wayne State University, 2727 Second Ave., Detroit 48201; (313) 577-4848
CoC:	600 S. Walnut St., Lansing 48933; (517) 371-2100
SCORE:	Detroit—c/o SBA, 477 Michigan Ave., Room 515, 48226; (313) 226-7947
	Kalamazoo—128 No. Kalamazoo Mall, 49007; (616) 381-5382
	Saute Ste. Marie—c/o Chamber of Commerce, 2581 I-75 Business Spur, 49783; (906) 632-3301
	Traverse City—202 E. Grandview Parkway, 49685; (616) 941-5736

MINNESOTA

DO:	900 American Center, 150 E. Kellogg Blvd., St. Paul 55101; (612) 296-3871; in state: (800) 652-9747
	Services: Business development, financial assistance, procurement assistance, minority/women opportunities; international trade (612) 297-4222
	Publications: *A Guide to Starting a Business in Minnesota, Minnesota Exporter's Assistance Guide*
SBA:	610 C Butler Sq., 100 North 6th St., Minneapolis 55403; (612) 370-2324
OFed:	FIC, Minneapolis (612) 370-3333
	IRS, St. Paul (612) 291-1422
	ITA, Minneapolis (612) 348-1638
	OSHA, (612) 296-2116
SBDC:	College of St. Thomas, Enterprise Center, 1107 Hazeltine Blvd., #245, Chaska 55318; (612) 448-8810
CoC:	300 Hanover Bldg., 480 Cedar St., St. Paul 55101; (612) 292-4650
SCORE:	Duluth—Duluth Arena, N. Pioneer, 325 Harbor Dr., 55802; (218) 722-5501
	Minneapolis—5100 Gamble St., #345, St. Louis Park, 55416; (612) 370-0839
	St. Paul—c/o Chamber of Commerce, 445 Minnesota St., #600, 55101; (612) 223-5010

MISSISSIPPI

DO:	3825 Ridgewood Rd., Jackson 39211-6453; (601) 982-6231
	Services: Business development, financial assistance, procurement assistance; international trade (601) 359-3444
	Publications: *How to Prepare a Business Plan, Mississippi Manufacturer's Directory, Exporter's Handbook, International Trade Directory*
SBA:	New Fed. Bldg., 100 W. Capitol St., #322, Jackson 39269; (601) 965-4378

OFed:	(Jackson)
	IRS, (601) 965-4526
	ITA, (601) 965-4388
	OSHA, (601) 965-4606
SBDC:	University of Mississippi, 3825 Ridgewood Rd., Jackson 39211; (601) 982-6760
CoC:	656 North State St., P.O. Box 1849, Jackson 39215-1849; (601) 969-0022
SCORE:	Biloxi—111 Fred Haise Blvd., 39530; (601) 863-4449
	Jackson—c/o SBA, New Fed. Bldg., 100 W. Capitol St., #322, 39269; (601) 960-5337

MISSOURI

DO:	P.O. Box 118, Jefferson City 65102; (314) 751-4982, (314) 751-8411
	Services: Business development, financial assistance, procurement assistance, minority/women opportunities; international trade (314) 751-4855
	Publications: *Existing Business Resource Directory, Starting a New Business in Missouri, A Missouri Export Directory, You Can Export*
SBA:	911 Walnut St., 13th Fl., Kansas City 64106; (816) 374-3605
OFed:	FIC, St. Louis (314) 425-4106; in state, outside of St. Louis (800) 392-7711
	IRS, St. Louis (314) 342-1040
	ITA, St. Louis (314) 425-3302; Kansas City (816) 374-3142
	OSHA, St. Louis (314) 263-2749; Kansas City (816) 374-2756
SBDC:	St. Louis University, 3674 Lindell Blvd., St. Louis 63108; (314) 534-7204
CoC:	P.O. Box 149, Jefferson City 65102; (314) 634-3511
SCORE:	Kansas City—1103 Grand Ave., Room 512, 64106; (816) 374-6675
	St. Louis—815 Olive St., Room 242, 63101; (314) 425-6600
	Springfield—620 S. Glenstone, #110, 65802; (417) 864-7670

MONTANA

DO:	1424 Ninth Ave., Helena 59620; (406) 444-3923; in state: (800) 221-8015
	Services: Business development, financial assistance, procurement assistance; international trade (406) 444-3923
	Publications: *A Guide to Montana's Economic Development and Business Assistance Programs, Montana Industrial Relocation Growth*

SBA:	301 S. Park, Room 528, Helena 59626; (406) 449-5381
OFed:	OSHA, (406) 657-6649
SBDC:	n.a.
CoC:	110 Neill Ave., P.O. Box 1730, Helena 59624; (406) 442-2405
SCORE:	Billings—P.O. Box 2519, 59103; (406) 245-4111
	Great Falls—P.O. Box 2127, 59403; (406) 761-4434

NEBRASKA

DO:	P.O. Box 94666, 301 Centennial Mall South, Lincoln 68509; (402) 471-4167
	Services: Business development, financial assistance, procurement assistance, minority/women opportunities; international trade (402) 471-4668
	Publications: *Resource Manual for Nebraska Business, International Trade Directory, Export Guide Manual*
SBA:	11145 Mill Valley Rd., Omaha 68154; (402) 221-4691
OFed:	(Omaha)
	FIC, (402) 221-3353
	IRS, (402) 422-1500
	ITA, (402) 221-3664
	OSHA, (402) 221-3182
SBDC:	University of Nebraska at Omaha, College of Business Administration Bldg., 60th & Dodge, Room 407, Omaha 68182; (402) 554-2521
CoC:	1320 Lincoln Mall, P.O. Box 95128, Lincoln 68509; (402) 474-4422
SCORE:	Lincoln—Southeastern Community College, 2929 S. 20th, 68520; (402) 471-3303
	North Platte—2101 Sunset, Box 1203, 69101
	Omaha—c/o SBA, 11145 Mill Valley Rd., 68154; (402) 221-3604

NEVADA

DO:	1100 East William, Suite 116, Carson City 89710; (702) 885-4602
	Services: Business development, financial assistance, procurement assistance, minority/women opportunities; international trade (702) 784-5203
	Publications: *Starting a Small Business in Northern Nevada, A Basic Guide to Exporting*
SBA:	301 E. Stewart St., #301, Las Vegas 89125; (702) 388-6611; 50 S. Virginia St., #238, Reno 89505; (702) 784-5268
OFed:	(Reno)
	ITA, (702) 784-5203
	OSHA, (702) 789-0380

SBDC:	University of Nevada Reno, College of Business Administration, Room 411, Reno 89557-0100; (702) 784-1717
CoC:	P.O. Box 3499, Reno, 89505; (702) 786-3030
SCORE:	Las Vegas—301 E. Stewart, Box 7527, 89125; (702) 385-6611
	Reno—c/o SBA, Room 308, 50 S. Virginia St., 89505; (702) 784-5477

NEW HAMPSHIRE

DO:	105 Loudon Road, Prescott Park, Bldg. 2, Concord 03301; (603) 271-2591
	Services: Business development, financial assistance, procurement assistance, minority/women opportunities; international trade (603) 625-4522
	Publications: *Starting a Business in New Hampshire, Business Planning Guide, So You Want to Export?*
SBA:	Post Office Bldg., 55 Pleasant St., #210, Concord 03301-1257; (603) 225-1400
OFed:	ITA, Boston, MA (617) 565-8563
	OSHA, Concord (603) 225-1629
SBDC:	University of New Hampshire, University Center, 400 Commercial St., Room 311, Manchester 03101; (603) 625-4522; (800) 322-0390
CoC:	23 School St., Concord 03301; (603) 224-5388
SCORE:	Berlin—P.O. Box 34, 03570; (603) 752-1090
	Manchester—Norris Cotton Fed. Bldg., 275 Chestnut St., Room 618, 03103; (603) 666-7561

NEW JERSEY

DO:	1 West State St., CN 835, Trenton 08625; (609) 984-4442
	Services: Business development, financial assistance, procurement assistance, minority/women opportunities; international trade (201) 648-3518
	Publications: "Startup Kits," *A Guide to Export Assistance, International Report* (monthly)
SBA:	60 Park Pl., 4th Fl., Newark 07102; (201) 645-2434
OFed:	FIC, Newark (201) 645-3600; Trenton (609) 396-4400
	IRS, Newark (201) 622-0600
	ITA, Trenton (609) 989-2100
	OSHA, Avenel (201) 750-3270; Camden (609) 757-5181
SBDC:	Rutgers University, 180 University St., 3rd Fl., Newark 07102; (201) 648-5950
CoC:	5 Commerce St., Newark 07102; (201) 623-7070

SCORE:	Camden—2600 Mt. Ephram Ave., 08104; (609) 757-5305
	Newark—60 Park Pl., 4th Fl., 07102; (201) 645-3982
	Vineland—Cumberland County College, P.O. Box 517, 08360; (609) 691-8600

NEW MEXICO

DO:	1100 St. Francis Drive, Santa Fe 87503; (505) 827-0300; in state: (800) 545-2040
	Services: Business development, financial assistance, procurement assistance, minority/women opportunities; international trade (505) 827-0283
	Publications: *Preparing a Business Plan, International Trade Directory*
SBA:	5000 Marble, NE, #320, Albuquerque 87100; (505) 262-6171
OFed:	(Albuquerque)
	FIC, (505) 766-3091
	ITA, (505) 766-2386
	OSHA, (505) 766-3411
SBDC:	Santa Fe Community College, P.O. Box 4187, Santa Fe 87502-4187; (505) 471-8200
CoC:	4001 Indian School Rd., NE, #333, Albuquerque 87110; (505) 265-5847
SCORE:	Albuquerque—5000 Marble NE, #316, 87110; (505) 262-6341
	Las Cruces—C&S National Bank, 1050 Cypress Ave., 88001; (505) 523-8254
	Santa Fe—U.S. Courthouse, Fed. Pl., Room 113, 87501; (505) 988-5302

NEW YORK

DO:	230 Park Ave., Room 834, New York 10169; (212) 309-0400
	Services: Business development, financial assistance, procurement assistance, minority/women opportunities; international trade (212) 309-0500
	Publications: *Your Business: A Management Guide for Small Business, Selling to Foreign Markets*
SBA:	26 Federal Plaza, Room 3100, New York 10278; (212) 264-2454; 100 S. Clinton St., #1071, Syracuse 13260; (315) 423-5383; 111 W. Huron St., #1311, Buffalo 14202; (716) 846-4301
OFed:	FIC, New York (212) 264-4464; Buffalo (716) 846-4010
	IRS, New York (212) 732-0100
	ITA, New York (212) 264-0634; Buffalo (716) 846-4191
	OSHA, New York (212) 264-9849; Buffalo (716) 684-3891

SBDC:	State University of New York (SUNY), SUNY Central Administration S-523, Albany 12246; (518) 473-5398
CoC:	152 Washington Ave., Albany 12210; (518) 465-7511
SCORE:	Albany—c/o SBA, 445 Broadway, #222, 12207; (518) 472-6300
	Binghamton—c/o Chamber of Commerce, Mutual Bldg., 13905; (607) 772-8860
	Buffalo—Fed. Bldg., 111 West Huron St., #1311, 14202; (716) 846-4516
	Jamestown—101 W. 5th, 14701; (716) 483-0485
	New York—c/o SBA, 26 Fed. Plaza, #3130, 10007; (212) 264-4507
	Rochester—601 Keating Fed. Bldg., 100 State St., 14614; (714) 263-6473
	Syracuse—1071 Fed. Bldg., 101 S. Clinton St., 13260; (315) 472-6300
	Utica—SUNY College, Mill Sq. Bldg. State & Court, Box 3050, 13501; (315) 792-7445
	Watertown—C.A.P.C. Office, Arcade P.O. Box 899, 13601; (315) 788-1200

NORTH CAROLINA

DO:	Dobbs Bldg., Room 2019, 430 N. Salisbury St., Raleigh 27611; (919) 733-7980
	Services: Business development, financial assistance, procurement assistance, minority/women opportunities; international trade (919) 733-7193
	Publications: *Big Answers to Small Business Questions, Guidelines on Starting a Business, Registering a Business Name and Organizing a Business Corporation in North Carolina, International Report* (bi-monthly)
SBA:	222 S. Church St., #300, Charlotte 28202; (704) 371-6563
OFed:	FIC, Charlotte (704) 376-3600
	ITA, Raleigh (919) 273-8234
	OSHA, Raleigh (919) 856-4770
SBDC:	University of North Carolina, 820 Clay St., Raleigh 27605; (919) 733-4643; (800) 258-0862
CoC:	336 Fayetteville St. Mall, P.O. Box 2508, Raleigh 27602; (919) 828-0758
SCORE:	Asheville—Fed. Bldg., Room 272, 28801
	Charlotte—c/o SBA, 222 S. Church St., #200, 28202; (704) 371-6567
	Kill Devil Hill—c/o Outer Banks Chamb. of Comm., P.O. Box 1757, 27984; (919) 261-2626
	Raleigh—Century P.O. Station, Box 406, 27602; (919) 856-4739

NORTH DAKOTA

DO: Liberty Memorial Bldg., Bismarck 58505; (701) 224-2810; in state: (800) 472-2111

Services: Business development, financial assistance, procurement assistance, minority/women opportunities; international trade (701) 224-2810

Publications: *Steps to Starting a Business, Manufacturer's Guide, North Dakota Guide to International Trade*

SBA: 657 2nd Ave. North, Room 218, Fargo 58102; (701) 237-5771, ext. 131

OFed: (Bismarck)
OSHA, (701) 225-4011, ext. 521

SBDC: University of North Dakota, 217 South 4th St., P.O. Box 1576, Grand Forks 58206; (701) 780-3403

CoC: 808 Third Ave., S., P.O. Box 2467, Fargo 58108; (701) 237-9461

SCORE: Fargo—Box 3086, 58108; (701) 237-5771

Grand Forks—c/o Chamber of Commerce, 202 N. 3rd St., 58206; (701) 795-6153

Minot—1821 11th St., SW, 58701; (701) 839-4678

OHIO

DO: P.O. Box 1001, Columbus 43266-0101; (614) 466-1876; in state: (800) 282-1085

Services: Business development, financial assistance, procurement assistance, minority/women opportunities; international trade (614) 466-5017

Publications: *Export Service Directory, International Business Opportunities* (monthly)

SBA: 85 Marconi Blvd., #512, Columbus 43215; (614) 469-6860; AJC Fed. Bldg., 1240 E. 9th St., #317, Cleveland 44199; (216) 522-4180; 550 Main St., #5028, Cincinnati 45202; (513) 684-2814

OFed: FIC, Cleveland (216) 522-4040; Columbus (614) 221-1014

IRS, Cleveland (216) 522-3000; Cincinnati (513) 621-6281

ITA, Cleveland (216) 522-4750; Cincinnati (513) 684-2944

OSHA, Cleveland (216) 522-3818; Cincinnati (513) 684-3784

SBDC: Columbus Chamber of Commerce, 37 N. High St., Columbus 43216; (614) 221-1321

CoC: 35 East Gay St., 2nd Fl., Columbus 43215-3181; (614) 228-4201

SCORE: Cincinnati—c/o SBA, 550 Main St., Room 5028, 45202;
(513) 684-2812
Cleveland—c/o SBA, 317 AJC Fed. Bldg., 1240 E. 9th St.,
44128; (216) 522-4196
Columbus—c/o SBA, Fed. Bldg., 85 Marconi Blvd., 43215
Toledo—1946 N. 13th St., Suite 352, 43624;
(419) 259-7598
Youngstown—Williamson School of Business, 410 Wick
Ave., Room 216, 44555; (216) 746-2687

OKLAHOMA

DO: 6601 Broadway Extension, Oklahoma City 73116;
(405) 521-2401
Services: Business development, procurement assistance,
minority/women opportunities; international trade
(405) 521-3501
Publications: *OSBDC Newsletter* (quarterly)

SBA: Fed. Bldg., 200 NW 5th St., #670, Oklahoma City 73102;
(405) 231-4301

OFed: FIC, Oklahoma City (405) 231-4868; Tulsa (918) 584-4193
ITA, Oklahoma City (405) 231-5302; Tulsa (918) 581-7650
OSHA, Oklahoma City (405) 231-5351

SBDC: Southeastern Oklahoma State University, Station A, Box
4194, Durant 74701; (405) 924-0277; (800) 522-6154

CoC: 4020 N. Lincoln Blvd., Oklahoma City 73105;
(405) 424-4003

SCORE: Oklahoma City—c/o SBA, 200 NW 5th St., Suite 673,
73102; (405) 231-4491
Tulsa—c/o Chamber of Commerce, 616 S. Boston, 74119;
(918) 585-1201

OREGON

DO: 595 Cottage St., NE, Salem 97310; (503) 373-1200; in
state: (800) 233-3306, (800) 547-7842
Services: Business development, financial assistance,
procurement assistance, minority/women opportunities;
international trade (503) 229-5625
Publications: *Services for Oregon Businesses, Oregon
Exporter's Handbook, International Trade Directory*

SBA: 1220 S.W. Third Ave., #676, Portland 97204;
(503) 294-5203

OFed: (Portland)
FIC, (503) 221-2222
IRS, (503) 221-3960
ITA, (503) 221-3001
OSHA, (503) 221-2251

SBDC: Lane Community College, Downtown Center, 1059
Willamette St., Eugene 97401; (503) 726-2250

CoC:	1149 Court St., N.E., P.O. Box 12519, Salem 97309; (503) 588-0050
SCORE:	Eugene—673 W. 10th, 97402 (503) 484-5485
	Portland—c/o SBA, 1220 SW 3rd Ave., Room 661, 97204; (503) 221-3441
	Salem—P.O. Box 2184, 97308; (503) 370-2896

PENNSYLVANIA

DO:	404 Forum Bldg., Harrisburg 17120; (717) 783-5700
	Services: Business development, financial assistance, procurement assistance, minority/women opportunities; international trade (717) 787-7190
	Publications: *Resource Directory for Small Business, Starting a Small Business in Pennsylvania, Export Opportunity Bulletin* (bi-monthly)
SBA:	100 Chestnut St., #309, Harrisburg 17101; (717) 782-3840; Philadelphia: Allendale Square, 475 Allendale Rd., #201, King of Prussia 19406; (215) 962-3700, (215) 962-3800
OFed:	FIC, Pittsburgh (412) 644-4636; Philadelphia (215) 597-7042
	IRS, Pittsburgh (412) 281-0112
	ITA, Pittsburgh (412) 644-2850; Philadelphia (215) 597-2866
	OSHA, Pittsburgh (412) 644-2905; Philadelphia (215) 597-4955
SBDC:	University of Pennsylvania, The Wharton School, 3620 Locus Walk, Philadelphia, 19104
CoC:	222 N. Third St., Harrisburg 17101; (717) 255-3252
SCORE:	Erie—3537 W. 12 St., 16505
	Harrisburg—101 Chestnut, Suite 309, 17101; (717) 782-3874
	Philadelphia—3535 Market St., 3rd Fl., #3210, 19104; (215) 569-5834
	Pittsburgh—c/o SBA, 5th Fl., 960 Penn Ave., 15222; (412) 644-5447
	Scranton—Washington Ave. & Linden, Fed. Postal Bldg., Room 334, 18503; (717) 347-4611

PUERTO RICO

DO:	Box S, 4275 Old San Juan Station, San Juan 00905; (809) 758-4747
	Services: Business development, financial assistance; international trade (809) 725-7254
SBA:	Fed. Bldg., Chardon Ave., Hato Rey 00919; (809) 753-4519
OFed:	n.a.

SBDC:	University of Puerto Rico, Mayaguez Campus, Box 5253, Mayaguez 00709; (809) 834-3590
CoC:	100 Tetuan St., Old San Juan 00904; (809) 721-6060
SCORE:	U.S. Fed. Bldg., Ave. Chardon, Room 691, Hato Rey 00918; (809) 753-4515

RHODE ISLAND

DO:	7 Jackson Walkway, Providence 02903; (401) 277-2601
	Services: Business development, financial assistance, procurement assistance, minority/women opportunities; international trade (401) 277-2601
	Publications: *Deadline, Starting a Business in Rhode Island, Guide to International Trade in Rhode Island, Export Quarterly*
SBA:	380 Westminster Mall, 5th Fl., Providence 02903; (401) 528-4561
OFed:	(Providence)
	FIC, (401) 331-5565
	ITA, (401) 528-5104
	OSHA, (401) 528-4669
SBDC:	Bryant College, 450 Douglas Pike, Smithfield 02830; (401) 232-6111
CoC:	91 Park St., Providence 02908; (401) 272-1400
SCORE:	Providence—c/o SBA, 380 Westminster Mall, 02903; (401) 528-4571

SOUTH CAROLINA

DO:	P.O. Box 927, Columbia 29202; (803) 737-0400; in state: (800) 922-6684
	Services: Business development, financial assistance, procurement assistance, minority/women opportunities; international trade (803) 737-0400
	Publications: *Business Formation & Expansion Manual*
SBA:	1835 Assembly St., #358, Columbia 29201; (803) 765-5376
OFed:	(Columbia)
	ITA, (803) 765-5345
	OSHA, (803) 765-5904
SBDC:	University of South Carolina, College of Business Administration, Columbia 29208; (803) 777-4907
CoC:	Bankers Trust Tower, 1301 Gervais St., #520, P.O. Box 11278, Columbia 29211; (803) 799-4601
SCORE:	Charleston—Fed. Bldg., 334 Meeting St., Room 505, 29403; (803) 724-4778
	Columbia—Fed. Bldg., 1835 Assembly St., Room 965C, P.O. Box 2786, 29202; (803) 765-5131

SOUTH DAKOTA

DO: Capital Lake Plaza, Pierre, SD 57501; (605) 773-5032; (800) 952-3625

Services: Business development, financial assistance, procurement assistance, minority/women opportunities; international trade (605) 677-5536

Publications: "Business Startup Kits"

SBA: Security Bldg., 101 S. Main Ave., #101, Sioux Falls 57102; (605) 336-2980, ext. 231

OFed: (Omaha)
ITA, (402) 221-3664

SBDC: University of South Dakota, Business Research Bureau, 414 E. Clarke St., Vermillon 57069; (605) 677-5272

CoC: P.O. Box 190, Pierre 57501; (605) 224-6161

SCORE: Rapid City—c/o Rapid City Chamber of Commerce, P.O. Box 747, 57709; (605) 343-1744

Sioux Falls—c/o SBA, Security Bldg., 101 S. Main Ave., #101, 57102; (605) 336-4231

TENNESSEE

DO: 320 6th Ave. N., 7th Fl., Rachel Jackson Bldg., Nashville 37219; (615) 741-2626; in state: (800) 872-7201

Services: Business development, financial assistance, procurement assistance, minority/women opportunities; international trade (615) 741-5870

Publications: *A Guide to Doing Business in Tennessee, International Trade Directory, Export Guide & Services Directory*

SBA: Parkway Towers, 404 James Robertson Pkwy., #1012, Nashville 37219; (615) 736-5881

OFed: FIC, Nashville (615) 242-5056; Memphis (901) 521-3285
IRS, Nashville (615) 259-4601
ITA, Nashville (615) 736-5161; Memphis (901) 521-4137
OSHA, Nashville (615) 736-5313

SBDC: Memphis State University, Fogelman Exec. Center, Central & DeLoach, Suite 220W, Memphis 38152; (901) 454-2500

CoC: 226 Capitol Blvd., #800, Nashville 37219; (615) 256-5141

SCORE: Knoxville—Farragut Bldg., 530 S. Gay St., Room 224, 37920; (615) 673-4534

Memphis—969 Madison Ave., Room 901, 38104; (901) 521-3588

Nashville—c/o SBA, Parkway Towers, 404 James Robertson Pkwy., #1004, 37219

TEXAS

DO: P.O. Box 12728, Capitol Station, 410 East Fifth St., Austin 78711; (512) 472-5059

Services: Business development, financial assistance, procurement assistance; international trade (512) 472-5059

Publications: *The Business Plan: A Suggested Model, Texas Small Business Minority Directory*

SBA: 1100 Commerce St., Room 3C36, Dallas 75242; (214) 767-0605; 2525 Murworth, #112, Houston 77054; (713) 660-4401; 7400 Blanco, #200, San Antonio 78216; (512) 229-6250

OFed: FIC, Austin (512) 472-5494; Dallas (214) 742-2440; Houston (713) 229-2552

IRS, Austin (512) 472-1974; Houston (713) 965-0440

ITA, Austin (512) 472-5059; Dallas (214) 767-0542

OSHA, Austin (512) 482-5783; Houston (713) 222-4305

SBDC: University of Houston, 401 Louisiana St., Houston 77002; (713) 223-1141; Community College, 302 N. Market, #300, Dallas 75202; (214) 747-0555

CoC: 206 West 13th, Suite A, Austin 78701; (512) 472-1594

SCORE: Austin—572 Fed. Bldg., 300 E. 8th St., 78701

Dallas—c/o SBA, 1100 Commerce St., 75242; (214) 767-0472

El Paso—c/o SBA, 10737 Gateway West, #320, 79935; (915) 541-7155

Houston—2525 Murworth, Suite 112, 77054; (713) 660-4401

San Antonio—c/o SBA, 7400 Blanco Rd., #200, North Star 78216; (512) 229-4535

UTAH

DO: 660 S. Second St., #418, Salt Lake City 84111; (801) 581-7905

Services: Business development, financial assistance, procurement assistance, minority/women opportunities; international trade (801) 533-5325

Publications: *Going into Business in Utah: Playing the Game, Business Planning Guide, Utah Export Directory*

SBA: Wallace F. Bennett Fed. Bldg., 125 S. State St., #2237, Salt Lake City 84138; (801) 524-3209

OFed: (Salt Lake City)

FIC, (801) 524-5353

ITA, (801) 524-5116

OSHA, (801) 524-5080

SBDC: University of Utah, 660 S. 200 E., Room 418, Salt Lake City 84111; (801) 581-7905

CoC:	175 E. 400th S., Suite 600, Salt Lake City 84111; (801) 364-3631
SCORE:	Salt Lake City—c/o SBA, 125 S. State St., Room 2237, 84138; (801) 524-5805

VERMONT

DO:	The Pavillion, 109 State St., Montpelier 05602; (802) 828-3221; in state: (800) 622-4553
	Services: Business development, financial assistance; international trade (802) 828-3221
	Publications: *Doing Business in Vermont, Vermont Buyer's Guide*
SBA:	87 State St., Room 205 (P.O. Box 605), Montpelier 05602; (802) 828-4422
OFed:	ITA, Boston, MA (617) 565-8563
SBDC:	University of Vermont, Extension Service, Morrill Hall, Burlington 05405; (802) 656-4479
CoC:	P.O. Box 37, Montpelier 05602; (802) 223-3443, (802) 229-0154
SCORE:	Burlington—c/o GBIC, 7 Burlington Square, 2nd Fl., 05402; (802) 862-5726
	Montpelier—Fed. Bldg., 87 State St., P.O. Box 605, 05602; (802) 828-4422

VIRGINIA

DO:	1000 Washington Bldg., Richmond 23219; (804) 786-3791
	Services: Business development, financial assistance, minority/women opportunities; international trade (804) 786-3791
	Publications: *Virginia Business Resource Directory, Establishing a Business in Virginia*
SBA:	Fed. Bldg., 400 N. 8th St., #3015, Richmond 23240; (804) 771-2617
OFed:	FIC, Norfolk (804) 441-3101; Richmond (804) 643-4928; Roanoke (703) 982-8591
	IRS, Richmond (804) 649-2361; Arlington (703) 557-9230
	ITA, Richmond (804) 771-2246
	OSHA, Richmond (804) 786-5873
SBDC:	(See **District of Columbia**)
CoC:	9 S. Fifth St., Richmond 23219; (804) 644-1607
SCORE:	Fredericksburg—c/o Chamber of Commerce, P.O. Box 7476, 22404; (703) 786-3235
	Richmond—400 N. 8th St., Room 3015, 23240; (804) 771-2765
	Roanoke—Fed. Bldg., Franklin Rd. & 2nd St., SW, P.O. Box 1366, 24011; (703) 982-4334

WASHINGTON

DO:
441 Todd Hall, Washington State University, Pullman 99164; (509) 335-1576

Services: Business development, financial assistance, procurement assistance, minority/women opportunities; international trade (206) 464-7076

Publications: *Starting a Business in Washington, Operating a Homebased Business in Washington, The Exporter's Guide*

SBA:
915 Second Ave., #1792, Seattle 98174; (206) 442-5534; 920 Riverside Ave., #651, Spokane 99201; (509) 456-3786

OFed:
FIC, Seattle (206) 442-0570

IRS, Seattle (206) 442-1040

ITA, Seattle (206) 442-5615; Spokane (509) 456-4557

OSHA, Bellview (206) 442-7520

SBDC:
Washington State University, 441 Todd Hall, Pullman 99164-4740; (509) 335-1576

CoC:
P.O. Box 658, Olympia 98507; (206) 943-1600

SCORE:
Seattle—c/o SBA, 915 Wind Ave., Room 1792, 98174; (206) 442-4518

Spokane—c/o SBA, West 601 1st Ave., 10th Fl. E., 99204; (509) 456-3786

WEST VIRGINIA

DO:
Capitol Complex, Charleston 25305; (304) 348-2960

Services: Business development, financial assistance, procurement assistance, minority/women opportunities; international trade (304) 348-0400

Publications: *Starting a Business in West Virginia*

SBA:
550 Eagan St., #309, Charleston 25301; (304) 347-5220

OFed:
(Charleston)

ITA, (304) 347-5123

OSHA, (304) 347-5937

SBDC:
1115 Virginia St., East Charleston 25301; (304) 348-2960

CoC:
1101 Kanawha Valley Bldg., P.O. Box 2789, Charleston 25330; (304) 342-1115

SCORE:
Charleston—2300 MacCorble Ave., SE, 25304; (304) 357-4880

Wheeling—c/o Chamber of Commerce, 1233 Main St., 26003; (304) 233-2575

WISCONSIN

DO: 123 W. Washington Ave., P.O. Box 7970, Madison 53707; (608) 266-0562; in state: (800) 435-7287

Services: Business development, financial assistance, procurement assistance, minority/women opportunities; international trade (608) 266-1480

Publications: "Wisconsin Business Startup Kits," *Wisconsin International Trade Handbook, Wisconsin International Trade Magazine* (bi-monthly)

SBA: 212 E. Washington Ave., #213, Madison 53703; (608) 264-5261; 310 W. Wisconsin Ave., #400, Milwaukee 53203; (414) 291-3941

OFed: (Milwaukee)

FIC, (414) 271-2273

IRS, (414) 271-3780

ITA, (414) 291-3473

SBDC: University of Wisconsin, 602 State St., 2nd Fl., Madison 53703

CoC: 501 E. Washington Ave., P.O. Box 352, Madison 53701; (608) 258-3400

SCORE: Eau Claire—Fed. Bldg., 510 So. Barstow St., Room B11, 54701; (715) 834-1573

Madison—802 W. Broadway, Suite L-4, 53713; (608) 264-5117

Milwaukee—c/o SBA, 310 W. Wisconsin Ave., Room 400, 53203; (414) 291-3942

WYOMING

DO: Economic Development and Stabilization Board, Herschler Bldg. 3-E, Cheyenne 82002; (307) 777-7287

Services: Business development, financial assistance, procurement assistance, international trade

SBA: 100 E. B Street, Room 4001, Casper 82602; (307) 261-5761

OFed: FIC, IRS, ITA, OSHA, (see **Colorado**)

SBDC: Casper Community College, 130 N. Ash, Suite 2A, 82601; (307) 235-4825

CoC: Contact local chambers in Jackson Hole, Rock Springs, and Sheridan

SCORE: Casper—c/o SBA, 100 E. B Street, Room 4001, 82602; (307) 261-5761

FEDERAL CONTACTS FOR MINORITY AND WOMEN'S BUSINESSES: THE OFFICE OF SMALL AND DISADVANTAGED BUSINESS UTILIZATION (OSDBU)

DEPARTMENT OF AGRICULTURE
OSDBU
14th St. & Independence Ave., S.W.
Rm. 126-W
Washington, DC 20250
(202) 447-7117

DEPARTMENT OF COMMERCE
OSDBU
14th St. & Constitution Ave., N.W.
Rm. H6411
Washington, DC 20230
(202) 377-3387

DEPARTMENT OF DEFENSE
OSDBU
Rm. 2A340, The Pentagon
Washington, DC 20301
(202) 697-1688

DEPARTMENT OF THE AIR FORCE
OSDBU
Rm. 4C255. The Pentagon
Washington, DC 20330
(202) 697-5373

DEPARTMENT OF THE ARMY
OSDBU
Rm. 2A712. The Pentagon
Washington, DC 20310
(202) 697-2868 695-9800

DEPARTMENT OF THE NAVY
NICRAD Program
5001 Eisenhower Ave.
Alexandria, VA 22333
(703) 274-9315

DEFENSE LOGISTICS AGENCY
OSDBU
Rm. 4B110. Cameron Station
Washington, DC 22314
(703) 274-6977

DEPARTMENT OF THE INTERIOR
OSDBU
18th & C Sts., N.W.
Rm. 2747
Washington, DC 20240
(202) 343–4907

DEPARTMENT OF JUSTICE
OSDBU
10th St. & Pennsylvania Ave., N.W.
Washington, DC 20530
(202) 724-6271

DEPARTMENT OF LABOR
OSDBU
200 Constitution Ave., N.W.
Rm. 5-1004
Washington, DC 20210
(202) 523-9151

DEPARTMENT OF STATE
OSDBU
Rm. 513 State Annex-6
Washington, DC 20520
(703) 235-9580

DEPARTMENT OF TRANSPORTATION
OSDBU
400 7th St., S.W.
Rm. 9414
Washington, DC 20590
(202) 426-1902

DEPARTMENT OF THE TREASURY
OSDBU
15th St. & Pennsylvania Ave., N.W.
Rm. 1320
Washington, DC 20220
(202) 566-9616

ADMINISTRATIVE OFFICE OF THE
    U.S. COURTS
Office of Supply and Equipment
719 13th St., N.W.
Rm. 500
Washington, DC 20544
(202) 633-6299

DEPARTMENT OF EDUCATION
OSDBU
400 Maryland Ave., S.W.
Rm. 2141
Washington, DC 20202
(202) 245-9582

DEPARTMENT OF ENERGY
OSDBU
100 Independence Ave., S.W.
Rm. 1E061
Washington, DC 20585
(202) 252-8214

DEPARTMENT OF HEALTH AND
    HUMAN SERVICES
OSDBU
200 Independence Ave., S.W.
Rm. 513D
Washington, DC 20201
(202) 245-7300

DEPARTMENT OF HOUSING AND
    URBAN DEVELOPMENT
OSDBU
7th & D Sts., S.W.
Rm. 10226
Washington, DC 20410
(202) 755-1428

AGENCY FOR INTERNATIONAL
    DEVELOPMENT
OSDBU
320 21st St., N.W.
Rm. 648
Washington, DC 20523
(202) 235-1840

BUSINESS SERVICE CENTER
7th & D Sts., SW
Rm. 1050
Washington, DC 20407
(202) 472-1804

OFFICE OF CIVIL RIGHTS
Urban Mass Transit Authority
Procurement Program (UMTA)
400 7th St., SE
Rm. 7412
Washington, DC 20590
(202) 426-2285

COMMODITY FUTURES TRADING
    COMMISSION
Office of Administrative Services
2033 K St., N.W.
Rm. 205
Washington, DC 20581
(202) 254-9735

U.S. CONSUMER PRODUCT SAFETY
    COMMISSION
EEO and Minority Enterprise
5401 Westbard Ave.
Washington, DC 20207
(202) 492-6570

ENVIRONMENTAL PROTECTION
    AGENCY
OSDBU
1921 Jefferson Davis Hwy.
Rm. 1108, Crystal Mall 2
Washington, DC 20460
(703) 557-7305

EXECUTIVE OFFICE OF THE
    PRESIDENT
Office of Administration
17th St. & Pennsylvania Ave., N.W.
Rm. 494
Washington, DC 20500
(202) 395-3314

FARM CREDIT ADMINISTRATION
Office of Administration
1501 Farm Credit Dr.
McLean, VA 22102-5090
(703) 883-4151

FEDERAL MARITIME COMMISSION
Administrative Services Activity
1100 L St., N.W.
Rm. 10409
Washington, DC 20573
(202) 523-5900

FEDERAL MEDIATION AND
   CONCILIATION SERVICE
Office of Administrative Services
2100 K St., N.W.
Rm. 100
Washington, DC 20427
(202) 653-5310

FEDERAL EMERGENCY
   MANAGEMENT AGENCY
Office of Acquisition Management
500 C St., S.W.
Rm. 728
Washington, DC 20472
(202) 646-3743

FEDERAL TRADE COMMISSION
Office of Procurement and Contracts
6th St. & Pennsylvania Ave., N.W.
Rm. 705
Washington, DC 20580
(202) 523-5552

GENERAL SERVICES
   ADMINISTRATION
OSDBU
18th & F St., N.W.
Rm. 6019
Washington, DC 20405
(202) 566-1021

UNITED STATES INFORMATION
   AGENCY
Office of Contracts
300 C St., S.W.
Rm. 1619
Washington, DC 20547
(202) 485-6404

INTERSTATE COMMERCE
   COMMISSION
Office of Procurement and Contracting
12th & Constitution Ave., N.W.
Rm. 1315
Washington, DC 20423
(202) 275-0893

NATIONAL AERONAUTICS AND
   SPACE ADMINISTRATION
OSDBU
600 Independence Ave., S.W.
Rm. 116
Washington, DC 20546
(202) 453-2088

NATIONAL ENDOWMENT FOR
   THE HUMANITIES
Office of Administrative Services
1100 Pennsylvania Ave., N.W.
Rm. 202
Washington, DC 20506
(202) 786-0233

NATIONAL LABOR RELATIONS
   BOARD
Office of Procurement
1717 Pennsylvania Ave., N.W.
Rm. 400
Washington, DC 20570
(Actual location)
1375 K St., N.W.
Washington, DC
(202) 633-0623

NATIONAL SCIENCE FOUNDATION
OSDBU
1800 G St., N.W.
Rm. 1260
Washington, DC 20550
(202) 357-7464

NUCLEAR REGULATORY
   COMMISSION
OSDBU
Rm. 7217, Maryland Natl. Bank Bldg.
Washington, DC 20555
(202) 492-4665

OFFICE OF PERSONNEL
  MANAGEMENT
OSDBU
1900 E St., N.W.
Rm. 1308
Washington, DC 20415
(202) 653-6300

PEACE CORPS
Office of Contracts
806 Connecticut Ave., N.W.
Rm. 300-P
Washington, DC 20526
(202) 254-3513

PENNSYLVANIA AVENUE
  DEVELOPMENT CORPORATION
Office of Real Estate
1331 Pennsylvania Ave. N.W.
Rm. 1220-N
Washington, DC 20004-1703
(202) 724-9091

U.S. GOVERNMENT PRINTING
  OFFICE
Office of General Procurement
North Capitol and H Sts., N.W.
Rm. A332
Washington, DC 20401
(202) 275-2470

Office of Printing Procurement
North Capital & H Sts., N.W.
Rm. C899
Washington, DC 20401
(202) 275-2265

U.S. POSTAL SERVICE
Office of Material Management
475 L'Enfant Plaza, S.W.
Rm. 1340
Washington, DC 20260-6201
(202) 268-4633

OFFICE OF PROCUREMENT AND
  GRANTS MANAGEMENT
1441 L St., N.W.
Rm. 219
Washington, DC 20416
(202) 653-6639

SMALL BUSINESS ADMINISTRATION
SBA District Office
1111 18th St., N.W.
Rm. 625
Washington, DC 20036
(202) 634-1805

SMITHSONIAN INSTITUTION
Office of Supply Services
955 L'Enfant Plaza, S.W.
Rm. 3120
Washington, DC 20024
(202) 287-3343

TENNESSEE VALLEY AUTHORITY
c/o Natural Resources and Economic
  Development
Rm. 2J107, Old City Hall
Knoxville, TN 37902
(615) 632-6030

VETERANS ADMINISTRATION
OSDBU
811 Vermont Ave., N.W.
Rm. 315
Washington, DC 20420
(202) 376-6996

SBA DIRECTORY OF BUSINESS DEVELOPMENT PUBLICATIONS

SBA Directory of Business Development Publications

"Building Excellence in Enterprise"

THANK YOU
for your interest in the U.S. Small Business Administration. We are pleased to offer you our extensive library of business publications.

FINANCIAL MANAGEMENT AND ANALYSIS

FM 1   ABC's OF BORROWING * _____
Some small business people cannot understand why a lending institution refused to lend them money. Others have no trouble getting funds but are surprised to find strings attached to their loans. Learn the fundamentals of borrowing ... $1.00

**FM 2   PROFIT COSTING AND
            PRICING FOR MANUFACTURERS _____**
Uncover the latest techniques for pricing your products profitably ... $1.00

FM 3   BASIC BUDGETS FOR PROFIT PLANNING * _____
This publication takes the worry out of putting together a comprehensive budgeting system to monitor your profits and assess your financial operations ... $0.50

FM 4   UNDERSTANDING CASH FLOW _____
In order to survive, a business must have enough cash to meet its obligations. The owner/manager is shown how to plan for the movement of cash through the business and thus plan for future requirements ... $1.00

**FM 5   A VENTURE CAPITAL PRIMER
            FOR SMALL BUSINESS * _____**
This best-seller highlights the venture capital resources available and how to develop a proposal for obtaining these funds ... $0.50

**FM 6   ACCOUNTING SERVICES
            FOR SMALL SERVICE FIRMS _____**
Sample profit/loss statements are used to illustrate how accounting services can help expose and correct trouble spots in a business' financial records ... $0.50

**FM 7   ANALYZE YOUR RECORDS
            TO REDUCE COSTS _____**
Cost reduction is not simply slashing any and all expenses. Understand the nature of expenses and how they inter-relate with sales, inventories and profits. Achieve greater profits through more efficient use of the dollar ... $0.50

FM 8   BUDGETING IN A SMALL SERVICE FIRM _____
Learn how to set up and keep sound financial records. Study how to effectively use journals, ledgers and charts to increase profits ... $0.50

**FM 9   SOUND CASH MANAGEMENT
            AND BORROWING _____**
Avoid a "cash crisis" through proper use of cash budgets, cash flow projections and planned borrowing concepts ... $0.50

FM 10   RECORDKEEPING IN A SMALL BUSINESS * _____
Need some basic advice on setting up a useful record keeping system? This publication describes how ... $1.00

**FM 11   SIMPLE BREAKEVEN
            ANALYSIS FOR SMALL STORES _____**
Learn how "breakeven analysis" enables the manager/owner to make better decisions concerning sales, profits and costs ... $1.00

**FM 12   A PRICING CHECKLIST
            FOR SMALL RETAILERS _____**
The owner/manager of a small retail business can use this checklist to apply proven pricing strategies that can lead to profits ... $0.50

**FM 13   PRICING YOUR PRODUCTS
            AND SERVICES PROFITABLY _____**
Discusses how to price your products profitably, how to use the various techniques of pricing and when to use these techniques to your advantage ... $1.00

GENERAL MANAGEMENT AND PLANNING

MP 1   EFFECTIVE BUSINESS COMMUNICATIONS _____
Explains the importance of business communications and how they play a valuable role in business success ... $0.50

**MP 2   LOCATING OR RELOCATING
            YOUR BUSINESS _____**
Learn how a company's market, available labor force, transportation and raw materials are affected when selecting a business location ... $1.00

**MP 3   PROBLEMS IN MANAGING
            A FAMILY-OWNED BUSINESS _____**
Specific problems exist when attempting to make a family-owned business successful. This publication offers suggestions on how to overcome these difficulties ... $0.50

**MP 4   BUSINESS PLAN
            FOR SMALL MANUFACTURERS _____**
Designed to help an owner/manager of a small manufacturing firm. This publication covers all the basic information necessary to develop an effective business plan ... $1.00

**MP 5   BUSINESS PLAN
            FOR SMALL CONSTRUCTION FIRMS _____**
This publication is designed to help an owner/manager of a small construction company pull together the resources to develop a business plan ... $1.00

**MP 6   PLANNING AND GOAL SETTING
            FOR SMALL BUSINESS * _____**
Learn how to plan for success ... $0.50

MP 7   FIXING PRODUCTION MISTAKES _____
Structured as a checklist, this publication emphasizes the steps that should be taken by a manufacturer when a production mistake has been found ... $0.50

MP 8   SHOULD YOU LEASE OR BUY EQUIPMENT? _____
Describes various aspects of the lease/buy decision. It lists advantages and disadvantages of leasing and provides a format for comparing the costs of the two ... $0.50

MP 9   BUSINESS PLAN FOR RETAILERS _____
Learn how to develop a business plan for a retail business ... $1.00

MP 10   CHOOSING A RETAIL LOCATION _____
Learn about current retail site selection techniques such as demographic and traffic analysis. This publication addresses the hard questions the retailer must answer before making the choice of a store location ... $1.00

**MP 11   BUSINESS PLAN
            FOR SMALL SERVICE FIRMS _____**
Outlines the key points to be included in the business plan of a small service firm ... $0.50

MP 12   CHECKLIST FOR GOING INTO BUSINESS * _____
This best-seller highlights important considerations you should know in reaching a decision to start your own business. It also includes a checklist for going into business ... $0.50

**MP 14   HOW TO GET STARTED
            WITH A SMALL BUSINESS COMPUTER _____**
Helps you forecast your computer needs, evaluate the alternative choices and select the right computer system for your business ... $1.00

**MP 15   THE BUSINESS PLAN
            FOR HOMEBASED BUSINESS * _____**
Provides a comprehensive approach to developing a business plan for a homebased business. If you are convinced that a profitable home business is attainable, this publication will provide a step-by-step guide to develop a plan for your business ... $1.00

MP 16   HOW TO BUY OR SELL A BUSINESS _____
Learn several techniques used in determining the best price to buy or sell a small business ... $1.00

---

* Denotes our best sellers

**Office of Business Development
U.S. SMALL BUSINESS ADMINISTRATION**

MP 17   PURCHASING FOR OWNERS OF SMALL PLANTS_____
Presents an outline of an effective purchasing program. Also includes a bibliography for further research into industrial purchasing ... $0.50

MP 18   BUYING FOR RETAIL STORES _____
Discusses the latest trends in retail buying. Includes a bibliography that references a wide variety of private and public sources of information on most aspects of retail buying ... $1.00

MP 19   SMALL BUSINESS DECISION MAKING _____
Acquaint yourself with the wealth of information available on management approaches to identify, analyze and solve business problems ... $1.00

MP 20   BUSINESS CONTINUATION PLANNING _____
Provides an overview of business owner's life insurance needs that are not typically considered until after the death of one of the business' principal owners ... $1.00

MP 21   DEVELOPING A STATEGIC BUSINESS PLAN * _____
Helps you develop a strategic action plan for your small business ... $1.00

MP 22   INVENTORY MANAGEMENT _____
Discusses the purpose of inventory management, types of inventories, record keeping and forecasting inventory levels ... $0.50

MP 23   TECHNIQUES FOR PROBLEM SOLVING _____
Instructs the small business person on the key techniques of problem solving and problem identification, as well as designing and implementing a plan to correct these problems ... $1.00

MP 24   TECHNIQUES FOR PRODUCTIVITY IMPROVEMENT _____
Learn to increase worker output through motiviating "quality of work life" concepts and tailoring benefits to meet the needs of the employees ... $1.00

MP 25   SELECTING THE LEGAL STRUCTURE FOR YOUR BUSINESS _____
Discusses the various legal structures that a small business can use in setting up its operations. It briefly identifies the types of legal structures and lists the advantages and disadvantages of each ... $0.50

MP 26   EVALUATING FRANCHISE OPPORTUNITIES _____
Although the success rate for franchise-owned businesses is significantly better than start-up businesses, success is not guaranteed. Evaluate franchise opportunities and select the business that's right for you ... $0.50

MP 27   STARTING A RETAIL TRAVEL AGENCY _____
Travel agencies are a rewarding yet challenging business. Learn how to start your own agency ... $1.00

MP 28   SMALL BUSINESS RISK MANAGEMENT GUIDE _____
Strengthen your insurance program by identifying, minimizing and eliminating business risks. This guide can help you secure adequate insurance protection for your company ... $1.00

MP 29   QUALITY CHILD CARE MAKES GOOD BUSINESS SENSE_____
Starting a childcare center involves all the challenges of any small business and also requires dedication to the well being of children. This comprehensive manual developed by childcare professionals in both private and public sectors, explains the business and academic dimensions of operating a childcare center... $2.00

CRIME PREVENTION

CP 1   REDUCING SHOPLIFTING LOSSES _____
Learn the latest techniques on how to spot, deter, apprehend and prosecute shoplifters ... $0.50

CP 2   CURTAILING CRIME — INSIDE AND OUT _____
Positive steps can be taken to curb crime. They include safeguards against employee dishonesty and ways to control shoplifting. In addition, this publication includes measures to outwit bad check passing and ways to prevent burglary and robbery ... $1.00

CP 3   A SMALL BUSINESS GUIDE TO COMPUTER SECURITY _____
The computer is a valuable and essential part of many small businesses and your computer related assets need protection. This publication helps you understand the nature of computer security risks and offers timely advice on how to control them ... $1.00

MARKETING

MT 1   CREATIVE SELLING: THE COMPETITIVE EDGE * _____
Explains how to use creative selling techniques to increase profits ... $0.50

MT 2   MARKETING FOR SMALL BUSINESS: AN OVERVIEW * _____
Provides an overview of "Marketing" concepts and contains an extensive bibliography of sources covering the subject of marketing ... $1.00

MT 3   IS THE INDEPENDENT SALES AGENT FOR YOU? _____
Provides guidelines that help the owner of a small company determine if a sales agent is needed and pointers on how to choose one ... $0.50

MT 4   MARKETING CHECKLIST FOR SMALL RETAILERS _____
This checklist is for the owner/manager of a small retail business. The questions outlined cover customer analysis, buying, pricing and promotion and other factors in the retail marketing process ... $1.00

MT 8   RESEARCHING YOUR MARKET* _____
Learn what market research is and how you can benefit from it. Introduces inexpensive techniques that small business owners can apply to gather facts about their customer base and how to expand it ... $1.00

MT 9   SELLING BY MAIL ORDER _____
Provides basic information on how to run a successful mail order business. Includes information on product selection, pricing, testing and writing effective advertisements ... $1.00

MT 10   MARKET OVERSEAS WITH U.S. GOVERNMENT HELP _____
Entering the overseas marketplace offers exciting opportunities to increase company sales and profits. Learn about the programs available to help small businesses break into the world of exporting ... $1.00

MT 11   ADVERTISING _____
Advertising is critical to the success of any small business. Learn how you can effectively market your products and services ... $1.00

PERSONNEL MANAGEMENT

PM 1   CHECKLIST FOR DEVELOPING A TRAINING PROGRAM _____
Describes a step-by-step process of setting up an effective employee training program ... $0.50

PM 2   EMPLOYEES: HOW TO FIND AND PAY THEM _____
A business is only as good as the people in it. Learn how to find and hire the right employees ... $1.00

PM 3   MANAGING EMPLOYEE BENEFITS _____
Describes employee benefits as one part of the total compensation package and discusses proper management of benefits ... $1.00

NEW PRODUCTS/IDEAS/INVENTIONS

PI 1   CAN YOU MAKE MONEY WITH YOUR IDEA OR INVENTION? _____
This publication is a step-by-step guide which shows how you can make money by turning your creative ideas into marketable products. It is a resource for entrepreneurs attempting to establish themselves in the marketplace ... $0.50

PI 2   INTRODUCTION TO PATENTS _____
Offers some basic facts about patents to help clarify your rights. It discusses the relationships among a business, an inventor and the Patent and Trademark Office to ensure protection of your product and to avoid or win infringement suits ... $0.50

> SBA collects a minimum donation for each publication it distributes. The minimum donation amount is indicated next to the publication description.

How to Order

1. Circle the publication numbers of the title you want. If you desire more than one copy of a publication, indicate the quantity on the line to the right of the publication title.

2. Complete the following:
   Total Number of publications ordered _____
   Amount Enclosed $ _____

3. Make your check or money order payable to: U.S. Small Business Administration
   (NOTE: No cash, credit cards or purchase orders please!)

4. Mail the entire form with your donation to:
   SBA-PUBLICATIONS
   P.O. Box 30
   Denver, Colorado 80201-0030

Thank You!

Name _____

Address _____

City, State _____

Zip Code _____

SBA REGIONAL AND DISTRICT OFFICES*

SBA REGIONAL OFFICES

Region 1   Boston

For Maine, New Hampshire, Vermont,
  Massachusetts, Rhode Island, and Connecticut
60 Batterymarch, 10th Fl.
Boston, MA 02110

Region II   New York

For New York, New Jersey, Puerto Rico, and the
  Virgin Islands
26 Federal Plaza, Room 29-118
New York, NY 10278

Region III   Bala Cynwyd

For Pennsylvania, Delaware, Maryland, Virginia,
  West Virginia, and Washington, D.C.
One Bala Cynwyd Plaza, West Lobby
231 St. Asaphs Rd.
Bala Cynwyd, PA 19004

Region IV   Atlanta

For North Carolina, South Carolina, Georgia,
  Florida, Mississippi, Alabama, Tennessee, and
  Kentucky
1375 Peachtree St. NE
Atlanta, GA 30367

Region V   Chicago

For Ohio, Indiana, Michigan, Illinois, Wisconsin,
  and Minnesota
230 South Dearborn St., Room 510
Chicago, IL 60604

Region VI   Dallas

For Louisiana, Arkansas, Texas, Oklahoma, and
  New Mexico
8625 King George Dr., Bldg. C
Dallas, TX 75235-3391

Region VII   Kansas City

For Missouri, Kansas, Iowa, and Nebraska
911 Walnut St., 13th Fl.
Kansas City, MO 64106

* Check the appropriate telephone directory under "U.S. Government" for telephone numbers.

Region VIII   Denver   For North Dakota, South Dakota, Colorado,
                                  Wyoming, Utah, and Montana
                               999 18th St., Suite 701
                               Denver, CO 80202-2395

Region IX   San Francisco   For California, Arizona, Nevada, Hawaii, Guam,
                                  Trust Territories, and American Samoa
                               450 Golden Gate Ave., Box 36044
                               San Francisco, CA 94102

Region X   Seattle   For Oregon, Washington, Idaho, and Alaska
                               2615 4th Ave., Room 440
                               Seattle, WA 98121

SBA DISTRICT OFFICES

Alabama
2121 8th Ave. N.
Suite 200
Birmingham, AL 35203-2398
205/731-1344

Alaska
701 C St.
Box 67
Anchorage, AK 99513
907/271-4022

Arizona
2005 North Central Ave.
5th Fl.
Phoenix, AZ 85004-4599
602/261-3737

Arkansas
320 W. Capital Ave.
Suite 601
Little Rock, AR 72201
501/378-5871

California
2719 N. Air Fresno Dr.
Suite 107
Fresno, CA 93727
209/487-5189

330 N. Brand Blvd.
12th Fl.
Glendale, CA 91203-2304
213/894-2956

880 Front St.
Suite 4-S-29
San Diego, CA 92188-0270
619/557-7269

211 Main St.
4th Fl.
San Francisco, CA 94105-1988
415/974-0590

901 West Civic Center Dr.
Room 160
Santa Ana, CA 92703
714/836-2494

Colorado
721 19th St.
Room 420
Denver, CO. 80202-2599
303/844-3984

Connecticut
One Hartford Square West
Hartford, CT 06106
203/240-4700

Delaware
Branch Office
844 King St.
Room 1315
Lockbox 16
Wilmington, DE 19801
302/573-6294

District of Columbia
1111 18th St. NW
6th Fl.
Washington, DC 20036
202/634-4950

Florida
1320 S. Dixie Highway
Suite 501
Coral Gables, FL 33134
305/536-5521

The Center Building
1st Fl.
7825 Baymeadows Way
Jacksonville, FL 32256
904/791-3782

Georgia
1720 Peachtree Road, NW
6th Fl.
Atlanta, GA 30309
404/347-2441

Hawaii
300 Ala Moana
P.O. Box 50207
Room 2213
Honolulu, HI 96850-4981
808/541-2973

Idaho
1020 Main St.
Suite 290
Boise, ID 83702
208/334-1696

Illinois
219 South Dearborn St.
Chicago, IL 60604-1779
312/353-4528

Indiana
575 N. Pennsylvania St.
Room 578
Indianapolis, IN 46204-1584
317/269-7272

Iowa
373 Collins Rd., NE
Room 100
Cedar Rapids, IA 52402
319/399-2571

210 Walnut St.
Room 749
Des Moines, IA 50309
515/284-4422

Kansas
Main Place Bldg.
110 East Waterman St.
Wichita, KS 67202
316/269-6571

Kentucky
Federal Office Bldg.
600 Dr. Martin Luther King, Jr. Pl.
Room 188
P.O. Box 3527
Louisville, KY 40202
502/582-5976

Louisiana
Ford-Fisk Bldg.
1661 Canal St., 2nd Fl.
New Orleans, LA 70112
504/589-6685

Maine
Federal Bldg.
40 Western Ave.
Room 512
Augusta, ME 04330
207/622-8378

Maryland
10 N. Calvert St.
3rd Fl.
Baltimore, MD 21202
301/962-4392

Massachusetts
10 Causeway St.
Room 265
Boston, MA 02222-1093
617/565-5590

Michigan
McNamara Bldg.
477 Michigan Ave.
Room 515
Detroit, MI 48226
313/226-6075

Minnesota
100 N. 6th St.
Room 610C - Butler Square
Minneapolis, MN 55403-1563
612/370-2324

Mississippi
First Jackson Center
101 W. Capitol St.
4th Fl.
Jackson, MS 39201
601/965-4378

Missouri
1103 Grand Ave.
6th Fl.
Kansas City, MO 64106
816/374-3419

815 Olive St.
Room 242
St. Louis, MO 63101
314/539-6600

Montana
Federal Office Bldg.
301 South Park St.
Room 528
Helena, MT 59626
406/449-5381

Nebraska
11145 Mill Valley Rd.
Omaha, NE 68154
402/221-4691

Nevada
Box 7527 - Downtown Sta.
301 East Stewart
Las Vegas, NV 89125-2527
702/388-6611

New Hampshire
55 Pleasant St.
Room 210
P.O. Box 1257
Concord, NH 03301-1257
603/225-1400

New Jersey
60 Park Pl.
4th Fl.
Newark, NJ 07102
201/645-3683

New Mexico
Patio Plaza Bldg.
5000 Marble Ave., N.E.
Suite 320
Albuquerque, NM 87110
505/262-6171

New York
26 Federal Plaza
Room 3100
New York, NY 10278
212/264-4355

Federal Bldg.
100 South Clinton, St.
Room 1071
Syracuse, NY 13260
315/423-5383

North Carolina
222 South Church St.
Room 300
Charlotte, NC 28202
704/371-6563

North Dakota
Federal Bldg.
657 Second Avenue, N.
Room 218
Fargo, ND 58108-3086
701/239-5131

Ohio
AJC Federal Bldg.
1240 E. 9th St.
Room 317
Cleveland, OH 44199
216/522-4180

Federal Bldg., U.S. Courthouse
85 Marconi Blvd.
Room 512
Columbus, OH 43215
614/469-6860

Oklahoma
200 N.W. 5th St.
Suite 670
Oklahoma City, OK 73102
405/231-4301

Oregon
222 S.W. Columbia St.
Suite 500
Portland, OR 97201-6605
503/326-2586

Pennsylvania
Allendale Square
475 Allendale Rd.
Suite 201
King of Prussia, PA 19406
215/962-3846

960 Penn Ave.
5th Fl.
Pittsburgh, PA 15222
412/644-2780

Puerto Rico/Virgin Islands
Federico Degatau Fed. Bldg.
Carlos Chardon Ave.
Room 691
Hato Rey, PR 00918
809/753-4002

Rhode Island
380 Westminster Mall
Providence, RI 02903
401/528-4586

South Carolina
1835 Assembly St.
Room 358
Columbia, SC 29202
803/765-5376

South Dakota
Security Bldg.
101 South Main Ave.
Suite 101
Sioux Falls, SD 57102-0577
605/330-4231, EXT. 231

Tennessee
Parkway Towers
404 James Robertson Pkwy
Suite 1012
Nashville, TN 37219
615/736-5881

Texas
1100 Commerce St.
Room 3C36
Dallas, TX 75242
214/767-0605

10737 Gateway West
Suite 320
El Paso, TX 79902
915/541-7586

222 E. VanBuren St.
Suite 500
Harlingen, TX 78550
512/427-8533

2525 Murworth
Suite 112
Houston, TX 77054
713/660-4420

1611 10th St.
Suite 200
Lubbock, TX 79401
806/743-7462

North Star Executive Center
7400 Blanco Rd.
Suite 200
San Antonio, TX 78216-4300
512/229-4535

Utah
125 South State St.
Room 2237
Salt Lake City, UT 84138-1195
801/524-3209

Vermont
87 State St.
Room 205
Montpelier, VT 05602
802/828-4474

Virginia
400 N. 8th St.
Room 3015
P.O. Box 10126
Richmond, VA 23240
804/771-2617

Washington
Federal Bldg.
915 2nd Ave.
Room 1792
Seattle, WA 98174-1088

Farm Credit Building
West 601 1st Ave.
10th Fl. East
Spokane, WA 99204
509/353-2800

West Virginia
168 West Main St.
5th Fl.
Clarksburg, WV 26301
304/623-5631

Wisconsin
212 E. Washington Ave.
Room 213
Madison, WI 53703
608/264-5261

Wyoming
Federal Bldg.
100 E. B St.
Room 4001
P.O. Box 2839
Casper, WY 82602-2839
307/261-5761

STATE SMALL BUSINESS CONFERENCES

Conference	State Office Location	Information Number
Alabama: Regional, November—December; Governor's conference, January; rural development, February.	Montgomery	(205) 263-0048
Alaska: Several regionals; statewide conference, Spring	Juneau	(907) 465-2017
Arizona: Rural development conference, September	Phoenix	(602) 255-5434
Arkansas: Joint rural development conference with SBA	Little Rock SBA office or Governor's office	(501) 682-2345
California: Annual commerce resource conference; annual Governor's Women-in-Business Conference	Sacramento	(916) 445-6545
Colorado: No formal conference; Small Business Council meets periodically; Women's Economic Summit meeting in March	Denver	(303) 892-3840
Connecticut: Small Business Advisory Council and others, including Small Business Services Expo, May	Hartford	(203) 566-2567
Delaware: Periodic conferences between Delaware Development Office and small business, September	Dover	(302) 736-4271
Florida: Small Business Regional Forums; one statewide Florida Conference on Small Business, variable dates	Bureau of Business Assistance, Tallahassee	(904) 488-9357
Georgia: Governor's Conference on Small and Minority Business; annually at various locations	Atlanta	(404) 656-1794

Hawaii: Annual Statewide Small Business Conference, since 1980, October	Honolulu	(808) 531-4111
Idaho: Conference on Small Business, January	Boise	(208) 376-8400
Illinois: State House Conference on Small Business, variable dates	Chicago (Office of the Lt. Gov.)	(312) 917-5220
Iowa: Small Business Issues Conference, annually in October, since 1987, Univ. of Iowa, Ames	Des Moines	(515) 281-8310
Kentucky: Emerging Business Conference, since 1987, variable dates	University of Kentucky, Lexington	(606) 257-8746
Louisiana: Informal procurement meetings by U.S. representatives from State, variable dates	Office of local U.S. Senator or Representative	
Maryland: Informal small business conference program, variable dates	Md. State Chamber of Commerce, Annapolis	(301) 269-0642
Massachusetts: State House Conference on Small Business, since 1987, June	Boston	(617) 727-2932
Michigan: Small Business Week, Department of Commerce, SBA, and associations, each May; Governor's Conference on Small Business for 145 State delegates, February	Lansing	(517) 373-7485 and (517) 373-8487
Minnesota: Conference on Small Business, 250 delegates from 17 regional meetings, March	Minnesota Dept. of Trade & Economic Development, St. Paul	(612) 296-3871
Montana: Access to Government for Small Business conferences in Helena and Glendive, May	Helena	(406) 449-5381
Nebraska: Variable conferences on exporting, government procurement, finance, management	Dept. of Economic Development, Lincoln	(402) 471-4167
Nevada: Annual economic development conference, variable	Carson City	(702) 885-4325
New Jersey: Governor's Conference on Small Business, since 1982, June	Trenton	(609) 984-4442
New Mexico: Conference on Small Business, since 1986, variable	Association of Commerce & Industry, Albuquerque	(505) 265-5847
New York: State Small Business Presentation, annually, variable date	Business Council NY National Federation of Independent Business	(518) 465-7511 (518) 434-1262

North Carolina: Governor's Small Business Conference, September		(919) 733-7980
Oklahoma: Governor's Conference on Small Business, annual, July	Oklahoma City	(405) 787-4833
Pennsylvania: Governor's Conference on Small Business, annual, July	Harrisburg	(717) 783-8950
Rhode Island: Governor's Conference on Small Business (financing and procurement), February; Nuts and Bolts of Exporting Conference, March; New England–Eastern Canada Trade Procurement Conference, May	Providence Bryant College, Smithfield Providence	(401) 277-2601 (401) 232-6111 (401) 277-2601
South Carolina: Entrepreneur Women Conference, each Fall; "Expo," a matchmaker conference, variable	Columbia	(803) 737-0400
South Dakota: Statewide Conference on Economic Development, February	Pierre	(605) 773-5032
Texas: Conference on Small Business, February and October; SBA Rural Development Conference, variable	Austin Austin (SBA)	(512) 472-5059 (512) 482-5288
Utah: Governor's Conference on Economic Development, February	Salt Lake City	(801) 538-3037
Vermont: Variable entrepreneurship forums through the Department of Economic Development	Montpelier	(802) 828-3221
Virginia: Governor's Conference on Small Business, variable	Virginia Chamber of Commerce, Richmond	(804) 786-3791 or 644-1607
Washington: Governor's Conference on Small Business, October	Seattle	(206) 343-2333
West Virginia: Governor's Conference on Small Business Development, September	Charleston	(304) 348-2960
Wisconsin: Governor's Conference on Small Business, November; prior regional meetings	Madison	(608) 266-3208